Additional Praise for *The Second Term of George W. Bush: Prospects and Perils*

"This collection of scholarship is timely and much-needed. It is a well-written, well-researched, and worthwhile addition to the scholarly literature on the presidency in general and on George W. Bush in particular. I believe this text is well-suited to advanced undergraduates as well as graduate students."
—Denise von Herrmann, University of Southern Mississippi

"This book lays to bare key questions and issues that plague all second term presidents and provides a powerful lens to understand the context, constraints and capacities which presidents must confront. This book will appeal to an advanced undergraduate audience and find a home in political science and history courses on the presidency."
—Victoria A. Farrar-Myers, The University of Texas at Arlington

The Evolving American Presidency Series

The Second Term of George W. Bush: Prospects and Perils
Edited by
Robert Maranto, Douglas M. Brattebo, and Tom Lansford

The Second Term of George W. Bush: Prospects and Perils

Book Editors

Robert Maranto
Associate Professor, Political Science
Villanova University

Douglas M. Brattebo
Assistant Professor, Political Science
United States Naval Academy

Tom Lansford
Associate Professor, Political Science
University of Southern Mississippi

THE SECOND TERM OF GEORGE W. BUSH

© Robert Maranto, Douglas M. Brattebo, Tom Lansford, 2006.

First published in 2006 by
PALGRAVE MACMILLAN™
175 Fifth Avenue, New York, N.Y. 10010 and
Houndmills, Basingstoke, Hampshire, England RG21 6XS
Companies and representatives throughout the world.

PALGRAVE MACMILLAN is the global academic imprint of the Palgrave Macmillan division of St. Martin's Press, LLC and of Palgrave Macmillan Ltd. Macmillan® is a registered trademark in the United States, United Kingdom and other countries. Palgrave is a registered trademark in the European Union and other countries.

ISBN 13: 978–1–4039–7291–0 (hardcover)
ISBN 10: 1–4039–7291–5 (hardcover)
ISBN 13: 978–1–4039–7514–0 (paperback)
ISBN 10: 1–4039–7514–0 (paperback)

Library of Congress Cataloging-in-Publication Data

The second term of George W. Bush : prospects and perils / book editors, Robert Maranto, Douglas M. Brattebo, Tom Lansford.
    p. cm.—(The evolving American presidency)
    Includes bibliographical references and index.
    ISBN 1–4039–7514–0
    1. United States—Politics and government, 2001. 2. Bush, George W. (George Walker), 1946–. 3. United States Foreign relations—2001–. I. Maranto, Robert, 1958–. II. Brattebo, Douglas M. III. Lansford, Tom. IV. Series.

JK275.S43 2006
973.931092—dc22   2005040164

A catalogue record for this book is available from the British Library.

Design by Newgen Imaging Systems (P) Ltd., Chennai, India.

First edition: June 2006

10 9 8 7 6 5 4 3 2 1

Printed in the United States of America.

Contents

Part I   The Setting

Part II   The Institutions

Part III   Domestic Policy

Part IV The Policies

Part V Foreign and Security Policy

Part VI Presidential Leadership

List of Figures

List of Tables

Series Foreword
Palgrave

The Evolving American Presidency

The American Presidency touches virtually every aspect of American and world politics. And the presidency has become, for better or worse, the vital center of the American and global political systems. The Framers of the American government would be dismayed at such a result. As invented at the Philadelphia Constitutional Convention in 1787, the Presidency was to have been a part of a government with shared and overlapping powers, embedded within a separation-of-powers system. If there was a vital center, it was the Congress; the Presidency was to be a part, but by no means, the centerpiece of that system.

Over time, the presidency has evolved and grown in power, expectations, responsibilities, and authority. Wars, crises, depressions, industrialization, all served to add to the power of the presidency. And as the United States grew into a world power, presidential power also grew. As the United States became the world's leading superpower, the presidency rose in prominence and power, not only in the United States, but on the world stage.

It is the clash between the presidency as invented and the presidency as it has developed that inspired this series. And it is the importance and power of the modern American presidency that makes understanding the office so vital. Like it or not, the American Presidency stands at the vortex of power both within the United States and across the globe.

This Palgrave series, recognizes that the Presidency is and has been an evolving institution, going from the original constitutional design as a Chief Clerk, to today where the president is the center of the American political constellation. This has caused several key dilemmas in our political system, not the least of which is that presidents face high expectations with limited constitutional resources. This causes presidents to find extra-constitutional means of governing. Thus, presidents must find ways to bridge the expectations/power gap while operating within the confines of a separation-of-powers system designed to limit presidential authority. How presidents resolve these challenges and paradoxes is the central issue in modern governance. It is also the central theme of this book series.

Michael A. Genovese
Loyola Chair of Leadership
Loyola Marymount University
Palgrave's The Evolving American Presidency, Series Editor

Notes on Contributors

Douglas M. Brattebo, Ph.D. and J.D., is Director of the Education Policy Fellowship Program at the Institute for Educational Leadership in Washington, D.C. Prior to this position, he served as an Assistant Professor of Political Science at the U.S. Naval Academy in Annapolis, Maryland from August 1999–August 2005. He is also a member of the Maryland Bar. In May of 2002 he was the winner of the Naval Academy's prestigious Apgar Award for Teaching Excellence. Brattebo is the author of numerous articles and book chapters and is guest editor of a special edition of the journal *White House Studies* (4:4, June 2004), organized around the theme of "The Presidency, the Navy, and the War on Terror." His book of the same name will appear later in 2005.

Robert Maranto is Associate Professor of Political Science, at Villanova University, previously served in government during the Clinton administration a mere twelve levels below POTUS, and has taught at numerous institutions including the University of Virginia and the U.S. Federal Executive Institute. In concert with others he has produced several dozen scholarly works, including *School Choice in the Real World: Lessons from Arizona Charter Schools* (2001), *Radical Reform of the Civil Service* (2001), and *Beyond a Government of Strangers: Career Executives, Political Appointees, and Presidential Transitions* (2005).

Tom Lansford is an Associate Professor of Political Science, and Assistant Dean of the College of Arts and Letters, at the University of Southern Mississippi. He has published articles in journals such as *Defense Analysis, The Journal of Conflict Studies, European Security, International Studies, Security Dialogue*, and *Strategic Studies*. Dr. Lansford is the author of a number of books, including *The Lords of Foggy Bottom: The American Secretaries of State and the World They Shaped* (2001), *All for One: NATO, Terrorism and the United States* (2002), and *A Bitter Harvest: US Foreign Policy and Afghanistan* (2003).

Jeffrey E. Cohen, professor of political science, Fordham University, received his Ph. D. from the University of Michigan in 1979. His major areas of interests are the presidency, public opinion, and public policymaking. He is the author of several books, including *Presidential Responsiveness and Public Policy-Making* (1997), which won the 1998 Richard E. Neustadt Award, as well as articles in numerous journals, including the *American Political Science Review*, the *American Journal of Political Science*, and the *Journal of Politics*.

Jack Covarrubias is a graduate student at Old Dominion University.

Roger H. Davidson is Professor Emeritus of Government and Politics at the University of Maryland, College Park and Visiting Professor of Political Science at the University of California, Santa Barbara. Dr. Davidson is author or coauthor of numerous books, monographs, and articles dealing with politics and policymaking. Among his books are *Congress and Its Members* (10th ed., 2006), the leading textbook on the subject; *Congress Against Itself* (1977); *The Role of the Congressman* (1969); *The Politics of Comprehensive Manpower Legislation* (1972); and *A More Perfect Union* (4th ed., 1989).

Michael A. Genovese currently holds the Loyola Chair of Leadership Studies and is a Professor of Political Science, and Director of the Institute for Leadership Studies at Loyola Marymount University. Professor Genovese has written fifteen books, including *The Paradoxes of the American Presidency* (co-authored by Thomas E. Cronin), 2nd ed. (2004); *The Presidency and Domestic Policy*, (with William W. Lammers), 2000, *The Power of the American Presidency 1789–2000* (2001, The *Presidential Dilemma*, 2nd ed. (2003, and *The Encyclopedia of the American Presidency*, Facts-on File, 2004. He has won over a dozen university and national teaching awards.

John Robert Greene is the Paul J. Schupf Professor of History and Humanities at Cazenovia College, Cazenovia, NY, where he has taught for the past twenty-five years. He is also the chair of the Division of Social and Behavioral Sciences, and serves as the College Archivist. Dr. Greene's teaching and writing specialty lies in American Political History, particularly the American presidency. He has written or edited fifteen books—including one on the election of Dwight Eisenhower, one on the Nixon presidency, three on the Ford presidency, and his most recent, a critically acclaimed study of *The Presidency of George Bush*.

Jeremy Johnson is a graduate student at Brown University.

Lori A. Johnson, assistant professor of political science, Wellesley College, received her Ph.D. from the University of California, Berkeley in 2003. She earned a law degree from the University of Virginia School of Law, practiced employment law, and clerked for a judge on the U.S. Court of Appeals for the 4th Circuit. She has published work on comparative regulatory policy and the politics of procedural rulemaking. Her book project, *Who Governs the Courts? The Politics of Policymaking for the Federal Courts*, examines the interaction between the judicial and legislative branches in making important policy decisions that shape the work of the federal courts.

Anne M. Khademian is an associate professor with the Center for Public Administration and Policy in the School for International and Public Affairs at Virginia Tech. She is the author of numerous articles in *Public*

Administration Review, the *Journal of Public Administration Research and Theory*, *Governance*, the *International Public Management Journal*, and the *Journal of Public Policy Analysis and Management*. Her books include *Working with Culture* (2002), *Checking on Banks* (1996), and *The SEC and Capital Market Regulation* (1992). Her chapter, "Strengthening State and Local Government Terrorism Prevention and Response" is included in the Century Foundations Report (2004) *The Department of Homeland Security's First Year: A Report Card*.

Ann M. Lesch is Dean of Humanities and Social Sciences at the American University in Cairo and a professor of political science. Her publications include *Political Perceptions of the Palestinians on the West Bank and Gaza Strip* (1980), *Israel, Egypt and the Palestinians* with Mark Tessler (1989), *Transition to Palestinian Self-Government* (1992), and *Origins and Development of the Arab-Israeli Conflict* with Dan Tschirgi (1998). She has written extensively on Egypt and the Sudan, including *The Sudan: Contested National Identities* (1998), *Battle for Peace in Sudan: An Analysis of the Abuja Conferences* (2000), and "Domestic Politics and Foreign Policy in Egypt," in *Democracy, War and Peace in the Middle East* (1995).

Bradley Patterson is one of the nation's foremost authorities on the organization and functioning of the White House staff. He served fourteen years on the staff, as the Assistant Cabinet Secretary under President Eisenhower, as the executive assistant to Leonard Garment under President Nixon and an Assistant Director of the Presidential Personnel Office under President Ford. He is the author of two books about the White House staff, including *The White House Staff: Inside the West Wing and Beyond* (Brookings, 2001). Winner of the Arthur S. Flemming Award for 1960 as One of the Ten Outstanding Young Men in Federal Service, he was President of the American Society for Public Administration and a Senior Fellow of the National Academy of Public Administration.

Stanley A. Renshon is Professor of Political Science and coordinator of the Interdisciplinary Program in the Psychology of Social and Political behavior at the City University of New York Graduate Center, and a certified psychoanalyst. He is the author of 90 professional articles and 12 books, including his psychological biography of the Clinton presidency, *High Hopes: The Clinton Presidency and the Politics of Ambition*, which won the 1997 American Political Science Association's Richard E. Neustadt Award and the National Association for the Advancement of Psychoanalysis' Gradiva Award for the best published biographical work. His new book *In His Father's Shadow: The Transformations of George W. Bush*, was published in 2004.

Andrew Rudalevige is Associate Professor of Political Science at Dickinson College, and during 2004–2005 a Visiting Scholar at the Center for the Study of Democratic Politics at Princeton University. His first book,

Managing the President's Program: Presidential Leadership and Legislative Policy Formulation (2002), won the 2003 Richard E. Neustadt Award. He has also written on congressional elections, the legislative processes underlying recent education reform, the structure of the Executive Office of the President, and the role of the Office of Management and Budget in the presidential management of the wider executive branch.

Amy Steigerwalt is Assistant Professor of Political Science at the University of New Orleans. Dr. Steigerwalt recently completed her Ph.D. at the University of California, Berkeley, and her dissertation, *Cultivating Controversy*, examines the role of senators and interest groups in politicizing federal judicial confirmations. Her work also focuses on informal interest group activity in the legislative process and the role of courts in the national policymaking. She has published entries in the *Encyclopedia of the Supreme Court* as well as pieces in *The Berkeley's Women Law Journal* and *The California Supreme Court Historical Society Yearbook*. She was an American Political Science Association Congressional Fellow in 2004–2005.

Shirley Anne Warshaw (Ph.D. Johns Hopkins University) is Professor of Political Science at Gettysburg College. She has written extensively on the president's cabinet and the White House staff in the modern presidency and is the author of seven books on the presidency including *Powersharing: White House-Cabinet Relations in the Modern Presidency* and *The Domestic Presidency: Policy Making in the White House*. Her most recent books include *The Presidency of William Jefferson Clinton* and *The Keys to Power: Managing the Presidency*, second edition. She is a frequent commentator for National Public Radio, *USA Today*, and other media outlets.

Part I

The Setting

Chapter One

Are Second Terms Second Best? Why George W. Bush Might (or Might Not) Beat the Expectations

Jeremy Johnson, Douglas Brattebo, Robert Maranto, and Tom Lansford

[For Bush] there is only one possible governing strategy: a quiet, patient and persistent bipartisanship . . . .

—Joe Klein after the 2000 election

They misunderestimated me.

—George W. Bush, November 6, 2000

Introduction

Facing a worsening situation in Iraq, a relatively jobless economic recovery, large budget deficits, mixed media coverage, a united and well-funded Democratic opposition, mediocre performance in two of the three presidential debates, and a relatively pessimistic public mood, President George W. Bush nonetheless won reelection in 2004, by a surprising popular and Electoral College vote majority over Massachusetts Senator John Kerry.[1] Indeed, Bush won the first popular vote majority since his father's win over another Massachusetts liberal, Michael Dukakis, in 1988.

Still, the Bush victory should in no way be interpreted a mandate. As table 1.1 shows, seven times in the twentieth and twenty-first centuries an incumbent president has won reelection to a second term.[2] Usually the reelection victory has been decisive with a mean of 55.3 percent of the popular vote and 13.6 percent popular vote margin, clearly reaffirming the president's leadership. Along with Woodrow Wilson's narrow 1916 victory, President George W. Bush's reelection marks an exception. Both men won reelection by small popular vote percentages (49.2 percent and 50.7 percent) and narrow popular vote margins (3.1 percent and 2.5 percent), with

Table 1.1   Reelected presidents of the twentieth and twenty-first centuries

President	Year reelected	Reelection % of popular vote	Change in % of popular vote from initial election	Reelection popular vote % margin over opponent	Electoral college vote breakdown	Gain or loss of seats in U.S. house	Gain or loss of seats in U.S. senate
Woodrow Wilson (D)	1916	49.2	+7.4	3.1	277 (D) −254 (R)	−21	−3
Franklin D Roosevelt (D)	1936	60.8	+3.4	24.3	523 (D) 8 (R)	+11	+6
Dwight Eisenhower (R)	1956	57.4	+2.5	15.4	457 (R)− 73 (D)− 1 (Other)	−2	0
Richard Nixon (R)	1972	60.7	+17.3	23.2	520 (R)− 17 (D)−	+12	−2
Ronald Reagan (R)	1984	58.8	+8.1	18.2	525 (R)− 13 (D)	+14	−2
Bill Clinton (D)	1996	49.2	+6.2	8.5	379 (D)− 159 (R)	+9	−2
George W. Bush (R)	2004	50.7	+2.8	2.5	286 (R)− 252 (D)	+7	+4

the possibility that the shift of a single state in the Electoral College could have altered the outcome.

It is still not clear in what precise measures Bush's victory reflected a vote of confidence in the president's policies; skepticism about his opponent (Senator John Kerry), concerns about an overly liberal Democratic party,[3] the wizardry of Bush's political strategist Karl Rove, or some combination of these factors. It is clear, however, that the answer to this query may not interest Bush much, since he demonstrated in his first term a willingness to proceed with a substantial and controversial agenda, even without any popular mandate. Indeed, the President already has expressed his view that, by winning reelection narrowly, he has accumulated a store of political capital that he intends to spend. As conservative journalist Fred Barnes puts it:

> [Bush] hates to fool around with small measures. They bore him. Another explanation, offered half-seriously by a White House aide, is that he's a Texan. For Texans, the aide says, the bigger the project, the better. In addition, the president regards himself as a problem-solver. "If there's a problem . . . I have responsibility to lay out potential solutions," he told the *Wall Street Journal*. When you combine an inclination to take on problems with a penchant for grand proposals, "you get George W. Bush," the aide says.[4]

Similarly, as political scientist Steven E. Schier has put it in the title of his own edited volume, Bush is a president of *High Risk and Big Ambition* seeking to "entrench a conservative regime among a public beset by even partisan divisions and without a stable Washington governing coalition."[5]

Contrary to popular perception, the president is not alone in policymaking and leadership. Rather he is one among several players empowered by the Constitution. The Congress, the Courts, as well as the federal system that grants states many powers are all "checks and balances" that limit the president's ability to act unilaterally. In addition, since the 1930s a large national bureaucracy has acted to hinder (and sometimes aid) presidential leadership. In sum, the constraints on the president are so formidable that President Lyndon Johnson once lamented that "the only real power, which I own, is the nuclear one, and it is the one which I can't make use of."[6] A president is thus forced to compensate, according to noted political scientist Richard Neustadt, through his ability to persuade rather than command;[7] hence, the "rhetorical presidency."[8]

Bush faces a formidable array of challenges in his second term. The insurgency in Iraq, fears about terrorism, a mixed economy, and looming long-term entitlement and health care fiscal issues as baby boomers near retirement are substantial roadblocks to his second term agenda.[9] However, a highly experienced cabinet and a president with a knack for turning success from less than promising circumstance may prove enough for these issues. What of these factors will determine the likelihood of success for the second term of George W. Bush?

Structural Explanations

As political scientist Stephen D. Krasner has joked, in the 1960s and 1970s prominent political science professors would teach their classes that leadership didn't matter since policies were determined by structural forces alone, while at the same time bragging to those same classes about time spent advising political leaders, who presumably did not matter![10] More recently, political science had grown more sophisticated about determining when leadership matters, and when it is constrained by the broader political environment. *Structural explanations* such as Stephen Skowronek's *political regime theory*, although not previously applied to transitions, implicitly suggest a framework for analyzing transitions.[11] The term "regime" refers to the dominant political coalition of an era.[12] Some transitions are more successful because the "political time" calls for more activism, permitting presidents greater *possibilities* of success, with the mass public and policy-making elites more open to persuasion by a determined president.

Skowronek suggests that second terms almost always fall into the category of regime continuation. Even those presidencies that represent a "regime shift" tend to lose their momentum after the initial stages of the first term. Franklin Roosevelt's most ambitious reforms occurred during the famous Hundred Days, and Reagan's major legislative initiatives passed during his first year in office. This would suggest a lackluster second George W. Bush term, yet Skowronek also notes that the presidency functions best when used as a "battering ram" to tear down existing structures.[13] President

George W. Bush's actions during the second term transition strongly indicate that he will pursue an aggressive agenda including Social Security reform and eventually tax reform, taking on not one but two of the "third rails" of American politics.[14] Bush aims to elude the typical second-term lethargy.

Another structural approach, articulated by James A. Stimson, focuses on how public opinion shapes politics. He notes that the American polity as a whole tends to be more moderate than either political party. Hence, when one political party takes control, there is usually a public backlash. This theory posits that most of a president's power to shape policy thus comes in the early stages of his first term. This was indeed the case for Ronald Reagan in 1981, with much of the rest of his time in office backsliding from his "Revolution." The reaction against Bill Clinton's liberalization in 1993 was swift and decisive—health care reform was defeated and Democrats suffered an historic electoral repudiation in the 1994 congressional elections.[15] This theory suggests that after an initial burst of activity in the first term, a president's second term legacy consists mostly of avoiding backsliding on first term accomplishments. By implication, a second-term president is not in a position to move radical legislation forward. Since George W. Bush wants to achieve big things in his second term, he is swimming against the structural tide.

A related structural approach developed by Paul Light similarly points out that presidential power depends in part on such short-term variables (political resources) as the size of the president's electoral victory, whether that victory had coattails, and control of Congress—all short-term variables that reflect the status of the political regime.[16] As noted above, Bush's electoral victory of less than three percentage points is dwarfed by the 49-state reelection victories of Nixon (1972) and Reagan (1984). Yet Bush became the first presidential candidate in 16 years (since his own father in 1988) to win a majority of the popular vote. Moreover, Bush won reelection in a highly unfavorable political environment.

President George W. Bush also had apparent coattails in several U.S. Senate elections, though not in the U.S. House or state and local races. As table 1.1 shows, unlike other recent second-term winners, Bush picked up Senate seats, becoming the first Republican president reelected with gains in both houses of Congress in 80 years. Given that 17 Democratic Senators face reelection in 2006, Congress should stay Republican through at least the 2008 congressional election cycle.[17] Yet Bush may find his political allies more of a problem than his political opponents. The Speaker of the House of Representatives, Dennis Hastert (R-IL), has articulated a policy of advancing legislation favored only by a majority of the majority caucus in the House. In other words, legislation apparently will not be allowed to come up for a vote, even if it could be enacted mainly with Democratic votes, if most House Republicans do not support it. This has already occurred, with House Republican members initially thwarting the 9/11 bill overhauling the intelligence community until the seemingly ambivalent president finally weighed in strongly to help secure its passage. The Senate's political independence may also give the president difficulty. Senate Democrats have enough votes to exercise a filibuster (which can only be halted by a 60-vote majority) to stymie legislation, though as chapter 5 of this volume details, Senate Majority Leader Bill Frist (R-TN) has threatened to change the rules to end this traditional bastion of minority power.

While some Presidents, such as Franklin D. Roosevelt (FDR) and Reagan, seemed to have mandates, Bush's reelection is structurally more muddled. In some ways, he most resembles Woodrow Wilson who was reelected by a slender majority and tried to impose bold ideas (such as the League of Nations) on the world during his second term. On the other hand, the structural similarities to Wilson are missing since Wilson was a Democratic president in a Republican era, while Bush seems to be the regime continuer to what admirers label the "Reagan Revolution." A plethora of recent works argue that American and to a lesser degree international public policy ideas and institutions have shifted in a pro-market direction in recent years, particularly since the fall of Communism.[18] Thus unlike Bill Clinton, whose main achievements (NAFTA, welfare reform, deficit reduction, reinventing government) were conservative, and Richard Nixon, whose main achievements (Détente with the USSR, rapprochement with China, wage and price controls, the Environmental Protection Agency, affirmative action) were liberal, George W. Bush may be a president at least partly in synch with an advancing political regime, an argument made by Stanley Renshon in chapter 13 of this volume.

A second-term president is also a "lame duck" with reduced political resources to pass major initiatives. Washington actors, including the vice president, are today likely to aspire to the presidency, and thus seek to distinguish themselves from the shopworn incumbent. In part George W. Bush will prove to be an exception, inasmuch as Vice President Cheney clearly lacks presidential ambitions. Yet Republican Senators, including John McCain (R-AZ) and Majority Leader Bill Frist (R-TN), harbor presidential ambitions that may not always align with the sitting president's interests.[19]

Managerial Approaches

Supplementing structural theories, *managerial approaches* suggest what presidents can do within the broader constraints of structural variables. James Pfiffner, Peter Burke, and others suggest that a transition's success depends upon the technical decisions and adjustments made during the pre- and post-inauguration period.[20] The managerial approach can include issues such as the facilitating of new policy initiatives, the appointment of White House staff, cabinet, and other positions, and also relationships with the media and Congress. It is generally agreed that the most successful modern transition was that of Ronald Reagan in 1980–1981. Reagan had a focused transition team ready with just a few key policy initiatives, in dramatic contrast to Jimmy Carter whose "laundry list" of proposals floundered during the 1976–1977 transition.

Carter's and Bill Clinton's transitions were among those most ineffectually managed. Burke argues that such problematic transitions feature many common characteristics:

> errors made during the pre-election period, too much attention to the appointment of cabinet members compared to the White House staff, conflicts between various 'camps' during the transition process that carried over once the administration was in office, problems in communication and the division of labor between Washington-based operations and the president-elect's home-base . . . wherever it may be.[21]

These problems have been extensively examined in the presidency literature, which also advises how to avoid such managerial debacles. James Pfiffner notes that presidents are most effective if they "hit the ground running," or work assiduously to implement policy as early as possible in their presidencies.[22] Presidents, like Reagan, who have just a few major agenda items, are the most successful in getting their programs passed. In contrast, Charles Jones suggests a more cautious approach, because the country may not be ready for such substantial change.[23] A good example of this would include Clinton's health care and gays in the military initiatives. The work of Pfiffner and Jones in some respects dovetails with Skowronek's: perhaps "hitting the ground running" applies most in a time of regime transition.

Pfiffner's "hitting the ground running" does not normally apply to second terms, in part because a president's agenda has been substantially exhausted. Jones's incremental approach would seem more viable. Here, George W. Bush could prove an exception. He has a robust domestic agenda that he did not try to implement in his first term, and he may have the political resources, combined with a seemingly workable Republican majority in Congress, to try to implement major change. As the first 100 days of the second term show, President Bush intends to spend political capital on Social Security reform before trying to simplify the tax code.[24] So far, the President has enjoyed relatively little success. As conservative journalist Andrew Ferguson argues, it may be that Bush's over-broad agenda has caused a public backlash by showing the same sort of lack of restraint that once characterized liberalism. On the other hand, liberal columnist Paul Krugman suggests that Bush's soft poll numbers simply indicate a public wary of his conservative vision.[25] Indeed, as of May 2005, President Bush suffers the lowest public standing of his administration.[26] Yet Bush is likely to keep trying to push his agenda, and before his presidency ends may well enjoy additional successes.

In addition to managing legislation and public opinion, a key part of the managerial presidency literature examines *The Administrative Presidency*, a term coined by political science professor and former Nixon and Reagan political appointee Richard P. Nathan in his book of that name.[27] Smart presidents will select competent appointees who share their goals, delegate widely to those appointees, and foster teamwork. Presidents will not micro-manage appointees, nor appoint a team that lacks consensus. Presidents will also have the ability to come to closure on key decisions. Political scientist Donald F. Kettl makes the case in *Team Bush*[28] that perhaps because of the president's past White House experience, or because of his background as an MBA business-person, he has in fact mastered the basics of leading the executive branch, a claim largely agreed to by some of our authors, most notably Bradley Patterson, Robert Greene, and to a lesser degree Shirley Anne Warshaw. Yet as Kettl and Warshaw respectively fear, too much consensus and too much focus on results can lead to groupthink, as the president fails to sufficiently consider alternative policies and impediments to his preferred plans.

Partisan Learning Theory

Another theoretical element relevant to explicating the behavior of newly elected presidents is Charles E. Walcott's and Karen M. Hult's concept of *partisan learning theory*.[29] Simply put, new presidents often model their White House staffs after those of predecessors of their own party. Kennedy, for example, looked back to the Truman administration for guidance, whereas Nixon and George H. W. Bush relied on the Eisenhower administration as a model. Clinton followed the same pattern, modeling his transition after those of Carter and Johnson, instead of taking his cues from more effective predecessors' transitions.[30]

Politically, this tendency of new presidents to imitate the transitions of recent predecessors of their own party seems logical. Kennedy understandably wanted to make a fresh start from the perceived torpor of the Eisenhower administration by dismantling the elaborate national security policymaking apparatus Ike had built and replacing it with one that would put the new president more visibly at center stage. A generation later, Clinton, who as a teenager had met JFK in the White House Rose garden, no doubt believed his own presidential transition should have more in common with that of his boyhood idol than with those of Republicans Eisenhower, Reagan, and George H. W. Bush. The problem, of course, is that this approach risks throwing out tested, effective approaches and structures in the rush to put one's own stamp on a new administration.[31]

It is no secret that recent Republican presidents-elect have done a better job than their Democratic counterparts in profiting from the transitions of predecessors of both parties. As they entered upon the office of the presidency, Ronald Reagan, George H. W. Bush, and George W. Bush were all less concerned about demonstrating change from the status quo than with paving the way for effective governance. Indeed, it would be fair to say that George W. Bush's 2000–2001 transition was in this sense quite unlike those of Carter and Clinton, and that this was fortunate given the impending events of

September 11, 2001. Instead, George W. Bush's transition was a model of efficiency that helped overcome some of the controversy associated with the 2000 election.[32]

Interestingly, one might argue that while learning the ins and outs of White House organization from working in his father's White House, George W. Bush modeled much of his rhetorical and policy strategy after Ronald Reagan, in direct opposition to his own father. George H. W. Bush was a centrist president who respected experts and sought consensus. He could master policy details, but had trouble developing goals and selling those goals to the American people.[33] In contrast, the younger Bush seems dismissive of expert opinion, and seemingly wants to fashion a new consensus rather than work within existing norms.[34]

The Unhappy Fates of Recent Second-Term Presidents

Of course, the boldness shown by George W. Bush holds perils. Traditionally, the hubris that accompanies winning a second term may lead to political overreaching or to scandal. The most common problem for second terms is the tendency to overreach. This is especially true of presidents who could be judged to have had successful first terms. Instead of being able to translate past accomplishments into future successes, the most likely trend among second terms is a diminishing of political clout and capital as public support dwindles and key staffers often leave the administration. Nine of fifteen members of Bush's first term cabinet have resigned. While such a turnover rate is normal for the early second term—Nixon, Reagan, and Clinton all lost or dismissed from 46 to 64 percent of their cabinets in the time period[35]—President Bush nominated replacements associated with some of his most controversial policies. Alberto Gonzales, the nominee for Attorney General, has been criticized for his role in narrowing the definition of torture of detainees, and Condoleezza Rice, the nominee for Secretary of State, is intricately linked with the ongoing war in Iraq. (As Stanley Renshon writes in the last chapter of this volume, this reflects Bush's tendency to confront political obstacles: "right back at you.") Also, the botched appointment of Bernard Kerik as Secretary of Homeland Security, after a slipshod vetting process failed to uncover damaging personal details of his career, sends signals of disarray in the usually disciplined Bush White House. So while all modern second term presidencies have been initiated with a cabinet reshuffling and the new appointees might exude new administrative energy, they could also turn out to be sycophants or yes-men who prove uninspiring, or worse, engage in corruption. There is also usually a concurrent loss of midlevel personnel as staffers seek to reap the rewards of their service through more prestigious or higher paying positions in the private sector. These factors often lead to problems in selling and implementing the second-term agenda.

Consider the twentieth-century presidents who won a second term in their own right: Woodrow Wilson, Franklin Roosevelt, Dwight Eisenhower, Richard Nixon, Ronald Reagan, and Bill Clinton. With the possible exceptions of the second-term Wilson, who led America away from isolationism, and the second-term Nixon, who attempted to reorient the institutions of government (bureaucracy, courts) to the right, each of these presidents was at this point in his presidency a regime continuer rather than a regime changer. Other than Wilson and Nixon, each had largely exhausted his agenda. (Of course, much of Wilson's agenda would unravel as a result of opposition in Congress and his health problems.) The drive by Congress to exert its power and authority during second terms is a trend that has progressed, regardless of party affiliation of the chief executive, and regardless of party control of the legislature.[36]

Just as Walcott and Hult's partisan learning theory accurately explains the experiences of many modern presidents heading into their first terms, it also has insights regarding second terms. President Nixon's first term taught him to develop the "administrative presidency" in his second term, an attempt at Reaganesque domestic policy regime change years before the political time was right.[37] Conversely, after Clinton's health care reform proposal came to naught during his first term; he learned to stress micro-initiatives and incremental policymaking as part of a broader "triangulation" political policy strategy during his second term.[38] In addition, like others before him, Clinton endeavored to concentrate more on foreign policy issues in his second term. As a result, Clinton enjoyed some success and was even able to gain bipartisan support for operations in the Balkans and against Iraq.[39] Interestingly, George W. Bush seems to have drawn the opposite lesson from Clinton, claiming a general mandate and undertaking bold second-term policy initiatives on the heels of a slender reelection victory. As noted above and in the chapters to come, initial results suggest that this may in fact constitute overreaching.

The general reticence of second term presidents to undertake sweeping domestic initiatives reflects the general trend in presidential politics whereby the chief executive enjoys far greater power and control of foreign policy as opposed to domestic agendas.[40] The division between the domestic and foreign policy presidencies has been well analyzed by numerous scholars, most notably Aaron Wildavsky and Richard Ellis.[41] Although, in general, Eisenhower's second term is not rated as highly as his first term, he left office with popularity, mainly because of his foreign policy. Likewise, Reagan was given accolades for ending the Cold War, even though his tenure was concurrently marred by the Iran–Contra Scandal.

Some scholars argue that second terms can be liberating for presidents since they are freed from the need to govern from the center or seek reelection. This factor certainly enhances the potential for presidents to overreach on policy initiatives. Second terms may allow presidents to address issues that they otherwise would avoid. For instance, in the case of Eisenhower, late in his second term the former general promulgated his famous warning about the rise of the military-industrial complex. Yet, history demonstrates that while presidents may elevate their rhetoric on new issues, they must continue to deal with the lingering repercussions of past policy decisions, preventing bold action. Despite his rhetoric, Eisenhower's administration did in fact support the military-industrial complex, though to a lesser degree than Truman and Kennedy.[42]

In contrast, based on their relative first term successes, Presidents FDR, Eisenhower, and Reagan essentially tried more of the same even as their fading political resources made a continuation of first term strategies problematic. Eisenhower was further handicapped by ill health and the resultant public perceptions of weakness during his second term.[43] Wilson (League of Nations), FDR (court-packing), Nixon (Watergate, and the administrative presidency), and Reagan (Iran–Contra) all arguably overreached in their second terms, perhaps in part out of hubris.

While first term presidents must worry about reelection, second term presidents must consider their legacy. Part of this entails exerting influence over the choice of who shall succeed the president as standard-bearer of his party. In some cases, presidents have essentially hand-picked their successors, as was the case with Theodore Roosevelt and William Howard Taft or Reagan and Bush.[44] In other cases, second-term presidents find themselves in the unenviable position of either tacitly opposing their possible successor, as in the case of Eisenhower and Nixon in 1960, or being marginalized as the campaign elevates the status of their potential successors, as with Clinton in 2000.

The Second-Term Potential of Bush

Bush thought he started his second term with strong political resources as a result of winning reelection. He declared after the November election, "I earned capital in the campaign, political capital, and now I intend to spend it."[45] Bush also has the advantage of being the first president since the Twenty-Second Amendment of 1951, which limited presidents to two terms, to be returned to office with his party in control of both Houses of Congress. Furthermore, although Bush has endured the usual post election cabinet shakeup, he has managed to retain many of his key advisors within the administration, including Andrew Card and Karl Rove. Other aides, such as Rice and Gonzales, have shifted positions but will remain in important posts, thus shortening the administration's learning curve.

Yet, after the first 100 days of Bush's second term, there are signs that like so many of his predecessors, this president may have overreached. While achieving significant victories by signing into law tort and bankruptcy reforms, Bush has boldly made Social Security personal/private accounts the centerpiece of his domestic agenda. Yet, the public has shown substantial resistance to these proposals, which may become more intense now that Bush has proposed freezing social security benefits at their current buying power for future middle and upper income retirees. Three months into his second term, Bush is suffering from the worst poll numbers of any second-term president in a comparable period.[46] The president may have exhibited hubris by nominating John Bolton as ambassador to the UN, a nominee strongly opposed by Democrats and many in the international community. Furthermore, the president was insisting on a showdown on Senate filibuster rules over a few of his judicial appointments.

Even so, the president has overcome many obstacles before, and may as yet be able to make substantial progress toward achieving his goals. As Stanley Renshon details in the book *In His Father's Shadow*,[47] a psychological portrait of George W. Bush, the president is someone who pushes ahead with potentially controversial initiatives even in the face of opposition. Bush spends rather than husbands his political capital; thus, it seems likely that Bush will attempt to reorient and partly privatize Social Security in his second term. With partisanship running high, the 2006 midterm elections looming, and chronic budget and trade deficits apparent, it is uncertain whether Bush can enact broad or sweeping new domestic programs. Finally, presidents cannot anticipate foreign policy intrusion. The assertive foreign policy of Bush's first term may force the president to devote resources and political capital to international affairs in such a manner as to undermine domestic initiatives.

Plan of the Book

Social scientists develop theories and make predictions based on those theories. Of course, the old saying goes that it is risky to make predictions, especially about the future. Good social scientists should always be willing to change their theories as new information comes forth; thus good social scientists must know the difference between self-contradiction and changing one's mind as new evidence arrives. A good social scientist must seek to avoid the former, but always stay open to the latter.[48]

So it is with presidency studies. The lead editor of this volume, Robert Maranto, thought Ronald Reagan a failed president during the 1980s, chiefly because of large budget deficits and an overly aggressive foreign policy. After serving in Washington in the 1990s at the Brookings Institution and in the Clinton administration, however, Maranto came to believe that Reagan's leadership played decisive roles in ending the Cold War and in restructuring the economy in painful but necessary ways. Maranto's short-term judgments were seemingly disproved by later events. In short, while none of us is free from judgment (or bias), we must be humble enough to acknowledge that history may disprove our views, however strongly held.

The same modesty should hold for evaluations of the George W. Bush presidency. Volumes such as this cannot explain what to think about this president's success, but can give clues as to what to think *about*. The following chapters, some favorably disposed toward Bush and others decidedly unfavorable, both summarize relevant scholarly literature on the presidency and apply the lessons of history and theory to the second term of George W. Bush. With the exception of the chapters in Section I ("The Setting," which includes this chapter and chapter 2 examining the 2004 presidential election), and the portrait of Bush's leadership in chapter 13, each chapter of the book addresses a particular institution or policy area, as described below. Most of the authors have sought to summarize how recent presidents have used the transition period to put their stamp on institutions and policies, describe how presidents often have distinguished themselves from their predecessors, and explore how early successes and failures influenced the course of a presidential administration. In these areas, particular attention is paid to previous second-term transitions and administrations, and the authors also examine how George W. Bush's first term likely will influence the 2005–2009 presidential term. Second, authors describe aspects of pre-transition planning and policy, as well as the most probable efforts to formulate and implement policy. Third, and finally, authors speculate about what the transition says about the course of the presidency from 2005 to 2009, paying special attention to potential pitfalls. Of course, as noted above, making predictions can be tricky.

The book is divided into three broad sections. "The Setting," comprised of this chapter and chapter 2, explores the broad patterns of presidential transitions. Chapter 2, Roger Davidson's "Public Opinion, Presidential Elections, and Presidential Governance," uses the 2004 election as a case study to elucidate broad patterns of public opinion as they affect presidential elections and campaign strategy. Davidson's main contention is that modern presidential elections are best understood through the exploration of the intensity of public attitudes among both the elites and the general public.

Section II, "The Institutions," examines the institutions and how presidents generally and George W. Bush, in particular, shape and are shaped by the institutions within the executive branch, as well as Congress and the courts. Bradley Patterson analyzes the White House staff in chapter 3, "The Bush White House Staff in the Second Term: New Structures? New Faces? New Processes?" Patterson traces the enduring continuity of the organizational structure in the chief executive's staff, and suggests that a second Bush term will continue to emphasize this consistency of purpose and function even through changes in the political environment. Chapter 4, "Choices for the President: Structuring the Second Term Cabinet of George W. Bush," by Shirley Anne Warshaw, examines Bush's cabinet choices, and how they reflect his broader electoral and governing strategy. Chapter 5, Andrew Rudalevige's "George W. Bush and Congress in the Second Term: New Problems-Same Results?" presents the main themes of presidential-congressional relations over the last four years and how the patterns that developed will affect the next term. Specifically, Rudalevige traces how both actors, the presidency and the Congress, manage interbranch relationships. Chapter 6, "Crusade: the Rhetorical Presidency of George Bush," by John Robert Greene, delves into the main aspects of the rhetorical presidency, including press relations, public relations, and speechwriting. The chapter discusses the interplay between rhetoric and policy through an overview of the role of White House press operations and presidential speechwriters. The Chapter 7 is "Judges, Courts, and Policy in President George W. Bush's Second Term" by Amy Steigerwalt and Lori Johnson. The essay begins by tracing the growing importance of the courts in the policy process and the increasing use of the judicial system by presidents, members of Congress, interest groups, and concerned citizens to implement or overturn policy. The chapter explores the contemporary ability of the executive branch to influence the judiciary and analyzes how the president's judicial nominees will fare before Congress and the general court of public opinion.

Section IV, "The Policies," explores the likely course of action that Bush will take in several significant policy areas during his second term. Chapter 8, Michael Genovese's "Domestic Policy in the Second Bush Term: the Un-Hidden Hand Leadership of a Conviction President," begins by discussing the differences between domestic and foreign policy and then explores the president's strategic policy options in the context of public support, legislative imperatives, and budget and economic constraints. The chapter also presents Bush's domestic agenda and its prospects for success. "Economic Policy: Responsibility But With Limited Authority," Jeff Cohen traces the role of public opinion as it relates to economic policy. He further presents the main economic priorities of the administration and appraises the likely success or failure of these goals and of Bush's economic team. In Section V in Chapter 10. Chapter 9, "Homeland (In?) Security," by Anne M. Khademian, provides an overview of the main issues in Homeland Security facing the Bush administration, and the administration's strategy and vision for securing the United States. The chapter also examines potential challenges and speculates as to the ability of the president to use his management style to navigate around political roadblocks. Security is also the focus of chapter 12, "Problematic Policies Toward the Middle East," in which area expert Ann M. Lesch examines the war on terror in the context of U.S. policy toward the Middle East and the broader trends in Bush's foreign policy. Lesch identifies the key diplomatic and security elements of the first term and analyzes whether the administration's key doctrines will remain through 2009, emphasizing how the Bush foreign policy is viewed by those in the region, who increasingly question both the administration's intent and its effectiveness.

Chapter 11, "The Best Defense? Iraq and Beyond," by Tom Lansford and Jack Covarrubias, details the main elements of Bush's defense policy within the context of domestic and international constraints. The chapter places Bush's defense priorities within the broad continuities of U.S. security policy and analyzes the impact of the military campaigns in Afghanistan and Iraq on U.S. defense policy.

Finally, in chapter 13, "George W. Bush: A Transformational Leader at Midterm," Stanley A. Renshon makes the case that Bush's personal psychology as a leader seeking big results, combined with the decay of the dominant governing paradigm, *interest group liberalism*, particularly after

9/11, makes it likely that Bush will become a highly successful president who will usher in a new political era. Key to Renshon's argument is the idea that a transforming president must first divide the nation in order to later unite it under a new political regime.

Conclusion

In short, there are no clear answers, at least not yet, as to how President Bush's second term will turn out. This is only natural given the divided nature of the electorate. Many presidents, including Truman and Reagan, experienced declines in popularity in their second term, but were rehabilitated by historical hindsight. As in the case of Truman, it may well be that the extremes of judgment and opinion of the Bush presidency will fade over time and move closer to a central, objective middle. Bush has consistently exceeded expectations in elections and policy matters, although he has often failed to gain significant political victories. Instead, Bush has demonstrated a capacity to win, though not by a large or commanding margin. The Bush administration defeated Afghanistan and Iraq, but then faced a significant insurgency in Iraq. It captured Saddam Hussein, but not Osama Bin Laden. Bush's electoral victories in 2000, 2002, and 2004 were small but historic given the underlying political dynamics.[49] The Iraqi elections held on January 30, 2005 mark an event of historical significance in the Middle East, but whether they will really lead to a transformation of the region remains open to doubt.

This trend of achieving small victories in both policy and management will likely continue in the second term. The range of assessment of Bush in this book reflects the unsettled or cloudy nature of his accomplishments, as well as the controversial nature of his goals. For instance, Lesch faults Bush's foreign policy on a range of levels, while Lansford and Covarrubias find successes in many of the same areas. Other contributors, such as Renshon or Patterson, give Bush high marks for leadership or organizational management, although the president's relations with Congress or the courts are criticized in succeeding chapters. Robert Maranto and Tom Lansford predict that history may mark the Bush presidency as a "C+" or "B−"; a grade that is above average, but one that fails to achieve greatness, in part since the president attempts great achievements, such as remaking Social Security and democratizing the Middle East, while committing insufficient political and financial resources for resounding success. Doug Brattebo expects that Bush will rank in the "C" to "C−" range. Meanwhile, the lead author of this chapter, Jeremy Johnson, maintains that the Bush administration's troubled economic and international policies in concord with its ethical lapses results in a grade no higher than a "D."

In the end, only history can tell who comes nearer the mark. Stay tuned.

Notes

1. As conservative columnist Charles Krauthammer reports, the Project for Excellence in Journalism found that in the first two weeks of October 2004, a key period in the presidential race, 59 percent of stories about President Bush but only 25 percent of stories about Senator Kerry had a negative tone. In addition, 34 percent of Kerry stories were positive, contrasting only 14 percent-positive stories for Bush. See Charles Krauthammer. "Rather Biased" (2005) via http://www.townhall.com/columnists/charleskrauthammer/ck20050114. shtml.
2. Since William McKinley was reelected in 1900, just before the twentieth century started, he is not counted in the list.
3. See, for example, Peter Beinart, "Self Image," *New Republic* (August 2, 2004), p. 6, which laments that while the conservative GOP highlighted moderates at its convention, Democrats promoted liberals at theirs.
4. Fred Barnes, "Double or Nothing: Bush's High-Stakes Second Term," *The Weekly Standard*, January 31, 2005, pp. 10–12, p. 10.
5. "Introduction: George W. Bush's Project," in *High Risk and Big Ambition*, ed. Steven E. Schier, pp. 1–14 (Pittsburgh: University of Pittsburgh Press, 2004), p. 9.
6. Hartmut Wasser, "Politics and Politicians in Current Democratic Systems or: Democracy and its Discontents," paper presented at the International Conference on Democracy and the New Millennium, Malibu. Center for Civic Education (2000), via http://www.civiced.org/german_conference2000_wasser.html.
7. Richard Neustadt, *Presidential Power and the Modern Presidents: The Politics of Leadership from Roosevelt to Reagan* (New York: Free Press, 1990).
8. Jeffrey K. Tulis, *The Rhetorical Presidency* (Princeton: Princeton University Press, 1987).
9. Kenneth T. Walsh, "Bush 2.0," *U.S. News and World Report* 138: 3 (January 24, 2005), pp. 16–22.
10. *Defending the National Interest* (Princeton: Princeton University Press, 1978), p. xi.
11. Stephen Skowronek, *The Politics Presidents Make: Leadership from John Adams to George Bush* (Cambridge, Massachusetts: Harvard University Press, 1997).
12. Skowronek divides American political history into the Jeffersonian (1800–1828), Jacksonian (1828–1860), Republican (1860–1932), and New Deal (1932–1980) regime periods. Of course, each era featured presidents not of the dominant political coalition.
13. Skowronek, *The Politics Presidents Make*, pp. 27–28.
14. Walsh, "Bush 2.0."
15. James A. Stimson, *Tides of Consent: How Public Opinion Shapes American Politics* (New York: Cambridge University Press, 2004).
16. Paul C. Light, *The President's Agenda: Domestic Policy Choice from Kennedy to Clinton* (Baltimore: The Johns Hopkins University Press, 1999).
17. Terence Samuel, "Democrats Still Get a Vote," *U.S. News and World Report* 138: 3 (January 24), p. 22.
18. John Micklethwait and Adrian Wooldridge, *The Right Nation: Conservative Power in America* (New York: Penguin Press, 2004), and for market-related ideas in particular, Daniel Yergin and Joseph Stanislaw, *The Commanding Heights* (New York: Simon & Schuster, 1998). For an empirical treatment of how this impacts the Washington bureaucracy, see Robert Maranto and Karen

M. Hult, "Right Turn? Political Ideology in the Higher Civil Service," *American Review of Public Administration* 34: 2 (June 2004), pp. 199–222.

19. Duncan Currie, "And They're Off!," *The Weekly Standard* (January 31, 2005), pp. 18–19.

20. James P. Pfiffner, *The Strategic Presidency: Hitting the Ground Running* (Lawrence: University Press of Kansas, 1996).

21. John P. Burke, *Presidential Transitions:From Politics to Practice* (Boulder, CO: Lynne Rienner, 2000), pp. 3–4.

22. James P. Pfiffner, *The Strategic Presidency: Hitting the Ground Running.* (Lawrence: University Press of Kansas, 1996).

23. Charles O. Jones, *The Presidency in a Separated System* (Washington: Brookings Institution, 1994).

24. Walsh, "Bush 2.0"; Barnes, "Double or Nothing". See also Andrew Ferguson "Operation Overreach: the downside of big-government conservatism," *The Weekly Standard* 10: 33 (May 16, 2005), pp. 12–14. The conservative Ferguson argues that Bush's over-broad agenda has caused a public backlash by showing the same sort of lack of restraint which once characterized liberalism.

25. Paul Krugman, "The Oblivious Right," *The New York Times*, April 25, 2005.

26. Andrew Ferguson, "Operation Overreach," pp. 12–14.

27. Richard P. Nathan, *The Administrative Presidency.* (New York: John Wiley, 1983); also see Robert Maranto, *Politics and Bureaucracy in the Modern Presidency: Careerists and Appointees in the Reagan Administration* (Westport, CT: Greenwood Press, 1993); Pfiffner, 1996, *The Strategic Presidency.*

28. Donald F. Kettl, *Team Bush* (New York: McGraw-Hill, 2003).

29. Charles E. Walcott and Karen M. Hult, *Governing the White House* (Lawrence: University Press of Kansas, 1995).

30. Ibid., p. 8.

31. Ibid., p. 258 and pp. 261–262. For a related discussion of recent transitions and partisan learning theory, see Douglas M. Brattebo, "The Failure to Govern Oneself: Partisan Learning and Clinton's Flawed Presidential Transition," *White House Studies* 3(3) (August 2003), pp. 291–302.

32. Joseph A. Pika, John Anthony Maltese, and Norman C. Thomas, *The Politics of the Presidency*, 5th ed. (Washington, DC: CQ Press, 2002), p. 401. See also John P. Burke, *Becoming President: the Bush Transition, 2000–2003* (Boulder, CO: Lynne Reinner, 2004).

33. See, for example, Robert Maranto, " 'Government Service is a Noble Calling': President Bush and the U.S. Civil Service," in *Honor and Loyalty: Inside the Politics of the George H. W. Bush Presidency*, ed. Leslie D. Feldman and Rosanna Perotti, pp. 97–108 (Westport, CT: Greenwood, 2002).

34. Franklin Foer, "Closing of the Presidential Mind," *The New Republic* 234(4) (July 5, 2004) pp. 17–21.

35. James W. Riddlesperger and James D. King, "Second Term Presidencies: Experience in Administrative Turnover in the Eisenhower, Nixon, Reagan, and Clinton Years," presented at the 1997 annual meeting of the American Political Science Association, Washington DC, August 28–31.

36. Alfred Zacher, *Trial and Triumph: Presidential Power in the Second Term* (Fort Wayne, IA: Presidential Press, 1996).

37. Richard P. Nathan, *The Plot that Failed* (New York: John Wiley, 1975); and Richard P. Nathan, *The Administrative Presidency.*

38. Dick Morris, *Behind the Oval Office: Winning the Presidency in the Nineties* (New York: Random House, 1997).

39. Ryan C. Hendrickson, *The Clinton Wars: The Constitution, Congress and the War Powers* (Vanderbilt: Vanderbilt University Press, 2004).

40. Paul E. Peterson, "The President's Dominance in Foreign Policy Making," *Political Science Quarterly* 109: 2 (Summer 1994), pp. 215–234.

41. On the division between the domestic and foreign policy presidencies, see Aaron Wildavsky, *"The Two Presidencies," in The Two Presidencies: A Quarter Century Assessment,* ed. Steven Shull, pp. 11–25 (Chicago, IL: Nelson-Hall, 1991); or Richard Ellis and Aaron Wildavsky, *Dilemmas of Presidential Leadership from Washington through Lincoln* (New Brunswick, NJ: Transaction Publishers, 1989).

42. Douglas Kinnard, *President Eisenhower and Strategy Management: A Study in Defense Politics*(Lexington: University of Kentucky Press, 1977).

43. Richard Neustadt, *Presidential Power and the Modern Presidents: The Politics of Leadership from Roosevelt to Reagan* (New York: Free Press, 1990).

44. Victoria A. Farrar-Myers, "The Collapse of an Inherited Agenda: George Bush and the Reagan Foreign Policy Legacy," *White House Studies* 1: 4 (2001); reprinted in Robert P. Watson, ed., *Contemporary Presidential Studies: A Reader* (New York: NOVA, 2002).

45. Terrence Hunt, "A Rocky First 100 Days for New Bush Term," *Washingtonpost. com*, April 29, 2005.

46. According to a May 3, 2005 Gallup Poll, only 48 percent of respondents approved of the president's overall performance.

47. Stanley Renshon, *In His Father's Shadow* (New York: Palgrave, 2004).

48. For example, see pp. x and 42 of Robert Maranto's *Beyond a Government of Strangers* (Lanham, MD: Lexington, 2005).

49. For example, the incumbent party normally loses seats in congressional midterm elections, but in 2002 the Republicans gained seats. Similarly, as noted above, the perceived state of the nation suggested a Gore win in 2000, and a Bush loss in 2004.

Chapter Two

Public Opinion, Presidential Campaigns, and Presidential Governance

Roger H. Davidson

"Public opinion stands out, in the United States, as the great source of power, the master of servants who tremble before it."[1] James Bryce, perhaps the most astute foreign observer of our political life, wrote those words in 1888. Among the "servants" controlled by opinion, Bryce noted, were the president, Congress, and the political parties' vast machinery. The systematic study of public attitudes, unknown in Bryce's day, emerged only in the late 1930s as the tools of market research were applied to the political arena. Today's candidates, officeholders, campaign committees, and media organizations devote vast sums to discovering and interpreting what citizens are thinking on all manner of political subjects.

The 2004 presidential contest was no exception. Journalists, pundits, and attentive citizens, not to mention the candidates and their handlers, understood the commanding role of public opinion and strived to understand and even to shape it. Using 2004 as a case study, this chapter will address enduring patterns of public opinion and their effects upon presidential elections and the dilemmas of campaign strategy and governance. The premise is that many of our concerns about contemporary presidencies can be better understood by recalling two of the most fundamental things we know about public opinion in the United States: first, how public attitudes are distributed within political elites and the general populace; and, second, how intensely those attitudes are held by each.

The broad contours of the 2004 presidential election are familiar and easily summarized. The race between President George W. Bush and Massachusetts Senator John F. Kerry was always viewed as a close call, with victory well within the grasp of either candidate.[2] Published surveys reported mixed results in predicting the outcome. The carefully choreographed party conventions yielded few dividends for Kerry in July but a measurable August "bounce" for Bush. In October's first televised debate, the president's lackluster performance gave Kerry a push. Although Kerry shone in subsequent appearances, Bush was able to refocus his appeals— and so in the end the two men's performances tended to even out. Daily tracking polls during the final month of the campaign showed the race "too close to call"; but the findings tilted toward Bush, with results that ranged from a tie to a 4–6 point lead for the president.[3]

When the actual votes were tallied, President Bush received 51 percent to Senator Kerry's 48 percent. The Electoral College margin was a bit wider: Bush, 286, Kerry, 252. Minor candidates, including Ralph Nader (who drew only a third of a percentage point), proved irrelevant to the outcome. It was a narrow but clear victory for the winner. (Four years earlier, Bush, the disputed Electoral College winner, trailed Al Gore by half a million votes.)

How divided is the nation?

Our nation is portrayed as politically and ideologically divided. Who has not seen the vivid electoral maps of red (Republican) states and blue (Democratic) states? Political commentators—scholars as well as journalists and survey researchers—mostly concur that Americans are split apart to a degree not seen since the Vietnam War era. Politically attentive citizens in 2004 were closely divided in their views (as they had been four years earlier), and those views were often passionately held. And the gap between Democrats and Republicans was measurably wider than at any time in the recent past. "The hard-fought 2004 fight for the presidency," analysts David S. Broder and Richard Morin concluded after the voting, "reflected both deep-seated social divisions in the country and the polarizing effects of Iraq, the economy and the war on terrorism."[4]

Indeed, the agreed-upon "story line" of the 2004 campaign and election was the deep rift within the U.S. public concerning pressing national concerns—the Iraq war and the state of the economy, not to mention such issues as abortion, gay marriage, and stem-cell research. This theme was repeated so often by reporters and commentators that it became the accepted description of contemporary politics. Indeed, after the 2004 balloting 72 percent of the citizens said the nation was more deeply divided on major issues than in recent years—up from 64 percent who felt that way after the truly disputed result four years earlier.[5]

At the same time, however, legitimate questions can be raised about the extent to which the U.S. public is really so divided over political and policy questions. To be sure, many students (including this one) have lamented the rigidity and coarsening of political dialogue among officeholders and staunch partisans. The 2004 outcome evoked gloating among Republicans; and among Kerry's supporters, recriminations and predictions of doom ("moving to Canada," though carelessly threatened, was hardly a serious option). After all, a sharper test had occurred four years earlier—when the election counts, the Electoral College, and the Supreme Court's intervention were all disputed. Yet the public accepted the result without visible protest.

So how acute is the great schism that is alleged? How widespread is it? How important is it? And, if we can pin it down, what is the explanation for it? Finally, what are the consequences for campaigning and governing?

Looking at the red and blue maps

Let's start with those ubiquitous national maps dividing the nation into red and blue states. The visually compelling 2004 Electoral College maps showed vast stretches of President Bush's red states—covering the entire South, Great Plains, and Rocky Mountain regions. Senator Kerry's blue states were clustered in the Northeast (every state north of the Potomac River), the upper Midwest, and the Pacific Rim (every state but Alaska). Such maps are of limited analytical validity, however, inasmuch as they emphasize landmass over population density.

Below the presidential level, the maps become more varied. After all, sizable numbers of liberals reside in red regions, and conservatives in blue domains. The U.S. Senate and House of Representatives are, of course, relatively closely divided between the two parties. State government control is equally widely distributed; nine states have divided-party control of their legislatures. Novelist Walter Kirn, a Montanan, noted wryly that "red Montana, like red Wyoming, red Arizona, and red Kansas, installed a blue leader, thus turning his state purple—a color the eastern analysts seem blind to, but which westerners recognized as the color of sagebrush."[6]

Looking at county-by-county returns, the map turns out to be even more complex and instructive. In only six states did the majority party win every county: the Republican strongholds of Nebraska, Oklahoma, and Utah, the Democratic bastions of Hawaii, Massachusetts, and Rhode Island. All the other states harbored pockets of resistance to statewide trends. Even in the now-solid Republican South, Kerry prevailed in many urban areas: Richmond and Norfolk, VA, Charlotte, NC, Atlanta, GA, Miami and Orlando, FL, New Orleans, LA, Austin, TX, Nashville and Memphis, TN, and Little Rock, AR. Other Democratic enclaves lay in heavily Black and Latino areas. The Grand Old Party (GOP) was strongest in rural areas, even within heavily Democratic states. Along the Pacific Coast, for example, Kerry's huge margins were confined mainly to the populous coastal counties. In reading national or state maps, in short, demography trumps pure geography.

The moderate majority

Surprising evidences of consensus can be found in citizens' political attitudes. Placing themselves on an overall ideological scale, citizens tend to follow a normal bell-shaped curve: most people fall somewhere in the middle, with motivated liberals and conservatives at the edges. The networks' 2004 exit polls found that a plurality of voters, 45 percent, classed themselves as moderates while 34 percent called themselves conservatives, and 21 percent said they were liberals.[7]

The National Election Survey (NES), for example, has since 1972 employed an item asking respondents to place themselves on a seven-point ideological scale running from "extremely liberal" on the left to "extremely conservative" on the right.[8] The responses from the most recent survey (2000) suggest two observations. First, as in prior years, the responses basically conform to a normal curve. Indeed, fully one-third of all respondents placed themselves in the exact center of the ideological spectrum.

Second, however, the curve is nowadays skewed slightly toward the right, or conservative, side of the spectrum. So contemporary Americans, while moderate, are also "a little right of center." If one considers voters rather than all respondents, the curve changes very little. And as Fiorina and his colleagues indicate, the differences between red and blue states, while generally in the predictable directions, are hardly extreme.[9]

Value-laden issues

Another theme in the commentary concerning the 2004 election was how "values" influenced voters' choices. An exit poll found that 22 percent of all voters ranked values at the top of seven options to the question, "Which one issue mattered most in deciding how you voted for president?" Four out of five of these voters went for President Bush.[10] This single response to a vaguely worded survey question ballooned into the favored post-election "story." CNN "Crossfire" co-host Tucker Carlson announced on November 5 that "it is clear that it was not the war on terror, but the issue of what we're calling moral values that drove President Bush and the Republicans to victory this week."[11]

How to interpret such a claim, however, is far from obvious. Terms like "morals" or "values" are not only vague but subject to virtually any interpretation one might give them. After all, everyone's political actions grow out of a foundation of values or priorities. Many pressing issue concerns named by voters in 2004—terrorism, the Iraq war, the economy, health care, or education—carry obvious ethical content. Indeed, when people were asked an open-ended question about what mattered most in their vote, other issues took precedence over "moral values."[12] A nationwide poll by Zogby International found that 42 percent of voters cited the war in Iraq as the "moral issue" that most influenced their candidate choice, more than triple the number who mentioned abortion (13 percent) and quadruple the number who mentioned same-sex marriage (9 percent). "While there may be a solid 20 percent who are very focused on abortion and gay marriage," remarked Tom Perriello, an organizer at the civic advocacy group Res Publica, "for most Americans of faith, there are other moral issues of greater urgency, and that's where the religious middle is."[13]

A sober rejection of the "values" explanation of the voting came from the conservative political scientist James Q. Wilson. Noting that a plurality of the voters—34 percent—cited terrorism and the Iraq war as their most important considerations, Wilson concluded:

> The nation did not undergo a rightward shift in 2004 any more than it had when it elected Reagan in 1980 and reelected him in 1984. The policy

preferences of Americans are remarkably stable, a fact that has been confirmed by virtually every scholar who has looked at the matter.[14]

Moral values are all too often identified with discrete issues that touch upon certain religious doctrines or teachings. In 2004 these included abortion, gay rights, and stem-cell research. Views on such issues, whether pro or con, obviously hinge upon one's ethical priorities. But these are examples of what are termed "wedge issues," in the sense that they have the potential of prying some voters away from their normal or traditional party loyalties. The Bush campaign and its allied groups, including conservative churches, actively mobilized people (including traditional Democrats) who opposed abortion and gay rights. The third issue, stem-cell research, was thought to favor the liberal cause, on the assumption that its potential benefits in medical research would outweigh ethical concerns.

Abortion

Even on seemingly controversial issues, however, broad areas of agreement can be found. Sizable majorities of Americans, for example, support abortion rights while at the same time condoning certain limits on abortions. Fiorina and his colleagues describe public consensus as, "I'm 'Pro-Choice,' But . . ."[15] As they explain,

> Americans are traditionally pragmatic, and they approach even an issue like abortion in a pragmatic fashion. They favor the right to choose, but only a small minority favors the right to choose in every conceivable circumstance.[16]

Citizens' attitudes toward the subject are relatively settled. Abortion, after all, has been on the policy agenda at least since 1973, the year of the Supreme Court's *Roe v. Wade* decision. Nearly two out of three citizens now think that decision should not be overturned. Minorities of people occupy the two extremes on the question: no more than three in ten say that abortion should be legal in all circumstances; fewer than two in ten believe it should be illegal in all circumstances. The majority are "Yes, but" people somewhere between the two extremes.

Inter-group differences on the subject are far narrower than generally believed, Fiorina and his colleagues contend. Most differences are in the expected direction: pro-choice support is higher within blue states (including California) than red states or the South; higher among mainline Protestants than among Catholics or Evangelicals; higher among the un-churched than among the churched; and higher among Democratic identifiers than among Republicans or Independents. But the variations are surprisingly minor. Nor is there a "gender gap" among the general public concerning abortion—even though men and women consistently differ in their attitudes toward a number of other political values.[17]

Continuing ambivalence concerning abortion, especially among core Republican voters and their allied groups, will ensure that additional restrictions will be proposed, voted upon, and perhaps (given a sympathetic White House) placed on the statute books. Courts will continue to face questions of whether such restrictions are compatible with the privacy rights established by *Roe*. The future fate of such cases is a core reason for battles over Senate approval of judicial nominees (recent Supreme Court rulings on the subject have been on 5-to-4 votes). At the same time, a complete reversal of *Roe* would seem beyond the grasp of the anti-abortion extremists—at least if the sentiments of a sizable majority of the U.S. public are kept in mind.

Gay Marriage

Another issue that seemingly divides Americans is the status of gays and lesbians. Many people, as shown by surveys throughout the years, are simply uncomfortable with the idea of same-sex relationships. Opinions are shifting, however, and the trend is toward greater recognition of, and tolerance toward, gays and lesbians. No doubt this has much to do with the fact that ever more gays and lesbians are deciding to "come out" to their families, friends, and fellow workers. Although coming out risks discrimination or isolation, the process is, more often than in the past, a positive experience. A long-established social science axiom is that people are more likely to treat minority-group members favorably if they are personally acquainted with someone of that group. It is especially uncharacteristic for people to shun a gay member of their own family—as has been demonstrated by several prominent political figures who are also parents of gay children.

An issue *du jour* in 2004 was the legalization of gay "marriage"—a controversy stoked when certain states began to recognize such rites. In retaliation, anti-gay groups in eleven states sponsored constitutional referendums—all of them successful—defining marriage as solely the union of a man and a woman. Overall, citizens were opposed to the notion of same-sex marriage: 57 percent opposed it, while 32 percent were in favor.[18] However, people varied in the importance they placed upon the issue. Nearly two-thirds of those polled said that gay marriage would be only somewhat or not at all an issue in their voting. But 34 percent—and 67 percent of regular churchgoers—ranked gay marriage as a very important issue.

People opposed to gay unions no doubt swelled the ranks of voters, especially in the eleven states where the issue was actually on the ballot. Their turnout no doubt had repercussions beyond the actual ballot measures on the subject. Although all of these ballot measures won handily, only three of the states were considered pivotal for the presidential contest: Michigan, Oregon, and Ohio. Kerry narrowly won the first two states, which leaves Ohio, where Bush won a slim, contested victory—making that state the 2004 equivalent of Florida four years earlier.

Stem-Cell Research

A final potentially divisive issue had to do with stem-cell research. On the one hand, research with stem cells is touted as a potential road to treatments for such debilitating diseases as Parkinson's or Alzheimer's. High-profile individuals—Nancy Reagan, Michael J. Fox, and the late Christopher Reeve—have joined the scientific community in stressing the life-enhancing possibilities of such research. On the other hand, some conservatives have sought to link the issue with pro-life concerns—under the theory that live stem cells are the products of aborted human embryos. The particulars of this debate surely elude most citizens; but the question was initially thought salient enough to benefit liberal candidates who advocated further stem-cell research.

Predictable divisions appeared over whether research should be permitted—liberals, college graduates, and non-churchgoers tended to favor it, while conservatives, evangelical Protestants and white Catholics tended to be opposed. For example, 72 percent of liberal Democrats supported such research; fewer than half that many conservative Republicans did.[19] However, sentiment has been shifting toward encouraging such research. By 2004, rising public awareness of the issue found a narrow majority (52 percent) favoring the use of stem cells, a gain of 9 percent from an earlier 2002 study. The positive shift held for all categories of respondents. In 2004, the issue simply lacked traction for either side of the debate; compared to other pressing issues, this one was simply not very compelling for the average voter. Growing support for stem-cell research, however, kept the issue alive beyond the election period.

Summary

All three of these issues could well have benefited Senator Kerry, if the views of the general public were the only ones at issue. A *Time* survey conducted two weeks before the election found pluralities of respondents saying that their views were closer to Kerry's than to Bush's on these three questions.[20] Concerning abortion, Fiorina and his colleagues find "nuanced popular views on the issue reflected in majority approval of regulating some aspects of abortion . . . and minimal partisan disagreement about the issue at the mass level as contrasted with vitriolic conflict at the elite level."[21] As for gay rights, they conclude on a hopeful note: despite current popular rejection of gay marriages or even civil unions, "we do not believe that many [Americans] have any wish for vitriolic conflict over the issue." Indeed, they suggest the possibility of "obvious compromises that we think might attract the support of majorities of Americans—most obviously the rights and duties of civil union without the name."[22]

It goes without saying, however, that gay rights, and probably abortion, are most salient for voters opposed to the issues—especially Republican stalwarts, political and religious conservatives, and voters age 65 and older.[23] Fiorina and his colleagues are careful to note that political elites exhibit "vitriolic conflict" over abortion, and that activist views would probably keep compromises on gay unions off the political agenda, at least in the near term. The 2004 pre-election *Time* and Pew surveys both noted that sizable minorities of people said that they could not vote for a candidate who disagreed with them on these very questions. A Pew Research Center study three months before the balloting showed that a huge proportion of certain Bush voters (78 percent) cited moral values as a high voting priority; but even they ranked abortion and gay marriage below terrorism, Iraq, the economy, and education. In contrast, relatively fewer swing voters (57 percent) or Kerry voters (55 percent) placed such emphasis upon moral values; among these respondents abortion and gay marriage ranked near the bottom of their issue concerns.[24]

Partisans and other true believers

Political activists—officeholders, volunteers, and strong partisan identi-fiers—cluster toward the left and right ends of the ideological spectrum. Ever since the 1950s, for example, studies have shown that delegates to the two parties' national nominating conventions are markedly to the left or to the right of the parties' voters, much less of the general voting public.[25] "At every Democratic convention," two analysts explained in 2004, "the dele-gates hold more liberal positions than the rank-and-file Democrats, just as Republican delegates are always more conservative than their voters. That is the nature of political activists."[26]

Four out of ten of the Democratic delegates, for example, considered themselves "very or somewhat liberal," compared with 33 percent of their party's voters and 20 percent of the whole voting public. Only 3 percent thought that the Iraq war was worth the loss of life and other costs, compared (at that time) to 12 percent of Democratic voters and 36 percent of the voting public. The delegates' opinions concerning abortion, gay marriage, the death penalty, and the war on terrorism differed markedly from those of the voting public, although on other issues the gap was less noticeable. The Republican convention's delegates—not so different from their Democratic counterparts in certain demographic respects—were at least as distant from average voters, but in a rightward direction.

Disparities between the party elites, and apparently between these elites and the general public, were by 2004 a gaping chasm. At a moment when citizens were still closely divided over the Iraqi war, no less than 93 percent of the 2004 Democratic convention delegates were convinced that the war was a mistake. Republican activists were at least as equally skewed to the right-hand side of the issues: Only four out of ten Republican loyalists in 2003 agreed that "government should help more needy people"—compared with 72 percent of Democrats and 50 percent of Independents.

Two things must be understood about these political activists. First, although we routinely describe these people as political "elites"—perhaps no more than 10 percent of the electorate—they are by no means a tiny or insignificant group. Media reporting of campaigns tends to focus on (what else?) expensive media advertising; but recent experience has taught campaign professionals that Get Out the Vote (GOTV) efforts are more effective in luring people to the polls. And while sophisticated methods can be employed (automated phone calls, for instance), there is no substitute for localized, personal contact with potential voters. According to Yale political scientists Donald P. Green and Alan S. Gerber, face-to-face canvassing raises turnout by 7 to 12 percentage points, and is more cost-effective than alternative media-based campaigns.[27]

Such personalized appeals require legions of volunteers. Democratic organizations and allied groups in 2004 mobilized hundreds of thousands of volunteers to canvass swing states.

Republicans were even more vigorous in recruiting volunteers. Party officials claimed after the balloting to have amassed "a corps of roughly 1.4 million party stalwarts who have proved they can offset traditional Democratic advantages at the grassroots level."[28] The party will build upon these recruits to wage campaigns in 2006 and beyond. These cadres may not look much like the old-fashioned party machines—many are not even formally attached to the party apparatus—but at the grassroots level they perform most of the traditional partisan functions.

Second, these activists constitute the "attentive public" for politics. As a class, they are more knowledgeable and outspoken in their views than the average citizen[29]; by definition they are more intense in their preferences and more fervently committed to their causes. Citizens who are activists are thus more likely to volunteer their time or donate their money to causes they espouse. If we array *intensities* of preferences, rather than simply the preferences themselves, on an ideological scale—left to right—the result is very different from the "normal" bell-shaped curve that describes the populace as a whole. People with intense convictions on political matters cluster at the edges of the scale. Such people might even be described as political "extremists," although in the United States the distance between the ideological poles is considerably narrower than, say, in European nations with vibrant socialist traditions countered by some groups that can best be described as quasi-fascist.

Politicians both covet and fear such voters, relying on their support while realizing that an errant statement or vote could easily destroy their loyalty. One result is that officeholders spend more time responding to their needs than to those of the less committed majorities. Especially between elections, Jacobs and Shapiro argue, contemporary presidents and legislators routinely ignore the public's policy preferences to follow their own political philosophies, and those of their party's activists, contributors, and interest group allies.[30] This is no doubt the reason that, for example, gun control legislation in the United States is infrequently pursued or successfully implemented. Even though some seven out of ten Americans favor restrictions on weapons, such initiatives are opposed by a vocal, narrowly focused, and well-financed minority. In other words, committed minorities normally trump indifferent majorities.

Partisan realignment—noticeable also in presidential voting patterns—is probably the root cause of the current surge in party loyalty. The Republican party is more uniformly conservative than it used to be. In the

South, the more conservative areas now tend to elect Republicans, not Democrats. Southern Democrats are increasingly confined to Black enclaves—in the cities and the rural Black belts. Outside the South, many areas once represented by GOP liberals—Northeastern and Mid-Atlantic precincts, for example—have been captured by Democrats. The decline of conservative Democrats and moderate Republicans, especially in the House, underlies much of the ideological cohesion within, and chasm between, today's national parties.[31] A prime victim of this partisan repositioning is the now-shrunken ideological center—the liberal Republicans and conservative Democrats who once could be relied upon to make the compromises, broker the deals, and build cross-party alliances to reach policy decisions.

To what extent have these ideological and policy cleavages of the political class seeped down to the rank-and-file party identifiers and the general public? If we can believe the surveys of rank-and-file party identifiers, it appears that their views are in fact more polarized than in past elections.[32]

Some analysts argue that the voters' partisanship mainly reflects the sharper partisan rhetoric in the political marketplace. If candidates send more partisan messages, if officeholders stake out more uncompromising positions—so the reasoning goes—then citizens have little choice but to line up on one side or the other. Also, citizens-who enjoy a richer media menu than in the past—can choose outlets . . . accounts of political events.[33]

Campaigning: core voters versus swing voters

Presidential campaigns must clearly mobilize the parties' most loyal followers—the "core voters." Such people are more committed to the parties' objectives; they are more likely to act upon their convictions—to volunteer, to donate money, to turn out on election day. Many campaign professionals, and more than a few political scientists, thus advise that campaigns focus primarily on raising the enthusiasm and the turnout of such loyalists.

However, in close elections—such as the most recent presidential contests—campaign managers can ill afford to ignore the uncommitted middle of the ideological spectrum. In June 2004 the Pew Research Center reported that about one-fifth of the "certain voters" were undecided about their choice. Later surveys and exit polls suggested that the number of true undecided voters had shrunk to between a quarter and half that number. Although a smaller portion of the electorate than in recent presidential election years, such voters are still numerous enough to sway election outcomes. These voters present a twofold challenge: they are more likely to be swayed by candidates than by the parties and their programs; and of course they are less likely than dedicated partisans to show up on election day.

Thus the campaigners' dilemmas are: How do you motivate your "base" without alienating undecided potential voters? And, how do you propel both kinds of citizens to the polling booths to vote for your ticket? Surveys are far less able to answer these questions than to record underlying attitudes.

In the 2004 campaign, the president's handlers opted for targeting core voters over swing voters, even in those states considered in play by both camps. As the late surveys indicated a dwindling number of undecided citizens (5 percent in some polls), the GOP strategy focused on getting out the vote in friendly precincts, and on mobilizing hordes of voters through churches, small businesses, gun owners, and so forth. Although Bush made inroads among swing groups, *Los Angeles Times* analyst Ronald Brownstein observed that "exit polls and voting results in key counties across the nation suggested he won his second term mostly by increasing the GOP strength in places where the party was already strong—especially rural, small-town and fast-growing ex-urban communities."[34]

Election totals and exit polls underscore the Bush campaign's success in mobilizing core GOP supporters (see table 2.1). Republican partisans,

Table 2.1   Exit poll: Groups' voting for president, 2004

Social / Political grouping	Bush %	Kerry %	% of all voters
Party affiliation			
Republican	94	6	39
Independent	48	49	19
Democrat	12	88	40
Party ideology			
Conservative Republicans	96	4	27
Other Republicans	13	89	13
Conservative Independents	77	22	6
Other Independents	36	60	13
Other Democrats	19	81	18
Liberal Democrats	5	95	22
Political ideology			
Conservative	82	18	39
Moderate	45	54	29
Liberal	19	79	32
Region			
East	42	57	24
Midwest	54	45	24
South	57	42	32
West	49	50	20
Locality			
City	43	56	36
Suburb	52	47	32
Small town	58	41	20
Rural	62	37	12

Continued

Table 2.1 Continued

Social / Political grouping	Bush %	Kerry %	% of all voters
Gender			
Men	53	46	49
Women	49	50	51
Gender and marital status			
Married men	59	40	31
Single men	40	58	16
Married women	57	42	30
Single women	35	64	19
Race / ethnicity			
White	57	42	79
Black	14	86	10
Latino	45	54	5
Asian	34	64	3
Age			
18–29	43	55	20
30–44	52	47	32
45–64	54	45	36
65 or older	55	45	12
Voting status			
First-time voter	42	57	11
Voted before	53	46	89
Education			
Less than college	54	45	48
College degree or more	49	50	52
Religion			
Protestant	61	38	51
Catholic	55	44	25
Jewish	26	74	4
Attendance at religious services			
Weekly or more	65	34	42
Less than that	42	57	58
Gun ownership			
Own guns	65	34	36
Don't own any	43	56	64
Do you think the country is on the right or wrong track?			
Right track	89	11	51
Wrong track	11	87	49
Do you think the situation in Iraq was worth going to war, or not?			
Worth it	88	12	50
Not worth it	14	84	50

Source: *Los Angeles Times* Exit Poll (5,154 voters interviewed in 136 polling places November 2, 2004, including 3,357 California voters in 50 polling places. Ronald Brownstein, "Democrats' Losses Go Far Beyond One Defeat," *Los Angeles Times* (November 4, 2004), pp. A1, 17.

especially those describing themselves as conservatives, were more faithful to their candidate than their left-wing opposites. Bush captured nearly two out of three votes in rural areas, three out of five in small towns, two out of three gun owners, and two out of three regular church-goers. He topped his 2000 performance among many social groupings, including white Protestants, Catholics, men, married people, whites, and older or more affluent voters, suburban dwellers, people making more than $50,000 a year, and those with less formal education (see table 2.2). Moreover, Bush picked up votes within several groupings traditionally

Table 2.2　Exit polls: How the presidential candidates fared 2000–2004: Bush's performance, 2004 compared with 2000

Overall	*Republicans*	*Democrats*
Total Vote	+ 3	0
Men	+ 2	+ 2
Women	+ 5	+ 3
Ideological identification		
Liberals	− 0	− 5
Moderates	+ 1	− 2
Conservatives	+ 3	+ 2
Race and Ethnicity		
Whites	+ 4	+ 1
Blacks	+ 3	+ 2
Hispanics	+ 12	+ 11
Age		
18 to 29	− 1	− 6
30 to 44	+ 4	+ 2
45 to 59	+ 2	0
60 or older	+ 7	+ 5
Family Status		
Married	+ 2	+ 2
Unmarried	+ 2	− 1
Have children under 18	+ 1	0
Gay, lesbian, or bisexual	− 2	− 3
Religion		
All Protestants	+ 1	0
White Protestants	+ 4	+ 2
Catholics	+ 5	+ 2
Jews	+ 6	+ 5
Weekly churchgoers	+ 2	0
Size of Place		
Cities over 500K	+ 13	+ 11
Cities, towns 50 K–500K	+ 9	+ 8
Suburbs	+ 3	0
Cities, towns 10K–50K	− 9	− 10
Rural areas	0	− 3
Education		
Not a HS graduate	+ 10	+ 9
HS graduate	+ 3	+ 1

Continued

Table 2.2 Continued

Overall	Republicans	Democrats
Some college	+ 3	− 1
College graduate	+ 1	− 1
Post-graduate education	0	− 3
Family Income		
Under $15K	− 1	− 6
$15K to $30K	+ 1	− 3
$30K to $50K	+ 1	− 1
$50K to $75K	+ 5	+ 3
$75 K to $100K	+ 3	0
$100K and over	+ 4	+ 2

Source: Marjorie Connelly, "How Americans Voted: A Political Portrait," *New York Times* (November 7, 2004), p. D4. The survey included 13,600 voters and was conducted by Edison Media Research and Mitofsky International for the National Election Pool, a consortium of ABC News, The Associated Press, CBS News, CNN, Fox News, and NBC News. The large sample size makes it possible to isolate views of some groups, such as Jews and Asians, whose share of the populace is too small for analysis by the usual telephone surveys.

linked to the Democratic party. Although he did not win these groups, he posted double-digit percentage gains among Hispanics and city dwellers, along with notable gains among women and Jews. Needless to add, GOP voters overwhelmingly supported the Iraq war and believed the nation was "on the right track"—the latter despite the widespread notion that conservatives were anguished over the nation's moral decline.

Democratic campaigners countered with efforts to register thousands of new voters, mainly young people. This no doubt paid off: new voters and those 18 to 29 years of age were among the strongest Kerry supporters. Within the traditional Democratic base, also, there were a few bright spots: Kerry improved upon Gore's performance among ideological liberals and moderates, small towns, rural Democrats, highly educated voters, and those whose family income placed them in the economic underclass. Among most other Democratic groupings, Kerry's performance lagged behind Gore's of four years before. Although women went narrowly for him, the so-called "gender gap" (the gap between men's and women's votes) was in 2004 a mere four points, far below that in recent elections. While losing the vote of men, however, Kerry actually won handily among single men and women. And as Bush gained proportionally among Democratic-leaning groups, Kerry fell behind—for example, among Blacks, Hispanics, Catholics, Jews, and city dwellers.

During the campaign the two contenders at one and the same time signaled to their most loyal supporters and to moderate or undecided members of the electorate. The most glaring example concerned the Iraq war. Anger over the war's rationale and its execution was a defining issue for Democratic loyalists, who initially bonded with former Vermont Governor

Howard Dean because he was so clearly a dissenter. Yet although Kerry—the eventual candidate—lambasted the administration's conduct of the war, he differed little from the president on key Iraq questions. After all, Kerry had voted for the war (who knows whether he later regretted it?)—a fact that hampered his appeals to anti-war Democrats. Nor did his prescriptions for future U.S. policy depart from the administration's evolving strategy: tough it out in Iraq, arm the troops more effectively, and hope for salvation when Iraqis themselves take charge.

Even on the seemingly divisive issue of gay marriage, Bush and Kerry were actually not so far apart. True, Bush backed a constitutional amendment banning gay marriage (a view not shared by Vice President Dick Cheney), and Kerry did not. But the amendment has little chance of adoption, so it served both candidates mainly as a device for signaling fealty to their core voters. Both candidates in fact supported "civil unions" though opposing legalizing of gay marriage—a distinction more of semantics than actuality, but again near the midpoint of public opinion. Exit polls revealed that 60 percent of voters favored some form of same-sex union (35 percent favored civil unions, 25 percent gay marriage), whereas 37 percent would deny gay couples any legal status.[35]

Both parties' camps succeeded impressively in persuading people to vote.[36] But the opposing parties' strategies diverged. The GOP action plan stressed repeated personal appeals within voting areas and groups already known to be loyal or leaning to the GOP.[37] The Kerry effort relied heavily upon friendly independent organizations like Rock the Vote (founded in 1990 by the music industry), MoveOn, Americans Coming Together (ACT), the New Voters Project, MTV's Choose or Lose, and something called Voter Virgin. The Democrats' campaign was buoyed by media and rock stars: on election eve, in pivotal Cleveland, Ohio, Kerry skipped walking precincts to appear at a rock concert headlined by Bruce Springsteen. Hundreds of thousands of people were added to the election rolls. Not all these registrants voted, and not all of the new voters were Democratic; but the survey numbers suggest that Senator Kerry benefited from the effort.

Nonetheless, observers judged that the Democratic effort lacked much of the neighbor-to-neighbor quality that was so successful in the 1990s. Before he was elected Democratic party chairman, Howard Dean remarked on "Meet the Press,"

> We [the Democrats] ran the best grassroots campaign that I've seen in my lifetime. They ran a better one. Why? Because we sent 14,000 people into Ohio from elsewhere. They had 14,000 people from Ohio talking to their neighbors, and that's how you win in rural states and in rural America.[38]

The Democrats' reliance on celebrities and "quick-hit canvassing," complained a progressive foundation official, is

> the central problem at the heart of the Democratic Party's political culture. [It] has no time or patience for the complex work needed to listen to Americans to

understand their range of views and positions, and to engage them on their deepest interests.[39]

The critique, in short, is that the Democrats failed to contend for the pivotal middle of the American electorate. Even if true, this shortcoming is arguably more a matter of technique than of structure: as we have noted, the Democratic elites are no farther from the vital center than are their Republican counterparts.

The Candidates: Bush versus Kerry

The final variable in the voting equation is the candidates themselves—their personalities, their character, their leadership strengths and weaknesses, their ways of connecting not only with committed partisans but also with average voters. Sitting presidents, and to a lesser extent non-incumbent challengers, are the subjects of intense media attention and coverage. Journalists all too rarely probe deeply into the candidates' attributes; often they fail to ask questions that might reveal basic leadership qualities, or they ask the wrong questions. Or the candidates evade the questions in order to restate their own themes. But even citizens distracted by non-political amusements or concerns (an all-too-common phenomenon these days) can glean general impressions of the candidates by watching them on television or hearing what is said about them. This is especially true for incumbent presidents, who are the most visible individuals in the world. Notably, only 2 percent of the respondents in the pre-election *Los Angeles Times* poll of likely voters had no opinion about President Bush's performance in office.[40]

What do voters expect from a president? Two leading possibilities are character/strength of leadership, and upholding issues deemed important by the voter. The *Los Angeles Times* poll mentioned above found that Bush and Kerry voters saw different qualities in their preferred candidates. Likely Bush voters emphasized character and leadership over stands on the issues by a margin of 48 percent to 26 percent; Kerry's supporters emphasized issue stands, 61 percent to 17 percent for personal characteristics. (Likely voters as a whole also chose issues over leadership, 44 percent to 32 percent.)[41]

Assessments of the two candidates on the part of likely voters just before the election are summarized in table 2.3 President Bush's performance ratings were not exceptional: citizens were equally divided on his job as president and troubled by his stewardship of the economy and the war in Iraq. A plurality of voters favored Kerry rather than Bush to handle leading domestic issues— even the presumed hot-button matters of abortion and gay marriage.

President Bush, on the other hand, won the image contest about keeping the nation safe from terrorism. Whatever the facts of his performance— critics held, for example, that the Iraq venture was a needless and even harmful diversion from the campaign against terrorism—a majority of voters regarded Bush as a strong leader who had the nation's safety at heart.

Table 2.3 Intended voters' views of the candidates

Question: How would you rate the president on handling

	Approve %	Disapprove %
The war on terrorism	53	44
His job as president	49	49
The situation in Iraq	48	50
The economy	47	51

Question: Which candidate would best handle

	Bush %	Kerry %	Both %	Neither %
Taxes	45	47	1	7
Social issues such as abortion, gay marriage	45	48	1	3
Creating jobs in the United States	40	51	1	5
The health care situation	39	50	1	7

Question: Which statement applies to George W. Bush or John F. Kerry?

Will keep the country safe from terrorism	53%	37%	3	6
Will be a strong leader for the country	51	44	2	2
Has honesty and integrity as president	47	44	3	5
Will develop a successful plan for Iraq	47	40	1	8
Will strengthen nation's economy	42	49	2	5
Will build respect around the world	42	50	1	5

Source: Los Angeles Times Poll of likely voters (October 21–24, 2004), Los Angeles Times (October 26, 2004), A13.

Conversely, Senator Kerry failed to convince a majority that he would be a steady, consistent leader—the very crux of his campaign task.

The president's positive image as a wartime leader was the payoff of a long-term, post-September 11, 2001, White House effort highlighted by declaring war on terrorists and portraying Bush as a wartime chieftain. Such a declaration, Jamieson and Waldman observe, was a notable instance of "framing" a public issue articulating and disseminating an interpretation, or way of thinking, that can be accepted by the press and the public.[42] Significantly, the White House vigorously exploited the wartime theme to cloak a variety of responses, extending from military assaults in Afghanistan and Iraq to singularly repressive actions involving alleged terrorists who were held indefinitely in a string of secret prisons for "detainees."

From the perspective of the Oval Office, wartime rhetoric had payoffs both immediate and long lasting. Especially in the immediate aftermath of a crisis event such as the terrorist attacks, a militant posture on the president's part would evoke a "rally" response from the general public. And in history's longer frame, wartime presidents are more apt to be accorded the laurels of greatness than those who serve in more benign times.

The very potency of the war metaphor, however, made it a high-risk venture that could undo those executives who utilize it. If major military assaults are contemplated, opposition will likely be heard (as happened prior to the Iraq venture) not only from anti-war groups but also from government bureaucracies whose cultures encourage skepticism about military deployments.

If there was a pivotal issue regarding the candidates themselves, it was leadership strengths and the ability to protect the nation from terrorist attacks. Here Bush, whether his policies were endorsed or not, projected strength and resolution—and in any event he was regarded as a known quantity. Kerry, for all his announced plans and policies, came across to many as a less resolute individual (the GOP's "flip-flop" portrayal of him may have taken its toll)—or, more charitably, as a more complex personality.

If Bush won points on image, Kerry seemed to have the edge on a majority of the issues on voters' minds. Voters, after all, expressed very mixed assessments of Bush's performance in office, and of his handling of the Iraq situation. Yet Kerry was preferred in dealing with such issues as the economy, job creation, health care, and even such signature Bush initiatives as Iraq policy, taxation, and social problems like abortion and gay marriage. As with Presidents Ronald Reagan and the elder George Bush, voters apparently endorsed the individual rather than his specific policies.

Governing: from the Center or from the Edges?

The same dilemma affects the winning candidate's governing strategy. Can presidents govern primarily from the middle, or must they appeal to the "extremes" represented by their most loyal supporters? Obviously presidents must at least appear to do both, sending cues and signals to both cadres of voters. But what is the most effective mixture, and what are the consequences for the nation's policies and future electoral politics?

Recent presidencies illustrate how difficult it is to achieve such a balance. Bill Clinton campaigned as a "new Democrat," which meant he was a moderate who was not afraid to break with his party's orthodoxies. He did so in several high-profile cases—for example, the North American Free Trade Agreement (NAFTA) in 1994, the Defense of Marriage Act (DOMA) in 1996, and welfare reform (also 1996). Yet the course followed by his administration was decidedly liberal—especially regarding the mid-level issues that normally fall below the radar screens of the national media. Needless to add, the Clinton presidency was extraordinarily divisive—even provoking a partisan attempt in 1998–1999 to remove him from office.

Clinton's successor, George W. Bush, campaigned in 2000 as a "compassionate conservative." Although the circumstances of his victory might well have dictated a middle-of-the-road course, he nonetheless pursued a rigorously ideological agenda, always aimed toward his most loyal supporters. With very few exceptions—the No Child Left Behind Act (2002) and the Medicare prescription drug plan (2003) among them—his legislative program was greeted with relentless partisan warfare. Needless to add, those decisions that lay largely beyond mass media scrutiny—sub-Cabinet and circuit court appointments, as well as regulatory policy changes (e.g., reversing Clinton-era environmental rules)—adhered strictly to economic or social conservatism.

The events of September 11, 2001, transformed Bush's presidency, and may well have saved him from his father's one-term fate.[43] Although his job ratings were sagging before the Trade Center attacks, they soared thereafter in a prolonged "rally effect." By early 2004, with the Iraq war seemingly bogged down, presidential approval again began a downward course. A *Washington Post / ABC* News poll in January 2004 found that, with the conspicuous exceptions of the fight against terrorism and the Iraq venture, the public believed Democrats would do a better job on a wide range of domestic issues—such as the economy, health insurance, Medicare, the budget deficit, immigration, and taxes.[44] Bush had even lost the advantage on education policy that he enjoyed the year before. On the question of who was trusted to handle the nation's leading problems, Bush enjoyed a 1-point advantage – down from 18 points.

Mandates of 2004?

What of Bush's second term? Unlike 2000, his victory in 2004 was clear and substantially unblemished. The president told reporters that his reelection was a ratification of his Iraq policy. "Well, we had an accountability moment," he said, "and that's called the 2004 elections."[45] Survey results, as we have seen, do not support the president's claim; and in any event, on the question of Iraq voters had little to choose between the candidates.

What was the 2004 election all about? Given the preceding discussion, the election was about many things. No single factor or issue was sufficient to explain the outcome, much less to interpret what the U.S. public said to those whom they placed in office. However, the citizens' concerns were fairly clearly expressed in a number of surveys and exit polls: safety from terrorism; the state of the economy, especially job creation; and, for a sizeable minority, the nation's moral condition.

Bush and his supporters quickly proclaimed an electoral "mandate" for a bold second-term agenda: privatizing Social Security accounts; further lowering (maybe even simplifying) taxes; limiting tort damage claims; stuffing the federal courts with judges who combined activism and conservatism; and installing democratic regimes in the Middle East. Core groups within the GOP orbit were equally quick to proclaim victory for their favorite agenda items, including a ban on same-sex marriage, further limits on abortion, looser environmental restrictions, entrepreneurial incentives, and "family values," among many others.

Claiming mandates comes naturally to politicians; but political scientists are just as naturally skeptical of the concept and the claims made for it. As Robert A. Dahl puts it, "[N]o elected leader, including the president, is uniquely privileged to say what an election means—nor to claim that the election has conferred on the president a mandate to enact the particular policies the president supports."[46]

The president's second-term prospects faded quite early. "What's been clear and surprising in the weeks after the election," said Democratic pollster Geoffrey Garin, "is that Bush got virtually no bounce and no honeymoon from his victory. 'What seems pretty clear is that there was nothing particularly healing about Bush's victory.' "[47] Skepticism was not limited to Bush's foes: by more than two to one, the general public—and even Republicans—rejected the idea of a 2004 Republican mandate.[48] And people were closely divided over whether the second Bush administration would deliver what was promised in 2000: to be a "uniter, not a divider." Asked about the prospect of the next four years, 48 percent said Bush would divide the country, while 40 percent thought he would bring America together. William Schneider summed up the problem: "the country remains divided—even over whether Bush will continue to divide the country."[49]

Bush's second-term agenda would not be an easy sell, on Capitol Hill or in the country at large. As a lame-duck president, his political clout is destined to fade. The Republican ranks, historically solid, are sure to balk at certain elements of the Bush agenda—particularly Social Security restructuring, budget cuts in popular programs, and the like. Democrats, despite their reduced forces, expressed undiminished resolve in opposing the president's initiatives, especially his federal court nominations. A prediction for the coming years would be: the same inter-party conflict, but even more so.

In the long term, too, Bush's war proclamation risks losing its potency over time. Public support for the Korean and Vietnam wars faded as the conflicts dragged on without demonstrable victory. The first President Bush presided over a brief and putatively successful war in Iraq in 1991; but the rally effect did not survive economic worries the following year, and he was turned out of office. Gradual erosion would seem the more likely threat to George W. Bush throughout his second term, and in history's ultimate judgment. The outcome, of course, hinges upon still unfolding events; but perhaps prophetic are the rising numbers of citizens who express doubt over the war's value. By year's end 2004, a clear majority (56 percent) of the public believed that the Iraq conflict's costs outweighed its benefits—although nearly six in ten saw no alternative to keeping our military forces there.[50]

Party Fissures

Internal divisions within the two parties pose other potential barriers for enactment of the president's unfinished agenda. In building their impressive majority coalition, the Republicans—like their predecessors, the

Jacksonians, the post-Civil War "Grand Old Party," and Franklin D. Roosevelt's New Deal coalition—have cobbled together a spectacularly mobilized but disparate combination of elements.

The party's main groups are the Economic Republicans and the Social Republicans. The economic wing forms the party's historic core, dating back to the nineteenth century's Gilded Age. Its interests are financial and entrepreneurial, and its policy prescriptions are written all over the Bush agenda: tax reductions, investment incentives, tightened bankruptcy rules, tort reform (especially limits on medical malpractice suits), privatized Social Security accounts, rollbacks of government regulations, and even amnesty for illegal immigrants (needed for jobs shunned by citizens). The Bush administration has benefited business entrepreneurs and higher-income Americans generally. Voting surveys show that these traditional Republicans handsomely reward the party's candidates with votes and financial support.

The party's second face is what one commentator calls " 'Sam's Club' Republicans."[51] These are middle or lower-income people who respond to the party's pledge to protect their families from terrorists and its seemingly shared traditional social and moral values of home and family. Not a few of these are voters from groups once loyal to the Democrats—for example, southern whites and conservative Catholics. Even if they are comforted by the party's professed values, these citizens have unmet material needs that recent tax cuts have not assuaged: higher pay, job security, affordable health care, strong schools, retirement benefits, and effective government services. Some liberals argue that the GOP's populist conservatism is little more than a con game that diverts such voters from recognizing their real economic and social interests.[52] This thesis is at least debatable; but the near-term challenge for the GOP will be to reconcile its conservative economic policy agenda with the needs of its under-class supporters and converts.

Some of the Bush administration's second-term roadblocks echoed this division in the GOP ranks. Bush's solution to the Social Security system's projected financial crisis was to shift people to private securities accounts— an option that would expose them to the vagaries of the stock market and that, as the White House was forced to admit, would do nothing to solve the system's financial problems. Although financial institutions stood to benefit from a massive influx of Social Security investments, the party's lower-income supporters remained apprehensive. Despite concerted White House efforts, including a campaign tour by the president, a *Washington Post*-ABC News survey in May 2005 found support for Bush's handling of the issue was just 31 percent.[53] A similar division occurred in the 2005 revision of bankruptcy procedures (P.L.109–31), a prize for banks and credit card companies that promised to make life more difficult for those in financial need.

The opposition Democrats—pushed into a deeper minority hole by the 2004 House and Senate contests—are by turns disheartened or panic-stricken. Like the Kerry campaign, the party's response to Bush is schizoid. One wing of the party counseled moderation—following Clinton's (and British Prime Minister Tony Blair's) "third way." Such a party would subordinate ideology in order to court centrist swing voters, advertising a brand of "tough-minded liberalism." Other Democrats—including most in the party's Capitol Hill caucuses—insisted that Bush's ideological program should be resisted at all costs. Such a message, of course, resonated with the party's core supporters—those who, for example, opposed the Iraqi war from the start and who view Bush as Darth Vader bent on destroying the federal programs they revere.

A harbinger of Bush's second term could be a House vote to ease the president's curbs on stem-cell research. The bill, pressed by a bipartisan coalition, was passed by a 238–194 margin—which included most Democrats and fifty Republicans. Party leaders claimed to have the votes to pass the measure in the Senate. Bush threatened to veto the bill (his first in five years), claiming that it "would take us across a critical ethical line."[54] Bush's resistance was in character; but it would prove unpopular: by this time a healthy majority of citizens favored conducting stem-cell research.[55] Democrats and Independents overwhelmingly favored such research, and for the first time Republicans were equally divided.

The Bush presidency may well encounter more such obstacles to its legislative objectives. Democrats will instinctively rally to oppose those initiatives and nominations that serve hard-line conservative goals. Perhaps more importantly for the president's record, his Republican allies could well diverge over measures that threaten to divide the party's economic elite from its legions of lower- and middle-class supporters.

Notes

1. James Bryce, *The American Commonwealth, Vol 1* (New York: Capricorn Books ed., 1959), p. 296.
2. Adam Nagourney and Janet Elder, "Poll Shows Tie: Concerns Cited on Both Rivals," *New York Times* (October 19, 2004), p. A1; Ronald Brownstein, "Voters Still Split Sharply, and Evenly," *Los Angeles Times* (October 26, 2004), p. A1.
3. "Charting the Campaign," *Washington Post*, October 26, 2004, washington-post.com; Pew Research Center for the People and the Press, "Survey Report: Kerry Support Rebounds, Race Again Even," September 16, 2004.
4. David S. Broder and Richard Morin, "Four Years Later, Voters More Deeply Split," *Washington Post*, November 3, 2004, p. A1.
5. Cited by William Schneider, "Divided We Stand," *National Journal* 36, December 4, 2004, p. 3644.
6. Walter Kirn, "What Color Is Montana?" *New York Times Magazine*, January 2, 2005, p. 14.
7. Cited in E. J. Dionne, Jr., "The New Liberalism," *Washington Post*, January 14, 2005, p. A19.
8. The National Election Studies (NES) is a survey and data-dissemination organization that since 1952 has conducted biennial election-year surveys since 1952. Unless otherwise specified, NES data in this chapter are from the 2000 survey.
9. See Morris P. Fiorina with Samuel J. Abrams and Jeremy C. Pope, *Culture War? The Myth of a Polarized America* (New York: Pearson Longman, 2005), pp. 27–30.

10. Dick Meyer, "The Anatomy of Myth," *Washington Post*, December 5, 2004, p. B 1.
11. Cited in ibid.
12. Pew Research Center for the People and the Press, "Voters Like Campaign 2004, But Too Much Mudslinging," November 11, 2004, p. 2.
13. Alan Cooperman, "Liberal Christians Challenge 'Values Vote'," *Washington Post*, November 10, 2004, p. A7. Zogby's nationwide telephone poll for more than 10,000 voters was sponsored by three progressive groups: Res Publica, the Catholic peace group Pax Christi USA, and the Center for American Progress.
14. James Q. Wilson, "Why Did Kerry Lose? Answer: It Wasn't "Values'," *On the Issues* (Washington, DC: American Enterprise Institute for Public Policy Research, November 2004), p. 1.
15. Fiorina et al., *Culture War?* p. 52, and ch. 4 generally.
16. Ibid., p. 64.
17. Ibid., pp. 54 ff.
18. Ibid., pp. 7–8.
19. Pew Research Center, "The 2004 Political Landscape," pp. 3–4.
20. Cited by Karlyn Bowman, "POLLitics," *Roll Call* (October 19, 2004), p. 12. On abortion, 45 percent of the respondents claimed to be closer to Kerry's position and 34 percent closer to Bush's; on gay rights, 44 percent closer to Kerry, 41 percent closer to Bush; on stem-cell research, the division was 49 percent tilted toward Kerry, 34 percent toward Bush.
21. Fiorina et al., *Culture War?* p. 79.
22. Ibid., pp. 91–93.
23. Pew Research Center for the People and the Press, "Survey Report: Gay Marriage a Voting Issue, But Mostly for Opponents," February 27, 2004, p. 1.
24. Figures in this paragraph are from: Pew Research Center for the People and the Press, "Survey: GOP the Religious-Friendly Party," August 24, 2004, p. 7.
25. Herbert McClosky, Paul Hoffman, and Rosemary O'Hara, "Issue Conflict and Consensus among Party Leaders and Followers," *American Political Science Review* 54 (1960), pp. 406–427.
26. CBS-*New York Times* Poll. David E. Rosenbaum and Janet Elder, "Delegates Lean Left and Oppose the War," *New York Times* (July 25, 2004), Section 15, p. 1. See also Pew Research Center, "The 2004 Political Landscape," p. 6.
27. Donald P. Green and Alan S. Gerber, *Get Out the Vote! How to Increase Voter Turnout* (Washington, DC: Brookings Institution Press, 2004).
28. Ethan Wallison, "GOP Looks to Bush's Grass Roots for Help in '06," *Roll Call* (November 29, 2004), p. 3.
29. Sidney Verba and Norman H. Nie, *Participation in America: Political Democracy and Social Equality* (New York: Harper & Row, 1972); and Michael X. Delli Carpini and Scott Keeter, *What Americans Know about Politics and Why It Matters* (New Haven, CT: Yale University Press, 1996), esp. ch. 4.
30. See Lawrence R. Jacobs and Robert Y. Shapiro, *Politicians Don't Pander* (Chicago: University of Chicago Press, 2000).
31. See Sarah A. Binder, *Stalemate: Causes and Consequences of Legislative Gridlock* (Washington DC: Brookings Institution Press, 2003), especially ch. 4.
32. Pew Research Center, "The 2004 Political Landscape"; and "Voters Like Campaign 2004, But Too Much Mud-Slinging," p. 6.
33. Pew Research Center, "Voters Like Campaign 2004, But Too Much Mud-Slinging," p. 1; John R. Hibbing and Elizabeth Theiss-Morse, *Congress as Public Enemy: Public Attitudes toward American Political Institutions* (New York: Cambridge University Press, 1995).

34. Ronald Brownstein, "Democrats' Losses Go Far Beyond One Defeat," *Los Angeles Times*, November 4, 2004, p. A1.
35. Cited in Paul Samuelson, "The Politics of Self-Esteem," *Washington Post*, November 10, 2004, p. A27.
36. A record-shattering 122 million people went to the polls—but that represented only 55 percent of the voting age population (VAP). Martin P. Wattenberg, "Turnout in the 2004 Presidential Election," *Presidential Studies Quarterly* 35 (March 2005), pp. 138–146.
37. Richard W. Stevenson, "GOP Building Army of Volunteers to Get Out the Vote," *New York Times*, December 20, 2003, p. A12.
38. E. J. Dionne, "The Democrats' Rove Envy," *Washington Post*, December 14, 2004, p. A27.
39. Michael Gecan, "In a Clueless Party," *Washington Post*, December 29, 2004, p. A19.
40. *Los Angeles Times* Poll (conducted October 21–24, 2004). Reported in Brownstein, "Democrats' Losses," p. A13.
41. Ibid.
42. Jamieson and Waldman, *The Press Effect*, pp. 151–152.
43. James P. Pfiffner, "The Transformation of the Bush Presidency," in Pfiffner and Roger H. Davidson, eds., *Understanding the Presidency*, 3rd ed. (New York: Longman, 2003), pp. 453–471.
44. Richard Morin and Dana Milbank, "Americans Dissatisfied with Bush's Domestic Agenda," *Washington Post*, January 19, 2004, p. A1.
45. Jim VandeHei and Michael A. Fletcher, "Bush Says Election Ratified Iraq Policy," *Washington Post*, January 16, 2005, p. A1.
46. Robert A. Dahl, "The Myth of Presidential Mandate," *Political Science Quarterly* 105 (Fall 1990), pp. 355–366.
47. Dan Baltz, "Democrats United in Plans to Block Top Bush Initiatives," *Washington Post*, January 10, 2005, p. A1.
48. Cited by Schneider, "Divided We Stand."
49. Ibid.
50. Christopher Muste, "Poll: Most Americans Think Iraq War Not Worth Fighting," *Washington Post*, December 20, 2004, washingtonpost.com.
51. Reihan Salam, "The Crisis of 'Sam's Club' Republicans," *Los Angeles Times*, January 11, 2005, p. B13.
52. A recent argument was: Thomas Frank, *What's the Matter with Kansas?* (New York: Metropolitan Books, 2004).
53. John F. Harris and Jim VanderHei, "Doubts about Mandate for Bush, GOP," *Washington Post*, May 2, 2005, A1.
54. Richard Alonso-Zaldivar, "House Defies the President on Stem Cells," *Los Angeles Times*, May 25, 2005, A1.
55. Pew Research Center for the People and the Press, "More See Benefits of Stem-Cell Research," May 23, 2005, pp. 1–4.

Part II

The Institutions

Chapter Three

The Bush White House Staff in the Second Term: New Structures? New Faces? New Processes?

Bradley H. Patterson

What flexibility does a newly elected, or re-elected, president have to alter the organization of the White House? Is not the White House—like all important federal institutions—born in and framed by statute? Would a president have to get laws amended to change the structure of the White House? To respond to the chapter's title and to these three initial questions requires a look-back of sixty-nine years, and produces a surprising answer: the White House staff is not a creation of law but is almost entirely the product of executive action.

The Birth Certificate of the White House Staff

On November 14, 1936 the newly re-elected Franklin Roosevelt met with his Committee on Administrative Management (the Brownlow Committee) and laid out for them the principles which he wanted them to highlight in recommending an expanded personal presidential staff. The following January 10, Roosevelt convened an extraordinary press conference at which he unveiled the Brownlow Committee's report with its proposals for "not more than six" administrative assistants and sent Congress draft legislation to give statutory authorization to this new White House staff. For two years the Congress huffed and puffed but took no final action to meet the president's request.[1]

On April 3, 1939, however, the Congress did enact the Reorganization Act of 1939 which began:

SECTION 1. (a) The Congress hereby declares that by reason of continued national deficits beginning in 1931 it is desirable to reduce substantially Government expenditures and that such reduction may be accomplished in some measure by proceeding immediately under the provisions of this Act. The President shall investigate the organization of all agencies of the government and shall determine what changes therein are necessary to accomplish the following purposes:

[. . .]

(2) to increase the efficiency of the operations of the Government to the fullest extent practicable within the revenues;

[. . .]

(b) The Congress declares that the public interest demands the carrying out of the purposes specified in subsection (a) and that such purpose may be accomplished in great measure by proceeding immediately under the provisions of this title, and can be accomplished more speedily thereby than by the enactment of specific legislation.[2]

President Roosevelt took up that invitation to "proceed immediately." On April 25, he submitted Reorganization Plan Number One, which the Congress approved; it became effective on July 1. This Plan did include authorization for an institutional staff unit entitled "Executive Office of the President"[3] but it was silent about any White House office.

Taking these two congressional enactments together, Roosevelt saw his opportunity: On September 8, 1939, he issued his own Executive Order 8248 which begins:

By virtue of the authority vested in me by the Constitution and Statutes, and in order to effectuate the purposes of the Reorganization Act of 1939 . . . and of Reorganization Plan[s] No[s] I . . . it is hereby ordered as follows . . . ." "There shall be within the Executive Office of the President the following principal divisions, namely: (1) The White House Office . . . ."

Part II, Section 1 of the Order went on to specify that this new Office was to be composed of "Secretaries to the President," "The Executive Clerk," and "The Administrative Assistants to the President." The Order listed their respective duties in only general terms (and added a warning against the Administrative Assistants interposing themselves between the President and the head of any department or agency).

"The White House" in Statute

Since its first usage in the appropriations act for FY 1940, "The White House Office" appears often in statutes in the years following 1939, but not in the sense of creating or establishing any part of the White House staff.

There are three exceptions to this statement. The first is in the National Security Act of 1947 which established the National Security Council (NSC). The Act specifies that the Council "shall have a staff to be headed by a civilian executive secretary who shall be appointed by the President . . . [and who may] appoint . . . such personnel as may be necessary to perform such duties as may be prescribed by the Council . . . ."[4] The second instance of congressional creation of presidential staff is in the

Homeland Security Act of 2002, which creates the Homeland Security Council (HSC) and also specifies that "The Council shall have a staff, the head of which shall be a civilian Executive Secretary, who shall be appointed by the President."[5] While the National Security Council in its statutory formation in the 1940s, and the Homeland Security Council, in its 2002 legislation, are located in the Executive Office of the President, the staffs of both Councils have *de facto* migrated to become part of the personal staff of the president, namely at the White House. For the NSC staff the evidence of this migration comes from (a) its direct supervision by the Assistant to the President for National Security Affairs, a senior White House officer, (b) the fact that of its currently listed 212 staffers, 21 have presidential titles (e.g. "Special Assistant to the President and Senior Director"),[6] and (c) the wording of the U.S. Court of Appeals for the D.C. Circuit in the *Armstrong* case of 1996: "The close working relationship between the NSC and the President indicates that the NSC is more like 'the President's immediate personal staff' than it is an agency exercising authority, independent of the President."[7] As for the Homeland Security Council, the Executive Secretary's full title is "Special Assistant to the President and Executive Secretary" and is located within the Office of the Homeland Security Advisor at the White House.[8] On government organization charts, both sets of Council staffs are depicted as being in the Executive Office, but their *de facto* presence in the White House makes them exceptions to the opening statement of this section.

The third statutory requirement affecting the White House staff is the law which makes it mandatory that the president and the vice president be protected by the U.S. Secret Service—and those special, protective units are elements within what can properly be defined as the White House staff community.

The most comprehensive statute about staff assistance to the president is the 1978 enactment "To clarify the authority of personnel in the White House Office and the Executive Residence at the White House [and] to clarify the authority for employment of personnel by the President to meet unanticipated needs . . . ."[9] The president is "authorized to appoint and fix the pay of employees in the White House Office without regard to any other provision of law regulating the employment or compensation of personnel in the Government service." As to what the staff is to do, the statute simply says that White House employees "shall perform such official duties as the President may prescribe." In addition, the president is authorized to expend "such sums as may be necessary" for the official expenses of the Executive Residence and the White House Office. Assistance is also authorized for the Domestic Policy Staff, the vice president, the spouse of the president and the spouse of the vice president. The same statute does impose limits on the numbers of super-grades to be employed in the White House Office, but for positions GS-16 and below permits "such number of other employees as he [the president] may determine to be appropriate." The hiring of experts and consultants is authorized. Finally, the 1978 law authorizes any executive branch agency to detail employees to the White House providing that the detailing agencies are reimbursed after 180 days and that the White House annually reports the numbers of detailees to the Congress for public disclosure. Significantly the key verb throughout this statute is "authorize," not "establish."

A 1994 act requires the White House to send to the House and Senate Governmental Affairs Committees each July 1 a list of all White House employees and detailees by name, position, and salary (excluding only individuals the naming of whom "would not be in the interest of the national defense or foreign policy)."[10]

The latest statute mentioning "the White House" is the consolidated FY 2005 Appropriations Act[11] which, like its predecessors (a) authorizes funds for the elements of the White House but (b) together with the House Appropriations Committee Report,[12] imposes some limitations and conditions upon the White House and also requires the White House to make certain reports to the Congress.

With the three noted exceptions, none of the above-cited statutes or appropriations acts by itself creates or abolishes units of the White House staff, or prescribes organizational structure or delineates the specific functions the staff is to perform for the president. The answer to the opening questions of this paper is: legally the president does have the flexibility to amend the structure and organization of his White House staff nearly completely. Only if he should wish (not at all likely) to abolish the staffs of the National Security or Homeland Security Councils, would he be required to seek changes in law.

The White House Staff: An Institutionalized Non-Institution

In the federal executive branch, the word "institution" connotes organizations formally established in law, their major organizational units delineated in statute with duties spelled out in legislation, staffed in the main by tenured personnel and headed by men and women who are confirmed by the Senate and answerable to the Congress and its committees.[13] Typically, the staffs of federal institutions spend billions of dollars, build major projects, own large areas of land and make sizable grants to state and local governments.

The White House definitely does not fit this description. Judged against the above characteristics, the White House staff is a non-institution.

It is truly institutionalized however: the modern White House is characterized by well-demarcated organizational elements, internal procedures some of which vary with each president, but others of which have long been firmly established, and a structure of surprising continuity since Eisenhower's time. In every case except the staffs of the NSC and the HSC, and the protective mandate of the Secret Service, the units of the modern White

House have been created not by statute, but by administrative action alone—occasionally by executive order but sometimes by nothing more formal than a press statement. It is not presidential whim that has brought each of them into being, but rather it is because each of them has been established to meet an indispensable need of the modern chief executive; collectively, and for precisely that reason, almost all of them endure from presidency to presidency. Over the past sixty-seven years those presidential needs, especially in the areas of outreach and communications, have expanded. Step by step, function by function, White House staff elements accordingly have multiplied. The White House Office of Homeland Security, established during his first term by a George W. Bush executive order,[14] is an example of that multiplication.

In addition to the core White House units there is a category of newer subgroups in which each incoming president will make subtractions (Bush's abolition of Clinton's "One America" office) or additions (Bush's establishment of the Office of Faith-Based and Community Initiatives)—reflecting his own priorities. If the staff additions last through more than one presidency (especially through a party change) expectations and traditions begin to form. The more often these offices are continued by successive presidents, the more certain it is that they will be confirmed as meeting that criterion of need and will become continuing elements in the White House establishment.

The staff structure of the White House at the inauguration of 2005 was thus the cumulative result of at least sixty-six years of step-by-step additions, shaped, to be sure, by a re-elected president's calculus of his needs but mightily reinforced by expectation and tradition. Thus non-institutions become institutionalized. So direct is the connection between presidential need and, over time, the White House's organizational response, and so potent have become those traditions and expectations, that it is most unlikely that the organization of George W. Bush's second-term White House staff will be amended in any significant fashion.

The Bush White House Staff in His Second-Term New Faces?

Everyone on the personal staff of the president at the White House serves at the president's pleasure; there is no one there with tenure in the job. Personnel changes are frequent; burnout is a common experience. Inauguration after re-election is typically a period of staff turnover. On this score, Richard Nixon went to an unusual length: he required every White House officer to submit two letters to him: one offering resignation, the second telling the president what the staffer's actual preference was. In 2000, President Bush did not replicate the Nixon requirement and while engineering some very important transfers, as discussed below, has not made any wholesale staff alterations. He personally asked Chief of Staff Andy Card to stay on.

New Second-Term Assignments— Transferring White House Staff Members to Cabinet Departments

Presidents are well aware of the swirls of conflicting pressures which tug at the loyalties of cabinet members: to the Congress, to interest groups, to the press, to the foreign offices of concerned nations. A frequently used antidote is employed: move some of the president's White House loyalists out into cabinet positions. Surely, it is thought, such recruits will help ensure that the president's policies and positions are more certain to be incorporated into departmental perspectives.

In his second term, President Bush used this technique: dispatching White House National Security Advisor Condoleezza Rice to be Secretary of State, White House Counsel Alberto Gonzales to be Attorney General, White House Domestic Policy Council chief Margaret Spellings to be Secretary of Education, Special Assistant to the President and NSC Senior Director Robert Joseph to be Undersecretary of State, and White House National Economic Council Director Stephen Friedman to chair the President's Foreign Intelligence Advisory Board. (Other White House staffers have been moved into departmental positions: they include Sean McCormack, James Wilkinson and Legal Adviser John Bellinger from the NSC staff to State, three senior members of the Counsel's staff to Justice with Mr. Gonzales, Deputy Press Secretary Claire Buchan to Commerce.) Referring to the whole second-term cabinet, Pulitzer–prize-winning columnist David Broder commented:

> There are some winners and losers in this bunch, but, overall, the president has assured himself that the lines of authority to the Oval Office will be unchallenged and that his wishes will be seen as commands.[15]

The intended suffusions of presidential loyalties are not, however, as neat or sure as the president hopes. However filled the new cabinet transplants may be with presidential gusto, their White-House-derived energies must now operate in much less receptive environments. They must pay attention to—aver to, and in fact demonstrate—loyalty to experienced and dedicated career staffs, to proud and committed bureaucracies. Condoleezza Rice will need support and cooperation from the men and women of U.S. Foreign Service, a corps with traditions from the time of Benjamin Franklin. Alberto Gonzales is dependent on his career departmental associates, such as the nationwide (worldwide in fact) operations of the 96-year-old Federal Bureau of Investigation. These former White House grandees will no longer be insulated behind a White House fence; they must appear in person before Congressional authorizing committees, will have to plead for funds before appropriations czars, and may often be subjected to aggressive congressional oversight. "Your accountability is no longer just to your friends and colleagues at the White House," Judiciary Committee member Senator Patrick J. Leahy reminded Attorney General candidate Alberto Gonzales. "Your responsibility is to the law and to the

American people." Contritely, Gonzales observed:

> I will no longer represent only the White House, I will represent the United States of America and its people. I understand the differences between the two roles. In the former, I have been privileged to advise the president and his staff. In the latter I would have a far broader responsibility to pursue justice for all the people of our great nation . . . [16]

New Structures?

As the second term began, the structure of the Bush White House staff was composed of some 133 separately identifiable elements: 58 principal policy offices, 26 supporting policy offices and 49 professional and technical units—the whole being what can be described as the White House Staff community. A summary listing follows, including estimates of the number of subordinate officers in each unit and the number of those officers whose title includes the word "president":[17]

The Office of the Vice President (21 elements, 86 staff members, 2 with presidential titles)

The Office of the First Lady (8 elements, 21 staff members, 2 with presidential titles)

Chief of Staff (10 staff members, 5 with presidential titles)

The Assistant to the President for National Security Affairs (including the Executive Secretary of the National Security Council, 21 other elements, 214 staff members, 21 with presidential titles)

Senior Adviser for Policy and Strategy (7 staff members, 3 with presidential titles)

Office of Strategic Initiatives (7 staff members, 2 with presidential titles)

Office of Public Liaison (12 staff members, 3 with presidential titles)

Office of Political Affairs (11 staff members, 2 with presidential titles)

Office of Intergovernmental Affairs (10 staff members, 4 with presidential titles)

Counsellor for Communications (3 staff members, 1 with presidential title)

Office of Communications (11 staff members, 2 with presidential titles)

Counsel to the President (26 staff members, 13 with presidential titles)

Office of Legislative Affairs (26 staff members, 18 with presidential titles)

Speechwriting (13 staff members, 4 with presidential titles)

Media Affairs (10 staff members, 1 with presidential title)

Office of Global Communications (6 staff members, 1 with presidential title)

White House Office of Homeland Security (including the Executive Secretary, Homeland Security Council and 5 additional elements, 45 staff members, 7 with presidential titles)

Domestic Policy Council (19 staff members, 7 with presidential titles)

National Economic Council (18 staff members, 8 with presidential titles)

Press Secretary (13 staff members, 3 with presidential titles)

Scheduling Office (12 staff members, 1 with presidential title)

Advance Office(20 staff members, 3 with presidential titles)

U.S.A. Freedom Corps Office (9 staff members, 3 with presidential titles)

The Presidential Personnel Office (29 staff members, 7 with presidential titles)

Office of National AIDS Policy (2 staff members)

Office of Faith-Based and Community Initiatives (10 staff members, 3 with presidential titles)

White House Office of Management and Administration (8 elements, 86 staff members, 2 with presidential titles, plus the 2,200-person Military Office (including 900 in the White House Communications Agency—WHCA), GSA's 133-person White House Service Delivery Team, the National Park Service's 100-person White House Liaison Office, and the U.S. Postal Service's 14-person White House Branch)

Staff Secretary (6 staff members, 2 with presidential titles, plus the 6-person Executive Clerk's Office, the 57-person Correspondence Office, 2 with presidential titles, and the 24-person Records Management Office)

Office of Cabinet Affairs (10 staff members, 3 with presidential titles)

The Executive Residence (96 staff members including the Chief Usher, the Calligrapher and the White House Curator)

The Office of Administration is in the Executive Office of the President, but it is estimated that one-half of its 230 listed staff members can be considered as part of the White House staff because they provide "administrative services which are primarily in direct support of the President."[18]

Some 100 interns, 700 volunteers and several White House Fellows work in the above offices. Dozens more work there as detailees from other agencies; their numbers are included in the figures listed.

The White House units of the U.S. Secret Service, including the presidential and vice- presidential protective details and the Uniformed and Protective Research Divisions are also a constantly close element of the White House staff community. Their numbers are kept confidential. In 2000 they were estimated at 1,200,[19] but there has clearly been a marked increase in the past four years.

The entire White House staff community listed above amounts to some 6,000 men and women. The current total budget for all of these elements, in the author's estimate, is $1 billion. President Bush has made minimal organizational changes in his second-term White House structure; the most significant alterations being a slimming down of the Office of Cabinet Affairs and the merger of the functions of the Office of Global Communications into the sphere of the staff of the National Security Council.

New Processes?

There are issues of relationships and procedures which will be the subject of intensive concentration by the White House leadership as the second term progresses and where innovation is going to occur.

Mitigating Cabinet Members' Feelings of Alienation

In Eisenhower's presidency, the cabinet met as a group practically every Friday morning. The White House staff prepared an agenda, distributed papers in advance, composed and circulated a presidential record of action afterwards. The discussions around the Cabinet table were open and frank, with Ike for his part being especially candid with the whole group about his priorities, his hopes, and his vision. Such meetings minimized the sense of institutional and personal distance which always tends to grow between the cabinet chieftains and the White House. Since Eisenhower left office, full cabinet meetings have almost evaporated, and feelings of alienation have become more intense.[20]

In the Bush second term a unique initiative is being undertaken: Cabinet members, especially those who, unlike Secretaries Rice, Rumsfeld, Gonzales and Chertoff, do not have occasion to be in the White House constantly, are being asked to spend at least four hours each week at the White House. A suite has been prepared in the Eisenhower Executive Office Building to accommodate two of them at a time, plus conference space. The Cabinet incumbents will thus have greatly increased opportunities to rub shoulders with the Chief of Staff and the other senior officers of the White House and to be more available to the president. They are being encouraged to make appointments with outside VIP visitors, telling the latter to "come to my office in the White House." While this creative arrangement does not confer any new legal or policy authority on the cabinet members, the symbolism for them will be powerful.

A New Assignment for the First Lady in the Second Term

President Bush employed an unusual device to outline a new area of responsibility for his spouse: his 2005 State of the Union Message.

> I propose a three-year initiative to help organizations keep young people out of gangs, and show young men an ideal of manhood that respects women and rejects violence. Taking on gangs will be one part of a broader outreach to at-risk youth, which involves parents and pastors, coaches and community leaders, in programs ranging from literacy to sports. And I'm proud that the leader of this nationwide effort will be our first lady, Laura Bush.[21]

While she will be depending on staff support primarily from the Departments of Justice and Health and Human Services, this will mean substantial travel for the first lady, visiting creative and successful community efforts as a means of calling attention to them as examples for other local initiatives.

National Security/Homeland Security/Intelligence Relationships

It was in 1947 that structured presidential machinery for national security decision making took shape. The statutory responsibility of the White House's National Security Council reads:

(a) . . . to advise the President with respect to the integration of domestic, foreign, and military policies relating to the national security so as to enable the military services and the other departments and agencies of the Government to cooperate more effectively in matters involving the national security . . .

[. . .]

(b) In addition to performing such other functions as the President may direct . . . to assess and appraise the objectives, commitments and risks of the United States in relation to our actual and potential military power, in the interest of national security . . . to consider policies on matters of common interest to the departments and agencies of the Government concerned with the national security. . . .[22]

In early October of 2001, following shortly after the 9/11 attack but prior to the creation of the Department of Homeland Security, the president by executive order established an Office of Homeland Security and initially labeled it as being in the Executive Office of the President. The order specified that the new office was to be headed by an Assistant to the President for Homeland Security and it also established a Homeland Security Council. The order gives the office a lengthy list of very broad responsibilities throughout the area of homeland security.[23] Each section of the list, however, begins with the verb "coordinate," or "ensure," or "facilitate," or "review," or "develop criteria"—in other words, *close monitoring* but not operational functions.

In his June, 2002 Message to Congress transmitting proposed legislation to create a Department of Homeland Security, the president referred to his 2001 order as having established the "White House Office of Homeland Security" and added the following paragraph:

Continued Interagency Coordination at the White House

Even with the creation of the new Department, there will remain a strong need for a White House Office of Homeland Security. Protecting America from terrorism will remain a multidepartmental issue and will continue to require interagency coordination. Presidents will continue to require the confidential advice of a Homeland Security Advisor, and I intend for the White House Office of Homeland Security and the Homeland Security Council to maintain a strong role in coordinating our government-wide efforts to secure the homeland.[24]

The Homeland Security Act, signed on November 25, 2002, created the Department of Homeland Security; its 17 titles repeat and expand the broad list in the 2001 executive order, but the verbs, as one would expect, establish *operational* authority. The 2001 order, however, is still extant, including the following sentence:

> The Assistant to the President for Homeland Security shall provide advice to the Director [of the Office of Management and Budget] on the level and use of funding in departments and agencies for homeland security—related activities and, prior to the Director's forwarding of the proposed annual budget submission to the President for transmittal to the Congress, shall certify to the Director the funding levels that the Assistant to the President for Homeland Security believes are necessary and appropriate for the homeland security-related activities of the executive branch.

Taken together, the executive order and the act set up a situation where a cabinet department, by statute, takes the lead in a huge interdepartmental field of urgent operations but the White House, by executive order, keeps in charge of coordinating and evaluating the whole of it. The new act puts the Homeland Security Council, with its broad membership of foreign-affairs and domestic departments, into law:

> for the purpose of more effectively coordinating the policies and functions of the United States Government relating to homeland security . . . [and to] (1) assess the objectives, commitments and risks of the United States in the interest of homeland security and make resulting recommendations to the President; (2) oversee and review homeland security policies of the Federal Government . . . and (3) perform such other functions as the President may direct.[25]

In its report accompanying the FY 2004 appropriations bill for the White House, the House Appropriations Committee focused on the request to fund the Office of Homeland Security, and opined that it was

> . . . not clear what work remains that cannot be effectively performed by the Department of Homeland Security. Although the Committee understands the President's need for policy support and advice, it is not clear why that would require 66 staff, given the existence and support of the Department of Homeland Security.[26]

The 9/11 Commission surveyed this somewhat confusing scene, and commented:

> . . . the problem of joint operational planning is often passed to the White House, where the NSC staff tries to play this role. The National security staff at the White House (both NSC and new Homeland Security Council staff) has already become 50 percent larger since 9/11. But our impression, after talking to serving officials, is that even this enlarged staff is consumed by meetings on day-to-day issues, sifting each day's threat information and trying to coordinate

everyday operations. Even as it crowds into every square inch of available office
space, the NSC staff is still not sized to be an executive agency . . .

[. . .]

. . . [a]serious danger is that as the NSC staff is consumed by these day-to-
day tasks, it has less capacity to find the time and detachment needed to advise
a president on larger policy issues. That means less time to work on major new
initiatives, help with legislative management to steer needed bills through
Congress, and track the design and implementation of the strategic plans for
regions [and] countries.[27]

The Commission added:

"To improve coordination at the White House, we believe the existing
Homeland Security Council should soon be merged into a single National
Security Council"—a merger which "should help the NSC staff concentrate
on its core duties of assisting the president and supporting interdepartmental
policymaking."[28]

In enacting the National Security Intelligence Reform Act of 2004, however, the Congress refused to accept the Commission's recommendation. In
that statute, the Congress did create a new, senior federal post, the Director
of National Intelligence, but specifically directed that this office "shall not
be located within the Executive Office of the President." The congressional
animus against including the new national intelligence directorate in the
Executive Office undoubtedly stems from a suspicion that even the statutory, non-White-House elements of the Executive Office are vulnerable to
undue and improper political influence in their decision-making processes.

The new law specifies that the duty of the National Intelligence Director
is to:

be responsible for ensuring that national intelligence is provided
(A) to the President;
(B) to the heads of departments and agencies of the executive branch;
(C) to the Chairman of the Joint Chiefs of Staff and senior military commanders;
(D) to the Senate and House of Representatives and the committees thereof; and
(E) to such other persons as the Director of National Intelligence determines to
be appropriate".[29]

The new Director, who is expected to have a staff of some five hundred,
will not only be outside the Executive Office but is also legally excluded
from service as the Director of the Central Intelligence Agency "or as the
head of any other element of the intelligence community."[30]

Meanwhile, the staff of the National Security Council at the White
House still includes a "Special Assistant to the President and Senior Director
for Intelligence Programs."

Clearly this whole highly interrelated area of national security/home-
land security/national intelligence will be scrutinized by President Bush's

second-term White House leadership. The new Assistant to the President for National Security Affairs (Mr. Hadley), the new Secretary of Homeland Security (Mr. Chertoff), the newly reappointed Assistant to the President for Homeland Security (Ms. Townsend) and the new Director of National Intelligence (Mr. Negroponte) face the daunting tasks of coordinating their missions, meshing their personalities and working out their access to the president. With the above-quoted documents all on the record, however, it will be a dicey challenge to the practitioners of presidential public administration. It is, however, assured that the preference of all the modern presidents, especially including George W. Bush, for centralization of policy development, policy coordination and policy articulation in the White House will continue to be the underlying *motif* for whatever will turn out to be the eventual personal and organizational arrangements.

White House Systems for Informing the President

In 1956, President Eisenhower initiated a special, private system for helping ensure that the cabinet departments would keep him informed, especially about issues and actions which might present the president with unexpected problems. A memorandum went to all departments from the White House Staff Secretary: wanted were "brief informational notes on items within your field of interest which may bear upon past presidential decisions, *or which may flag especially important upcoming problems.*"[31] The system was unostentatiously labeled "Staff Notes" and Staff Secretary Andrew J. Goodpaster hired two new assistants in his immediate office to collect and edit the departmental contributions. The initial input was sparse; in cabinet meetings stern reminders were issued. But at the end of every day a short information sheet went into the oval office; Ike often underscored items that caught his attention, demanded more data, made acerbic comments. Kennedy continued the enterprise; what he asked for, explained Cabinet Secretary Frederick Dutton, was "naked candor." Thus was born an executive-branch-wide information system which has now developed into the weekly Cabinet Report—which the Secretary to the Cabinet now assembles from sheaves of material sent in from each department. The objective is still: keep the White House informed. "If you don't surprise us, we won't micromanage you," said Christine Varney, President Clinton's Cabinet Affairs chief. ("But we do it anyway," commented a Clinton White House senior.)

Contemplating the Bush second-term White House but looking back at the first four years, the author is struck by what appears to be inadequate information being funneled to the top. The estimates about the presence of weapons of mass destruction in Iraq, the early Red Cross finding that prisoners were being mistreated in Abu Ghraib (and the photographs), the questions later raised about the qualifications of Bernard Kerik to be Secretary of Homeland Security—these were instances of weakness in the White House warning systems. When they fail, the president is embarrassed and his credibility comes under attack. Whether through breakdowns in formal arrangements or the White House staff simply not doing enough personal sniffing among their own contacts and friends, such deficiencies injure the chief executive. With regard to the Kerik episode, a Democratic official commented "The most cursory checking would have shown this guy has more skeletons than a haunted house."[32] The second-term Bush White House can be expected to put more demands on its formal and informal information-gathering systems.

2006 and Beyond

The successes of Karl Rove and company in the 2004 presidential and congressional elections are not laurels on which the White House staff is going to rest. The aim is to keep on building the Republican Party for 2006 and for years into the future. As described in a 2003 essay:

> The real prize is creating a Republican majority that would be as solid as, say, the Democratic coalition that Franklin Roosevelt created—a majority that would last a generation and that, as it played itself out over time, would wind up profoundly changing the relationship between citizen and state in this country. [Quoting Rove himself]: ". . . somebody will come along and figure out a new governing scheme through which people could view things and could, conceivably, enjoy a similar period of dominance." Karl Rove clearly wants to be that somebody, and his relentless pressing for every specific advantage is in service of that larger goal.[33]

The second-term White House is gearing up to help ensure that "period of dominance." Its Director of Communications, Dan Bartlett, has been elevated to the Counselor level in the White House staff. A description of Tim Goeglein, Deputy Director of President Bush's White House Office of Public Liaison, characterizes him and other conservatives like him as "strategically positioned in the White House in positions of authority." Goeglein is quoted: "One of the principal roles of public liaison is not only explaining policies that have been decided, but to faithfully and accurately report into the White House bloodstream" the views of conservatives.[34]

That White House political bloodstream will be pumping red Republican electoral oxygen all the way until 2008.

Conclusion: Looking Into the Second Term

As described above, during his first term President Bush made one major and several other important additions to his personal staff: he established the White House Office of Homeland Security and created the offices of Faith-Based and Community Initiatives, of Strategic Planning, of Global

Communications and the White House Freedom Corps Office. As the second term begins, the president has downsized the White House Cabinet Affairs and shifted responsibilities for global communications oversight into the NSC. Chief of Staff Andrew Card has commented that "Far fewer [people have departed] than I would have anticipated."[35] While President Bush, in early 2005, had the authority, under law, to cut back and/or drastically unscramble/reorganize his personal White House staff (except for the staffs of the National Security Council and of the National Homeland Security Council), this was not done to any major extent.

The president not only would not, but in truth he in effect could not. The 133-element, 6000-person contemporary White House staff is the cumulative outcome of sixty-six years of building a structure of help for the chief executive—help which has successfully demonstrated its value. Growing simultaneously with that buildup and stemming from that success, have arisen customs, traditions and expectations—too strong for even a president to disassemble, as President Clinton discovered, after vainly promising to trim the staff by 25 percent.

If not cut back, could the staff be expanded? In his first term, President Bush saw the formal appropriations for the White House rise from $125,607,000 in FY 2001 to $185,651,000 in FYs 2005, most of the increase attributable to homeland security outlays in FYs 2002 and 2003.[36] It is anticipated that there will be a leveling off or perhaps a slight decrease of expenditures for the White House during the second term. There will be increased outlays to fund the new Directorate of National Intelligence and its expected staff of five hundred, but, as noted above, this is an arena outside the White House boundaries.

Notes

1. The author is indebted here to Matthew J. Dickinson, *Bitter Harvest: FDR, Presidential Power and the Growth of the Presidential Branch* (New York: Cambridge University Press, 1997), Pt. II, Sec. 3.
2. United States Statutes At Large, 1939, Vol. 53, P. 2, p. 561.
3. The Plan effectuated the transfer, into this newly minted Executive Office, of the Bureau of the Budget from the Treasury Department. Statutes At Large, 1939 p. 1423 ff.
4. 50 USC 401 *et seq.* of July 26, 1947.
5. Public Law 107–296 of November 25, 2002, Title IX, Secs. 901–906.
6. *Daily Report for Executives—White House Telephone Directory* (Bureau of National Affairs, Inc., Washington, DC), May 5, 2004, S-34–40.
7. United States Court of Appeals for the DC Circuit, case number 95-5057, *Scott Armstrong*, et al., *v. Executive Office of the President*, decided August 2, 1996, 25.
8. *White House Telephone Directory*, S-11 *et seq.*
9. Public Law 95–570 of November 2, 1978.
10. Public Law 103–270 of June 30, 1994.

11. 108th Congress, H.R. 4818, p. 439 ff.

12. 108th Congress, Second Session, House of Representatives, Committee on Appropriations, Report 108–671 of September 8, 2004, pp. 125–136.

13. See Patterson, "The Bush White House." in *George W. Bush: Evaluating the President at Mid-Term*, ed. Hilliard, Lansford, and Watson (Albany, NY: State University of New York Press, 2004).

14. Executive Order 13228 of October 8, 2001.

15. In Dave Broder's column "Tight Little Cabinet," in *The Washington Post*, December 15, 2004, p. A33.

16. Statement by Alberto Gonzales before the Senate Judiciary Committee at his confirmation hearing, *New York Times*, January 7, 2005, p. A14.

17. *White House Telephone Directory, S-7 et seq.*

18. Carter Executive Order 12028 of December 12, 1977, Section 3(a).

19. Patterson, Bradley H., *The White House Staff: Inside the West Wing and Beyond* (Washington, DC: Brookings Institution Press, 2000), pp. 348, 373–383.

20. See *Locked in the Cabinet*, by President Clinton's Secretary of Labor Robert Reich (New York: Albert A. Knopf, 1997).

21. *Weekly Compilation of Presidential Documents*, February 7, 2005. 41: 5, p. 130.

22. The National Security Act of 1947, 50 USC 101.

23. Executive Order 13228 of October 8, 2001.

24. Message to the Congress Transmitting Proposed Legislation To Create the Department of Homeland Security, *Weekly Compilation of Presidential Documents June 18, 2002–38*. No. 25, p. 1034ff.

25. Homeland Security Act of November 25, 2002, PL 107–296, p. 131.

26. U.S. House of Representatives, One Hundred Eighth Congress, First Session, Committee on Appropriations, *Report Number 108–243 re the Departments of Transportation and Treasury and Independent Agencies Appropriations Bill*, July 30, 2003, p. 163.

27. *The 9/11 Commisson Report, Authorized Edition* (New York: W. W. Norton and Company 2004), p. 402.

28. Ibid., p. 406.

29. The National Security Act of 1947 as amended by the National Security Intelligence Reform Act of 2004, Section 102A.

30. Ibid., Section 102(c).

31. Andrew J. Goodpaster, Memorandum of July 5, 1956, Staff Notes File, Dwight D. Eisenhower Library.

32. Marshall Wittman, quoted in "On Kerik Nomination, White House Missed Red Flags," *The Washington Post*, December 15, 2004, p. A4.

33. Nicholas Lemann, *The Controller, The New Yorker*, May 12, 2003.

34. Jim VandeHei, "Pipeline to the President for GOP Conservatives," *The Washington Post*, December 24, 2004, p. A15.

35. *New York Times*, February 8, 2005.

36. *Patterson*, White House Telephone Directory, S–7 et seq.

Chapter Four

Choices for the President: Structuring the Second-Term Cabinet of President George W. Bush

Shirley Anne Warshaw

With his second-term electoral victory in November, 2004, President George W. Bush was afforded an opportunity to reorganize his entire advisory structure. While presidents may tinker with changes in their cabinets throughout the first term, most presidential cabinets remain stable during the term. The major change in personnel is not likely to occur until a president is reelected.

If a president is reelected, all political employees, including the White House staff and cabinet, are asked for their resignations as a matter of course. Following tradition, the White House staff, cabinet and sub-cabinet political appointees submitted their resignations following the 2004 election. Few knew whether their resignations would be accepted, although several cabinet officers had intimated prior to the election of their intention to return to private life. Throughout November and December 2004, the second term cabinet was assembled, with President Bush retaining only four cabinet officers. Changes were made in eleven cabinet positions.

The question examined in this chapter focuses on the decisions that President George W. Bush incorporated into organizing his second-term cabinet. Among the issues examined are whether cabinet officers were chosen for their political ideology, their technical expertise, or their personal relationship with President Bush; whether the second-term cabinet reflected the same goals and objectives as the first-term cabinet; whether moving three White House staff into the cabinet was intended to gain tighter control over certain departments; and whether the President's commitment to a conservative political agenda was enhanced by his cabinet-building strategy. Central to this question is whether other considerations such as party bridge building and diversity of religion, gender, and ethnicity were also key to cabinet building during the second term. The chapter is organized in subsections that delve into each of these issues.

The Timing of Cabinet Nominations

Presidents have traditionally used cabinet building as a means to signal to the American public how they will approach governance. The long and arduous campaign provides little insight into the governance process, but leaves it to the brief transition period to define how the new administration will manage the government. The choices a president makes for the cabinet are the first window that the public has into understanding whose advice the president will seek in policymaking. Will that advice come from policy experts, political ideologues, or old friends? What implications in the policymaking process does the advisory structure of the cabinet have?

Presidential campaigns are aware of the statement that their policymaking structure has on the voting public, which explains why names are not provided or even floated until after the election. Not surprisingly, campaigns are reluctant to offer information on who the cabinet nominees will be, for fear of alienating any segment of the voting population. During the 2000 presidential campaign Governor George W. Bush hinted in early August of his intention to nominate Colin Powell as Secretary of State, but such preelection cabinet selections are not common practice.[1]

Colin Powell was the only name even hinted at by Bush during the campaign as a possible cabinet nominee. President Bush followed campaign protocol and did not formally announce any appointments to his cabinet until after the 2000 election. Table 4.1 outlines the first-term cabinet. His first formal announcement concerning the cabinet came soon after the December 13, 2000 Supreme Court ruling on Vice President Gore's challenge to the Florida electors. Not surprisingly, President-elect Bush named Colin Powell as his designee for Secretary of State.

During his re-election campaign in 2004, President Bush again refrained from any discussion of the cabinet nominations until after the election.

Table 4.1   President George W. Bush's first-term cabinet

Secretary of State	Colin L. Powell (2001–2005)
Secretary of the Treasury	Paul O'Neill (2001–2002); John W. Snow (2003–)
Secretary of Defense	Donald H. Rumsfeld (2001–)
Attorney General	John Ashcroft (2001–2005)
Secretary of the Interior	Gale Norton (2001–)
Secretary of Agriculture	Ann Veneman (2001–2005)
Secretary of Commerce	Donald Evans (2001–2005)
Secretary of Labor	Elaine Chao (2001–)
Secretary of Health and Human Services	Tommy G. Thompson (2001–2005)
Secretary of Housing and Urban Development	Mel Martinez (2001–2005)
Secretary of Transportation	Norman Y. Mineta (2001–)
Secretary of Energy	Spencer Abraham (2001–2005)
Secretary of Education	Roderick R. Paige (2001–2005)
Secretary of Homeland Security	Tom Ridge (2003–2005)
Secretary of Veterans Affairs	Anthony J. Principi (2001–2005)

Alexis Simendinger wrote in the *National Journal* in October, 2004 that "if [Andrew] Card knows Bush's plans for his second-term cabinet and staff, the chief of staff believes saying anything publicly would be appallingly presumptuous."[2] Even cabinet officers such as Tom Ridge, who were widely reported to be leaving the administration, refused to confirm their plans. Ridge did not resign until November 30, 2004.

The cabinet nomination process did not formally begin until November 11, 2004, six days after the election, when Alberto Gonzales was nominated as Attorney General to replace John Ashcroft. Ashcroft had resigned only a day earlier, leaving little question that the transition team had a plan in place that allowed Gonzales to be so quickly named. However, that plan was kept a tightly held secret. On the day that Ashcroft resigned, the administration continued to have no comment on naming a new Attorney General. The press cited a number of possible successors, including former Montana governor Marc Racicot, who had been the 2004 Bush campaign chairman; Larry Thompson, general counsel of PepsiCo; and Gonzales but the White House refused comment until the nomination was formally made.[3] Again, President Bush followed protocol by waiting until after the election to name his cabinet nominee, prior to his first term.

The Cabinet Selection Process: Jimmy Carter to George W. Bush

Although the nominations are withheld until after the election, presidential campaigns often develop a private list of names for each cabinet office. The process of developing names for the cabinet during the campaign generally is handled quietly among a small cadre of senior campaign advisors. The Carter campaign in 1976 had one of the most organized efforts to consider cabinet nominations. Led by Jack Watson, a senior campaign advisor and former staff member to Governor Jimmy Carter, the transition team had a clear picture of who would best serve the new president in the cabinet but never released any names.

Carter promised the nation that he believed in "Cabinet administration of government" and sought to build a cabinet that would be his primary advisory structure.[4] Carter demonstrated his commitment to a strong cabinet by declaring that his cabinet would:

1. Play a major role in policymaking.
2. Would be free to set their own priorities.
3. Would be free to choose their own staffs.
4. Would be able to administer their departments without White House interference.[5]

President Carter's commitment to a strong cabinet was in direct response to the Watergate crisis that led to President Richard Nixon's resignation and eroded public confidence in the presidency. Carter viewed Nixon's White

House staff as overly political and manipulative, features which Carter hoped to end with a stronger reliance on the cabinet for policy decisions. As such, the Watson team, formally known as the Talent Inventory Program (TIP), spent months during the campaign focusing on developing a pool of potential cabinet nominees that were experienced managers and policy experts, with the focus on policy expertise. Watson sought to create a cabinet with few ties to the Democratic Party or to Governor Carter in an effort to rebuild public confidence in presidential government.

The Carter experience with cabinet building was replicated to some extent in the Reagan campaign of 1980. Reagan asked E. Pendleton James, a long-time advisor and New York executive recruiter, to manage the transition process during the campaign. As had Carter, Reagan wanted a clear plan in place for potential cabinet nominees. The names developed by the transition team remained a closely guarded secret, with names bandied about within the campaign but never released to the public. The individuals whose names were discussed by the transition team were not contacted and remained names only on a list. The names were presented to President Reagan after the election for his decision, as had the names on the Carter transition team's list.

E. Pendleton James diverged from the Carter model by injecting significant political criteria into the decision process. While Jack Watson sought policy experts for the Carter cabinet, James sought political loyalists for the Reagan cabinet. The criteria established for the Reagan cabinet were:

1. Was he a Reagan man?
2. Was he a Republican?
3. Was he a conservative?
4. Was the conservative ideology properly represented?[6]

Thus, the personnel choices for the Reagan cabinet differed significantly from those of the Carter cabinet with the Reagan focus centered on the political backgrounds of the nominees. While Carter sought policy expertise as the primary criteria in cabinet building, Reagan sought political loyalty. He wanted not only Republicans for his cabinet, but also conservative Republicans who had worked for the Reagan campaign. Their goal was to reduce the size of the federal government, cut programs, and even eliminate the newly created Department of Education, all of which were goals supported by conservatives within the Republican Party. Political homogeneity in cabinet building was central to maintaining the administration's efforts to reduce federal spending by cutting the number of federal employees and federal programs.

By the 1988 campaign, which saw Vice President George Herbert Walker Bush running against Governor Michael Dukakis of Massachusetts, the focus on cabinet building which had been prominent in both the 1976 transition of Jimmy Carter and the 1980 transition of Ronald Reagan had all but disappeared. The Bush campaign had consciously stayed away from cabinet-building decisions for fear of alienating Reagan supporters. While the Bush campaign argued that "George Bush didn't come to the presidency to make a 180 degree turn, he came to build upon the successes"[7] of the Reagan years, they were reticent to make any decisions on the cabinet until elected.

Once elected, George H. W. Bush initiated a cabinet selection process that placed the cabinet at the center of the policymaking structure, noting that there would be a "new leadership style." While Reagan relied heavily on his White House staff, Bush intended to rely more heavily on his cabinet. The cabinet selection process put in motion differed from both the Carter model, directed at policy expertise, and the Reagan model, directed at ideological consistency. The process put in motion by George H. W. Bush centered on including friends of long-standing in his cabinet, including James Baker as Secretary of State and Nicholas Brady as Treasury Secretary. Baker and Brady, both friends from Texas, were named soon after the election.

In contrast to the early appointment of Baker and Brady, John Sununu was named White House Chief of Staff on November 17, nearly two weeks after the election. The focus on the cabinet as the center of policymaking and the focus on placing friends in the cabinet were the hallmark of the Bush administration's decision structure. Sununu, chosen to be the most senior member of the White House staff, was a relative newcomer to the Bush inner circle. As governor of New Hampshire, Sununu had been an early supporter of George H. W. Bush in the 1988 primary election and later became a key advisor during the general election. He was rewarded with his nomination as chief of staff, but he never became a Bush confidante. When Sununu was questioned in the press about violating the White House ethics code by using his official limousine for personal trips to stamp shows (his hobby), Bush did not hesitate to ask for his resignation in 1991.

The model created by the George H. W. Bush administration for cabinet building lacked the ideological framework that the Reagan administration had. George H. W. Bush created a cabinet-selection process that was woven together by networks of old friends and long-established working relationships. He felt comfortable with his cabinet and sought their advice in policymaking. As John Burke noted in his discussion of past presidential transitions in *White House World*, one of the distinctive features of the Bush cabinet was that "George H. W. Bush was skilled at selecting associates who were personally loyal to him".[8]

The Clinton transition team created another model for cabinet building in 1992. Led by campaign advisor Vernon Jordan, the Clinton transition team sought to develop a cabinet that had broad ethnic and gender diversity and policy expertise. The Clinton cabinet, although having distinct features in diversity, was closer to the Carter cabinet in composition than to either the Reagan or the George H. W. Bush cabinets.

The most significant decision that the Clinton transition team made was a public repudiation of the political criteria that Reagan had established. In an effort to shape a distinctively different cabinet than his two predecessors,

Clinton stated, "I don't want a cabinet of strangers but neither do I want people whose only criteria for having a job was that they had somehow been involved with me before."[9] What Clinton did want was a cabinet with broad racial and gender diversity that "looks like America" and with strong policy skills. Cabinet nominees did not need to have worked in his campaign, to be aligned with any part of the Democratic Party, or to have a commitment to any ideology. Clinton sought to build a cabinet of policy advocates to move his legislative agenda forward and to build a cabinet with a bold commitment to diversity.

After eight years in office, the Democrats lost the White House in 2000 to Republican George W. Bush, the son of former President George H. W. Bush. The obvious question was whether George W. Bush would follow his father's model for cabinet building by naming a coterie of old friends to the key cabinet positions or would follow the Reagan model by using ideological consistency as the model. Few speculated that the Clinton model for diversity or policy advocacy would become part of the George W. Bush model. After all, Bush was a Republican who would follow the Republican models of Reagan and his father and would certainly steer away from the Carter and Clinton models.

The model that George W. Bush followed in the first term was surprisingly not that of his father, but rather that of Ronald Reagan. The first-term Bush cabinet was composed of political ideologues, as the Reagan cabinet had been, rather than the network of old friends that the George H. W. Bush cabinet had been. The new Bush cabinet was politically homogeneous, overwhelmingly conservative and shared his commitment to the pro-life agenda. The only close friend that Bush named to the cabinet was Donald Evans as Secretary of Commerce. Evans had been a close friend to Bush for many years and was considered to be the person who brought Bush out of a downward personal spiral in the mid-1980s.

In summary, the cabinet selection process from Jimmy Carter to George W. Bush reflected the respective president's personal style but, more importantly, reflected his political base. Politics drives the cabinet selection process.

The Cabinet Selection Process:
George W. Bush's Second Term

As was true in the past, the cabinet selection process of George W. Bush in both the first and the second terms was driven by the need to build support within his political base. Not surprisingly, the appointment of politically conservative Republicans was the overarching theme for both the first- and the second-term cabinet building strategy.

However, one second-term cabinet officer was chosen primarily for his ethnic diversity rather than his political credentials. Carlos Gutierrez lacked the conservative political credentials of other second-term cabinet appointments. He was not an ally of, friend of, or strong political supporter of George W. Bush, although he had been a leader of the Bush campaign in Michigan in 2004. In spite of the casualness of their relationship, President Bush called Gutierrez to the White House for an interview after the election and immediately offered him the position of Commerce Secretary. The inclusion of Gutierriez, a Hispanic, provided depth to the Republican Party's courting of the Hispanic vote for the 2006 Congressional elections and the 2008 Presidential elections. The Hispanic vote had often gravitated toward Democratic rather than Republican candidates. Thus, the appointment of Gutierriez provided an opportunity for the Bush administration to be seen as sensitive to the Hispanic community.

Perhaps the most surprising appointments to the second-term cabinet were the elevation of three staff from the White House into the cabinet (Alberto Gonzales, Condoleezza Rice, and Margaret Spellings). Two of the three White House staff (Gonzales and Spellings) had worked for Bush while he was Governor of Texas and one (Rice) had worked on his presidential campaign. Although the appointment of the three White House staffers to the cabinet became the most commented-upon cabinet nominations within the press, their appointments clearly fit the pattern of maintaining political homogeneity. Their loyalty to the conservative agenda had been unfailing throughout the four years of the first term.

President Bush worked swiftly after the election to move forward new programs within his conservative agenda. Speaking at a press conference two days after the election, he noted that the mandate of a majority of voters supported his view and his conservative agenda. With his victory in the 2004 election, Bush felt empowered to move the conservative agenda forward. The selection of strong conservatives for the cabinet was a signal that the conservative agenda would be continued in the implementation of existing policy and the promotion of new policy.

Table 4.2 on the following page, indicates the background of the fifteen second-term cabinet officers. They tend to be politicians, who are politically connected, rather than policy experts. Kenneth Walsh of *U.S. News and World Report* commented that "Bush . . . is installing a Dubyacracy, populating the government with men and women who will carry out his conservative goals."[10] One notable feature of the second-term cabinet was the number of Republican politicians who made their reputations supporting conservative agendas.

Diversity in Cabinet Building

In addition to a cabinet-building strategy focused on ideological homogeneity, geographic, ethnic and gender diversity have been addressed. Geographic diversity, first used in 1789, has been addressed in every administration since then. Ethnic and gender diversity, while addressed only in modern administrations, has also become a critical building block in cabinet

Table 4.2   Background of second-term Bush cabinet

Second-Term cabinet officers	Background
Sam Bodman	Deputy Secretary of Commerce and Treasury, Executive at the Cabot Corporation
Elaine Chao	Married to Senator Mitch McConnell
Michael Chertoff	Political appointee to Justice Department, federal judiciary, Republican Senate Staff
Alberto Gonzales	Holdover, Texas State Judiciary Heritage Institute
Carlos Gutierrez	Michigan executive (Kelloggs)
Alphonso Jackson	Texas executive (Dallas Housing Authority)
Michael Johanns	Governor of Nebraska
Michael Leavitt	Governor of Utah
Norman Mineta	Holdover, Secretary of Commerce (Clinton)
Jim Nicholson	Former Chair, Republican National Committee
Gale Norton	Holdover, Attorney General of Colorado
Condoleezza Rice	2000 presidential campaign advisor
Donald Rumsfeld	Holdover, Secretary of Defense (Ford)
John Snow	Florida executive (CSX)
Margaret Spellings	Texas governor's office

building. The second-term Bush Administration adhered to these classic building blocks in cabinet building.

The oldest evidence of a president using cabinet building to build support for his administration came when George Washington used geographic diversity to broaden support for his administration in both the northern states and the southern states. Washington divided his cabinet in half geographically. He named two of his four appointments from the South and two from the North. He wanted to ensure that all citizens of the newly created republic felt represented in their government. This was a basic step in building political support for Washington's fledgling government. Although he was sure to alienate voters, he had built at least the bridge of representation to them.

Washington's bridge of representation was expanded in the twentieth century when women and minorities gained a seat in the Cabinet Room. The first woman in the cabinet was Frances Perkins, Secretary of Labor appointed by Franklin Delano Roosevelt. The Labor Building in Washington, DC bears her name. It was not a coincidence that Roosevelt named a woman, as women were moving into the workforce in the millions during the Depression and then during World War II. They were a voting bloc which became the criterion for representation in the president's cabinet. The major push for women in the cabinet coincided with the Equal Rights Movement of the 1970s and the passage of the Equal Right Amendment (ERA) in 1973. Women had by then emerged as a major force in American politics. Politicians coveted their vote. President Ford named the second woman cabinet officer and presidents subsequently routinely named one or two women to their cabinets.

Similarly, the civil rights movement brought political power to African Americans, leading Lyndon B. Johnson to name the first African American cabinet officer, Robert Weaver at Housing and Urban Development. By 1993 when President Clinton came to office, recent presidents had routinely named one or two women and one or two African Americans to their cabinets. But President Clinton saw an opportunity to build on the increasing political activism of women and minorities and symbolically stated through his cabinet, "the new Democratic Party is your party." He named more women and minorities to the cabinet than any president in history, including the nomination of the first female Attorney General and first female Secretary of State.

Ethnic and Gender Diversity in Cabinet Building

When President George W. Bush was inaugurated to his first term in January 2001, he clearly understood the political value of diverse representation in the cabinet. The strategy to continue broad ethnic and gender diversity was based on political necessity since the 2000 election failed to give President Bush a popular mandate. He had lost the popular vote in the 2000 election by 500,000 votes—Vice President Al Gore received 48.3 percent of the popular vote to George Bush who received 47.8 percent of the popular vote. Bush captured the Oval Office with the slimmest of victories, winning the Electoral College with 271 votes, one more than the necessary 270 electoral votes. As a result, the razor-thin victory was contested by Gore for over a month after the November election. Only after the Supreme Court ruled against Gore in *Bush v. Gore* in December did he concede.[11]

Because of the fragile state of his election, President-elect Bush attempted to build bridges to a broad spectrum of the voting public. He used the opportunity during the transition to build bridges through his cabinet selection process to include women and minorities and to ensure broad geographic breadth. The cabinet was designed to signal to the voting public that women and minorities would have a voice in the administration and that their interests would be given significant weight in the policymaking process. This strategy sought to reduce the tensions after the volatile 2000 election and to set the stage for the 2004 coalition that President Bush would need to engage for his reelection.

Not surprisingly, the first-term appointments to the Bush cabinet saw broad ethnic and gender diversity. The cabinet included not only women and African Americans, but also Hispanics and Asian Americans. There were two Asian Americans appointed to the cabinet, Elaine Chao at Labor and Norman Mineta at Transportation, and an Arab American, Spencer Abraham, at Energy. Of the fourteen original appointments, only seven were white males, or just over half of the nominees. This was not far from the Clinton cabinet of 1993 when six of the cabinet nominees were white

Table 4.3   Cabinet diversity of George W. Bush

Men	Women	African American	Hispanic	Asian
First-term cabinet 2001–2005				
Spencer Abraham	Elaine Chao	Alphonso Jackson		Elaine Chao
John Ashcroft	Gale Norton	Rod Paige		Norman Mineta
Don Evans	Ann M. Veneman	Colin Powell		
Alphonso Jackson				
Norman Mineta				
Rod Paige				
Colin Powell				
AnthonyPrincipi				
Tom Ridge				
Donald Rumsfeld				
John Snow				
Tommy Thompson				
80% Male	20% Female	20% African American	0% Hispanic	13% Asian
Second-term cabinet 2005–				
Sam Bodman	Elaine Chao	Alphonso Jackson	Alberto Gonzalez	
Alberto Gonzalez				
Norman Mineta				
Michael Leavitt	Gale Norton	Condoleezza Rice	Carlos Gutierrez	Elaine Chao
Carlos Gutierrez	Condoleezza Rice			
Alphonso Jackson	Margaret Spellings			
Mike Johanns				
Michael Chertoff				
Anthony Principi				
Donald Rumsfeld				
Jim Nicholson				
Norman Mineta				
73% Male	27% Female	13% African American	13% Hispanic	13% Asian

males. It is worth noting that both the Clinton and Bush cabinets were in stark contrast to the Nixon cabinet of 1969 that was 100 percent white male. According to Susan Page of *USA Today*, "Bush's appointments and his matter of fact approach to them signal a new stage in the racial history of the nation, one in which diversity is taken as a matter of course."[12] Whether such diversity becomes "a matter of course" remains to be seen, but it clearly built bridges to a divided electorate in 2001. It also built bridges to a divided electorate in 2005 (see table 4.3).

The second term is often an opportunity for presidents to relax their bridge building, but President Bush continued to use the cabinet to build bridges to women and minorities. There were for the second-term cabinet, eleven men and four women, an increase in gender diversity from the twelve men and three women in the first-term. Gender and ethnic diversity was evident with the appointment of seven white males, two white females, one Asian American male, one Asian American female, one African American male, one African American male, and two Hispanic males. As a comparison, the first-term cabinet had eight white males, two white females, one

Asian female, one Asian male, two African American males and one Arab male. The most significant diversity change was the addition of an African American woman in the cabinet.

Geographic Diversity in Cabinet Building

In addition to ethnic and gender diversity in his first- and second-term cabinet selections, President Bush included geographic diversity. During the first term, cabinet members were selected from each of the four regions of the county, such as Ann Veneman from California, Rod Paige from Texas, Paul O'Neill from Pennsylvania, John Ashcroft from Missouri and Tommy Thompson from Wisconsin. The cabinet, however, had a definite tilt toward the south and west. Few were from the northeast. The only first-term cabinet officer from the northeast was Paul O'Neill, although Tom Ridge of Pennsylvania was added following the creation of the Department of Homeland Security. It is worth noting that O'Neill was fired from the cabinet and John Snow of Florida added. Florida was pivotal to both the 2000 and 2004 elections.

Not surprisingly, the geographic diversity of the first-term cabinet was focused on building bridges to the south and west, the two regions that had given President Bush the strongest support during the 2000 election. There was virtually no effort to build bridges to the northeast, where the Democratic Party maintained its dominant foothold.

The second-term cabinet continued to have a tilt in its geographic diversity toward the south and west. Of the ten new nominees (that is, excluding the five holdovers—Chao, Rumsfeld, Norton, Mineta, and Snow) in the second term, we see the following geographic distribution:

- Mike Johanns—Nebraska
- Carlos Gutierrez—Michigan
- Margaret Spellings—Texas
- Sam Bodman—Massachusetts
- Mike Leavitt—Utah
- Michael Chertoff—New York
- Alphonso Jackson—Texas
- Alberto Gonzales—Texas
- Condoleezza Rice—California
- Jim Nicholson—Colorado

Note that only two of the ten cabinet nominees were from the northeast and only one from the Midwest—seven of the ten were from the south or west and three were from President Bush's home state of Texas. Thus we are beginning to see in the second term an effort to reward the "red states" (those states that voted Republican) for their 2004 electoral support.

While geographic diversity continued to be part of the strategic design to use the cabinet as a political tool, the focus was on building support within

Table 4.4   Relation between administration and key electoral states

Cabinet member	Electors represented
Sam Bodman—Massachusetts	12
Michael Chertoff—New York	31
Alberto Gonzales—Texas	34
Carlos Gutierrez—Michigan	17
Alphonso Jackson—Texas	34
Mike Johanns—Nebraska	5
Mike Leavitt—Utah	5
Jim Nicholson—Colorado	9
Condoleezza Rice—California	55
Margaret Spellings—Texas	34

certain geographic areas, particularly the south and the west. In this same light, the appointment of an African American from Texas and a Hispanic from Texas is a signal that the administration is seeking to solidify its base among the African American and Hispanic community in the south. The absence of a single African American from the northeast or midwest indicates that the administration and the Republican Party will be focusing their energies on the south and west. It is also worth noting that most of the new cabinet offices came from the states that the Republicans have targeted for the 2008 presidential election. Democratic margins in Michigan, New York, and California have been declining and both New York and California elected Republican governors. The effort to enhance the relationship between the administration and key electoral states is part of the Bush cabinet building strategy (see table 4.4).

Electoral Representation of Cabinet Members

The Presidential Orbit

Perhaps the most interesting analysis of the second-term cabinet involves the background of the nominees, particularly the number of nominees that are moving from the White House staff to the cabinet. Of the fifteen cabinet appointees, in the Second term. President Bush selected three from his White House staff: Margaret Spellings for Education, Alberto Gonzales for Justice, and Condoleezza Rice for State. Is this unusual for White House staff to move into the cabinet? The answer is no, since it has been done in recent administrations. We saw, for example, similar changes in the second term of the Reagan administration when Reagan moved two key White House staff to the cabinet. Ed Meese was moved by President Reagan from his position as White House domestic advisor to the Justice Department and Jim Baker moved from his position as chief of staff to the Treasury Department.

President Clinton moved Alexis Herman from the White House to the Labor Department after having moved Mickey Kantor to the Labor Department from the White House following the death of Ron Brown in a plane crash in Bosnia. And President Clinton tried but failed to move his National Security Advisor, Tony Lake, to the CIA but his nomination failed in the Senate confirmation process. So there is clearly precedent in recent second-term administrations for moving White House staff to the cabinet. The only difference between the Bush administration and other administrations is that Bush moved three White House staff at one time. There is however clearly precedent for moving White House staff into the cabinet in spite of the headlines we have been seeing.

The Conservative Agenda in Cabinet Building

We have looked at several of the more obvious components of the second-term Bush cabinet, specifically political ideology, ethnic and gender diversity, and geographic diversity. We also now want to look at the commitment by cabinet officers to the conservative agenda. In the first term, President Bush chose twelve of his fourteen cabinet officers from the ranks of the conservative wing of the Republican Party. There was little effort to build bridges to the moderate or liberal wing of the Republican Party. President Bush kept one Clinton cabinet officer, Norman Mineta, who was a Democrat, and he brought in Colin Powell, a moderate Republican. The political homogeneity of the Bush cabinet was one of its significant hallmarks—the cabinet was politically conservative, ideologically consistent, and generally pro-life and pro-business.

The single most important test of joining the Bush cabinet in 2001 was the commitment to the conservative political goals of the administration. Among these goals were the affirmation of the right to life agenda and the banning of homosexual marriage. The principles of the religious right of the Republican Party were evident in the cabinet appointments. Some members of the cabinet were so openly religious that they held regular prayer meetings in their departments once in office. John Ashcroft invited his senior staff in the Justice Department to morning prayer meetings and Donald Rumsfeld in the Defense Department invited Franklyn Graham to lead departmental prayer sessions. The first-term cabinet did not include a single non-Christian and most cabinet members were Evangelical Christians.

The second-term cabinet maintained the same commitment to conservative principles. It was again a cabinet composed primarily of born-again Christians from the conservative wing of the Republican Party. For example, in the second term Bush added Jim Nicholson, the former chair of the Republican National Committee (RNC), an outspoken conservative from Colorado. Both Mike Johanns of Nebraska and Michael Leavitt of Utah were also Christian conservatives within the Republican Party.

The dominance of conservatives in the cabinet who were also Christian conservatives continues the realignment of the Republican Party. During the Nixon, Ford, and Reagan administrations, the Republican Party sought to devolve government programs from the national to the state level through what Nixon called the "New Federalism." However, the Bush administration that came into office in 2001 began the transformation of the federal government as a vehicle for funding programs that were part of the conservative agenda. Such programs included faith-based initiatives, abstinence programs, and pregnancy counseling for adoption.

Political Ideology and the Sub-Cabinet in Cabinet Building

The Bush administration successfully filled its sub-cabinet appointments with political conservatives who were supportive of the president's conservative agenda. For example, many sub-cabinet appointees were born-again Christians. In addition, many of the appointees were pro-business conservative activists who had been lobbyists for companies they were now regulating. For example, Mark Rey, the Undersecretary of Agriculture for natural resources was a lobbyist for the timber industry and Michael Parker, Assistant Secretary of the Army for Civil Works, was a lobbyist for the barge industry who openly opposed Army Corps of Engineers projects, and Michael Jackson, Deputy Secretary of Transportation, was vice president of the trucking industry. Another striking feature of the sub-cabinet was the overwhelming number of white males and the inclusion of relatively few women and minorities. This can largely be explained by the focus on business and lobbying organization personnel to populate the sub-cabinet, a group that is traditionally dominated by white males. In contrast, when President Clinton filled the ranks of the sub-cabinet, he turned to advocacy groups that have much higher numbers of women and minorities.

Other examples of politically conservative appointments within the sub-cabinet were Kay Coles James from the Heritage Foundation and Pat Robertson's Regent University, Jay Leftowitz, a former law partner of Kenneth Starr, and Theodore Olson, a board member of the conservative *American Spectator* magazine. President Bush even nominated Eugene Scalia, the son of Justice Antonin Scalia, as chief counsel for the Labor Department. Because of his extreme conservative leanings, he was one of several appointments the Senate refused to confirm. The President later named him as a recess appointment.

Thus, although there is strong gender and racial diversity in both the first- and second-term cabinet, the sub-cabinet lacks such diversity. The geographic concentration of cabinet nominees in the south and west, the focus on Christian conservatives in the cabinet, and the conservative ideological orientation of the cabinet and sub-cabinet appointments paint a picture of governance aimed at a narrow segment of the American public.

Conclusion

This chapter began by noting that Presidents have traditionally used cabinet building as a signal to the American public regarding their approach to governance. Cabinet building is often the first opportunity that the nation has to assess the administration. As we look at the cabinet-building strategies of the first and second terms, the strategies appear identical. While there was strong gender and racial diversity in the cabinet, the sub-cabinet remained remarkably white and male. In addition, both the first- and second-term cabinets were drawn predominantly from the south and midwest, which was the base of the 2000 and 2004 elections for President Bush. Finally, both the first- and second-term cabinets were drawn from the conservative ranks of the Republican Party.

The major change in the second term was the absence of moderates in the cabinet. With the departure of Colin Powell and Tom Ridge, the two moderates in the first term, the cabinet became solidly conservative, with the exception of Democratic holdover Norman Mineta. The absence of moderates in the second term implied a narrower focus in the decision-making structure. This focus was enhanced by the appointment of three White House staffers to the cabinet who were not only conservatives but were presidential insiders. By increasing the number of both conservatives and loyalists in the second-term cabinet, President Bush reduced the number of differing opinions voiced in the policymaking process. The cabinet had become a unitary voice that was moving toward groupthink.[13] Cabinet officers in the first term rarely offered their own points of view in public. When they did, they faced White House retribution. Paul O'Neill, Secretary of the Treasury, was fired for arguing against economic policy emanating from the White House; Secretary of Health and Human Services Tommy Thompson often needed to be reined in by the White House. On his last day at Health and Human Services, Thompson again ran into trouble with the White House when he announced that the nation's food supply was vulnerable to terrorist attacks. Secretary of State Colin Powell also refused to follow the White House policy directives and was frequently at odds with official policy positions.

The dilemma for the Bush administration's second term will be how to build a cabinet that is loyal and that reaches out to core supporters without resulting in group think. Or will the second term be dominated by a narrow agenda focused on massaging the conservative wing of the Republican Party as the cabinet-building strategy seems to indicate?

The chapter began with the premise that presidents have traditionally used cabinet building as a means to signal to the American public how they will approach governance. It appears that the second-term cabinet of President George W. Bush is a strong indicator of how he will govern.

Notes

1. Jamie McIntyre, "Secretary Powell? Bush Hints of Former General's Role," CNN Web.
2. Alexis Simendinger wrote in the *National Journal* in October, 2004; Carl Cannon, "Which Bush?" *National Journal*, November 6, 2004, p. 3343.
3. Elisabeth Bumuller, "Ashcroft Quits Top Justice Post, Evans Going To," *New York Times*, November 1, 2004, p. A1.
4. Public Papers of the President, January 23, 1977, "Cabinet Swearing In Ceremony."
5. Ibid.
6. Dom Bonafede, "Reagan and His Kitchen Cabinet are Bound by Friendship and Ideology," *National Journal*, April 11, 1981, p. 608.
7. Janet Hook and Chuck Alston, "Mixed Signals, Agenda Gap Plague Bush's First Year," *Congressional Quarterly*, November 4, 1989, p. 2922.
8. John Burke, "Lessons from Past Presidential Transitions," in *White House World*, ed. Marthan Joynt Kumar and Terry Sullivan (College Station, Texas: Texas A&M Press, 2003).
9. Gwen Ifill, "Clinton's High Stakes Shuffle to Get the Right Cabinet Mix," *New York Times*, December 21, 1992, p. A1.
10. Kenneth Walsh, "Grand Ambitions," *U.S. News and World Report*, November 29, 2004.
11. *Bush v. Gore*, 531 U.S. 98 (2000).
12. Susan Page, "Bush is Opening Doors with a Diverse Cabinet," *USA Today*, December 10, 2004, p. A1.
13. Irving L. Janus, *Groupthink: Psychological Studies of Policy Decisions and Fiascoes*, 2d. ed. (Boston, MA: Houghton Mifflin, 1982).

Chapter Five

George W. Bush and Congress in the Second Term: New Problems—Same Results?

Andrew Rudalevige

When it comes to presidents and Congress, familiarity seems to breed contempt. Compare, for example, presidents' first and second term records on one common measure of legislative success. Presidents start out with ideas, energy, and sometimes even a mandate. But reelected, their clout fades, or so it seems. When examining contested roll calls on which the president took a position, each reelected president since Eisenhower did worse in his second term than in his first. The scope of the drop-off varies, House to Senate and president to president. But if postwar history is any guide, an average chief executive will see his success rate in each chamber plummet a full twenty percentage points in a second term.[1] By the end of their terms, as one aide said of Lyndon Johnson, they can't "get [a resolution honoring] Mother's Day through."[2]

This is simplistic, to be sure, and given the small sample size it is hard to make such calculations with any real exactitude. Yet the pattern is clear enough; nor are reasons for it hard to find. First and foremost, presidents have usually seen the size of their co-partisan legislative delegation diminish over time—Eisenhower, for example, enjoyed Republican control of Congress in 1953–1954, but not thereafter. Republicans led the Senate for the first six years of the Reagan administration, but lost that edge in 1987. Bill Clinton's Democratic majorities evaporated after 1994.

However, presidents themselves have helped their own demise. Reelected administrations often suffer from a sort of hubris that may lead to overreach (FDR's court-packing) or to scandal (Watergate, Monica Lewinsky). At the same time they may run short of new ideas, reduced to offering minor initiatives or to repackaging earlier proposals. A Reagan staffer warned that a 1987 State of the Union legislative "laundry list" might consist "mainly of sweat socks and old underwear."[3] It's worth noting too that since the passage of the 22nd amendment, presidents have been lame ducks from the moment they take their second oath of office. Members of Congress will face the voters again; the president cannot. Naturally enough those members' interests,

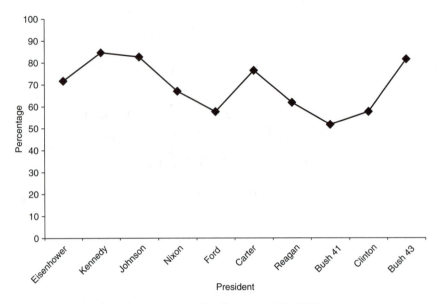

Figure 5.1   Presidential success on roll-call votes, 1953–2004

Source: *CQ Weekly Report* (December 11, 2004).

even those of the President's strongest loyalists, begin to diverge. Ambition, even if deferred for a time, begins once more to check ambition.

Does the same fate await President George W. Bush, reelected in 2004 after a first term marked by impressive success in the legislative arena? When the 108th Congress adjourned on December 8, 2004, Bush became the first full-term president in 175 years—since John Quincy Adams—not to have vetoed a single bill. The reason was simple: he didn't need to. When asked at a December 2004 press conference about using the veto to curb spending, the President sounded bemused: "they passed bills that met our budget targets. And so how could you veto a series of appropriations bills if the Congress has done what you've asked them to do?" Indeed, by at least one reckoning (see figure 5.1), Bush was more successful than any president since the heady Great Society days of the mid-1960s. And, if anything, as discussed later, this particular measure may well *under*estimate Bush's success in some ways.

From 2001 through 2004, indeed, Congress largely did what the president asked it to do. That included resolutions giving the president unfettered authority to take military action after 9/11 and against Saddam Hussein's Iraq, as well as three major tax cuts (plus two smaller ones), an expensive restructuring of Medicare, and significant expansion of the federal role in public education. It also included failing to pass measures the president opposed—not just affirmative attempts at legislation but efforts to overturn controversial actions taken unilaterally by the administration, from revising overtime rules to the indefinite detention of American citizens suspected in the war on terror. Bush and a steadfast Republican leadership in Congress, especially in the House, showed that a firm grip on the legislative and public agendas can produce meaningful policy change.

This chapter examines the prospects for extending this record in President Bush's second term. First it details what political scientists know about presidential-congressional relations generally. Subsequent sections review Bush's first-term success and the lessons he drew from it, briefly tracing his agenda, the strategies and contexts through which he sought to implement it, and what we might expect of developments to come.

The picture is mixed. In the 2004 election, the president won re-election as the GOP increased both its Senate and House majorities. These gains, all else equal, strengthen the Bush administration's hand in its legislative dealings, a hand already reinforced by the administration's record of working within, and manipulating, its political environment. However, the president's announced agenda for the 109th Congress was correspondingly more ambitious. The likelihood of partisan warfare over looming Supreme Court vacancies and gloomy news from Iraq, along with massive budget deficits, myriad competing policy priorities, and continued divisions among voters, cast long shadows over Capitol Hill. In short, the structural political context seemed far less favorable to presidential management, and thus to influence over legislative outcomes, than it did in the first term. Still, based on prior returns it would be wrong to underestimate either George W. Bush's determination to win—or the determination of his allies in Congress to help him do so.

Presidents and Congress

Though the Constitution vests legislative power in Congress, presidents have long been entrenched in the legislative process. Beyond the constitutional requirements that the Senate ratify treaties and confirm high-level appointments, presidents have the power to veto congressional enactments (and thus to bargain over them) as well as the responsibility to propose measures they think "necessary and expedient." Franklin Roosevelt took full advantage of this during his famous "hundred days" in 1933; his successors have institutionalized a presidential legislative program, an annual package of requests across the spectrum of national needs as the president sees them.

The president's success in persuading Congress to accept his programmatic proposals has become a key factor in assessing his overall success. As Carter and Clinton administration official Stu Eizenstat put it: "People judge strong presidents versus weak presidents on the basis of whether they perceive that the president is able to get the Congress to do what he wants. And brother, if you have the perception that you cannot, then regardless of how competent you may be you are not going to be judged competent in the office."[4]

That judgment is often unfair, given that political scientists have found actual presidential "competence"—in the limited sense of personal leadership skills, at least—to be a relatively minor component of legislative success. Who is president certainly matters: presidents' popularity, their use of the presidential pulpit to spotlight particular issues, and their ability to bargain effectively with key legislators are all useful tools. But these operate largely "at the margins."[5] Indeed, three things seem most important to presidential success: the broad political setting, the influence of external events, and presidential strategies of agenda setting and policy formulation.

The fundamental parameters of a given outcome are structured externally by the political context. Bush aide Karl Rove mused in early 2005 that "history has a way of intruding on you," and this is especially true of a president's opportunity to lead. The most important determinant is the number of seats held in Congress by the president's co-partisans, along with his ideological congruence with the House and Senate majorities. Presidents overseeing large majorities of like-minded partisans in both chambers (e.g., Lyndon Johnson in 1965–1966) will, not surprisingly, get more of what they ask for than presidents in divided government (e.g., Bill Clinton in 1995–1996) or even presidents where the label "unified" government disguises deep ideological fissures in the majority party (e.g., Jimmy Carter in 1977–1980).

Other aspects of the political world within which presidents must operate should be kept in mind as well. Broad expectations of government (is it a solution, or a problem?); the strength of party leadership in Congress; the relative unity of the president's electoral coalition, along with his mandate (if any); the size and disposition of the interest group universe; the state of the national economy—all these are things the president can affect, but rarely command. In short, where presidents fall in "political time," and their ability to discern the tenor of that time, gives them a better or worse chance of achieving policy change.[6]

A second set of factors stems from what scholars have called "focusing events." In times of national crisis, legislators are far more likely to defer to presidential initiative. The Congress, like the public as a whole, tends to "rally 'round the flag' " in wartime, and to respond readily to domestic natural or manmade disasters.

Presidents are hardly without strategic options, though. The makeup of their agenda is something presidents usually have a choice about (though it may well be influenced by events). Policy type matters too: presidents are often given more leeway in foreign affairs than in domestic matters. Further, large and complex proposals on average do worse than incremental changes.

Presidents also have a choice about how many issues to press—should they attempt a focused "rifle" or a widespread "shotgun" approach? And they can puzzle about how to manage policy formulation, since centralizing this process within the White House, without departmental input, tends to hurt a proposal's chances for success. Each of these strategies is selected within, then interacts with, the "intrusions of history" noted above.[7]

George W. Bush: The First Term, 2001–2004

Projections for the second Bush term must be leveraged from the lessons of the first. As noted above, the president had an enviable track record with the 107th and 108th Congresses. Several factors will be highlighted in this section: the president's focused initial agenda, disciplined Republican party majorities in the House, the shock (and aftershocks) of the September 11 attacks, and the administration's deft use of the political capital these contexts provided. In short, history dealt the president a good hand. But he played it adroitly.

Making a Mandate

On Election Day 2000, Democrat Al Gore won the popular vote. In the all-important Electoral College, though, there was no immediate winner, and it took more than a month—and an unprecedented 5:4 ruling by the Supreme Court—to determine the outcome. Even as President Bush won, Republicans lost four seats in the Senate to leave that body split evenly at fifty seats for each party, in GOP control only by virtue of the vice president's ability to break tie votes. In the House, the majority's margin was shaved to just ten seats, meaning that five Republican dissenters could stymie presidential initiatives. It appeared that the presidential honeymoon would more closely resemble a one-night stand.

However, the president behaved as though he had a mandate for the policies he had propounded during the 2000 contest, choosing to ignore the thin majorities and bitter disputes. Press clippings from early 2001 suggest that the new administration "relentlessly focused on the campaign agenda." Bush did have some advantages here. For one thing, he was the first Republican president to have *any* congressional majority in both chambers of Congress since Dwight Eisenhower in 1953–1954. His legislative allies were exultant and energized; as Texas Sen. Phil Gramm put it, "I've been waiting all my life to have a Republican president and a Republican Congress." At the same time the public was eager for closure after the campaign and the question of the president's legitimacy in office quickly faded. Bush took office famously claiming to be a "uniter, not a divider." He pointed to his record as Texas governor as evidence of his ability to cross party lines and work toward consensus on key issues.[8]

Though Social Security reform was relegated to a study commission (to reemerge as a major issue in 2005), the other components of the 2000 agenda—tax cuts, education reform, Medicare expansion, and support for faith-based social programs and charitable giving—were quickly sent to Congress. The faith-based initiative won some support but would ultimately be implemented largely administratively; amendments to Medicare would pass in 2003. Early on, education and taxes were the president's clear priorities, in terms of time and political capital. Both were important: the No Child Left Behind Act (NCLB) was the largest restructuring of the Elementary and Secondary Education Act since its passage in 1965; the 2001 tax cuts were the largest since 1981. And both were passed.

Both bills, further, were bipartisan—though they showed how elastic that descriptor can be. On NCLB, the president did indeed build a broad coalition of the willing. Bush worked with numerous Democrats, including liberal icon Ted Kennedy. In the end, the extreme right and extreme left broke away, but the center held. After an extended conference committee process reconciling House and Senate versions of the legislation, led by Kennedy, Representative George Miller (D-CA), Senator Judd Gregg (R-NH) and Representative John Boehner (R-OH), NCLB became law in early January 2002.[9]

The 2001 tax cuts also attracted some bipartisan support, but in effect rather than in approach.[10] That was mainly because they were very hard for Democrats to be against. The federal budget was in the black—the surplus was then projected at US$5.6 trillion over ten years—and the 2000 campaign had posed a choice between placing the surplus in a Social Security "lockbox" and spending it on tax cuts. After the election, Democrats found themselves constrained to arguing over the size and makeup of the package, not the fact of it. The president's proposal of US$1.6 trillion in tax relief over ten years, attained by cutting rates for all taxpayers, doubling the child tax credit, eliminating the estate tax (effectively renamed the "death tax" by the GOP), and lessening the marriage penalty for joint filers, passed in the House largely as written (its three sections attracting as many as sixty-four Democratic votes). In the Senate, Montana Senator Max Baucus, ranking Democrat on the Finance Committee, broke ranks with those who wanted to hold the package to US$900 billion or so and began working with Finance Republicans on a compromise. The US$1.35 trillion conference committee report, based largely on the Senate version, was signed into law in June. Since its stated cost was attained only by writing disingenuous sunset provisions into the plan, the president had attained largely what he wanted.

On issues with less crossover appeal at the outset, however, the president did not try very hard to attract new allies. The president's version of the HMO patients' "bill of rights" measure was a good example. It did not attract Democratic votes but was enough to stalemate a conference committee—not a bad outcome, from the president's point of view. Another was the industry-friendly energy bill, whose inclusion of exploratory drilling in the Alaskan National Wildlife Refuge helped make it one of the president's few outright legislative failures in the first term.[11] Bipartisanship, then, depended largely on the bill's starting point: Bush worked with any Democratic allies who presented themselves early in the process, but did not usually reach out further than he had to in order to gain converts along the way.

In one important case, in fact, the conversion went awry. In May, Republican Senator Jim Jeffords of Vermont became an independent, giving Democrats control of the Senate by a 50–49 margin. The shift did not affect NCLB or the tax bill, but as Labor Day approached, it was unclear how much additional success the president would have in the 107th Congress. Gridlock impended; it seemed that the president had lost control of the agenda.

But as it turned out, a new agenda was on its way.

Uniting America

The terrorist attacks of September 11, 2001, do not need to be revisited here in any detail. However, whether or not they "changed everything," they clearly changed the Bush presidency in a dramatic fashion. From a 50–50 split the week before the attacks, Bush's public approval ratings quickly brushed 90 percent. As Americans waited tensely for additional attacks, the president took charge. On September 20, he addressed a joint session of Congress. Afterwards, Representative Maxine Waters (D-CA), one of the most liberal members of the House, described the speech as a "home run, a ten. . . . Right now," she added, "the president of the United States has support for almost anything he wants to do."[12]

He wanted to do a lot. Even before the president spoke, Congress passed a joint resolution broadly authorizing President Bush to use "all necessary and appropriate force against those nations, organizations, or persons he determines planned, authorized, committed, or aided the terrorist attacks that occurred on September 11, 2001, or harbored such organizations or persons."[13] There was just one dissenting vote in the House and none in the Senate—most part of the Senate's discussion of the bill actually took place *after* the vote. Forty billion dollars in emergency aid was also provided, to be spent largely at the president's discretion. A Transportation Security Agency was created (though here, Senate Democrats were able to get the president to accept security screeners as federal employees). The president proposed another tax cut to stimulate business investment by accelerating depreciation deductions and amending the corporate alternative minimum tax (AMT); this became law in March 2002. Presidential trade promotion authority (a.k.a. "fast-track"), another Bush priority, was passed in August.

The process behind the October 2001 USA PATRIOT Act, which expanded federal law enforcement powers, exemplified the willingness of legislative leaders to defer to the president on issues linked to the war on terror. The administration draft received no hearings or committee consideration in the Senate, going directly to the floor—where it was to be considered under a unanimous consent order in the Senate that prohibited amendments or even discussion. Unanimous consent was denied by Senator Russ Feingold (D-WI); nonetheless, it was passed unamended after just four hours of debate, with only Feingold's vote against. On the House side, the normally polarized Judiciary Committee rewrote the administration's draft to provide increased protections for civil liberties. However, at the behest of the White House, the new version passed unanimously in committee vanished from consideration, replaced with language much closer to the administration's own proposal. The rule closed off all other amendments, and allowed just one hour for debate; no advance analysis was provided of the 187 pages of new text.[14] Still, it was passed, 337–79. It should be noted that in the conference committee the bill regained some of the checks that civil libertarians had urged. Most significant was a sunset provision for many (though not all) of the changes in the surveillance regime; they were to expire on January 1, 2006, unless extended.

The shockwaves of September 11 extended well into 2002, with the president doing his best to keep the agenda focused on what became known as the "global war on terror." The 2002 State of the Union address warned grimly of an "axis of evil" intent on undermining American security. And a new war was on the horizon—this time preventive rather than reactive. After condemning Iraq in an effective speech to the United Nations that fall, the president turned to Congress and requested a resolution authorizing the use of force to remove Saddam Hussein (an "axis" member) from power. The original administration draft authorized the president "to use all means that he determine[d] to be appropriate" in order to "restore international peace and security in the region"—a broad grant indeed, given the paucity of both those attributes in the Middle East. Congressional negotiators removed that phrase. But the bottom line changed little, and passed by margins of 77–23 and 296–133 in the Senate and House, respectively. Legislators, spooked by constant and seemingly persuasive (though ultimately inaccurate) warnings of Hussein's armory of chemical, biological, and nuclear weapons—and by the upcoming midterm elections— didn't want to vote against what the president said was a national security imperative.

The midterm elections also helped the president attain another legislative victory. After opposing creation of a new Department of Homeland Security (DHS), the president had changed his tune in June 2002, taking ownership of the idea by proposing a reorganization plan more expansive than the one before Congress.[15] In order to evade entrenched committee interests averse to the jurisdictional changes that a new department would require, the House created a new select committee chaired by Majority Leader Dick Armey to move the administration bill. However, while the Senate version met the president's structural preferences, it limited the administration's flexibility over personnel. Bush reacted with one of the few successful instances of presidential involvement in Congressional elections. Campaigning vigorously, the president made a record ninety appearances on behalf of House, Senate, and gubernatorial candidates. He battered Democrats opposing his homeland security bill, even painting them as unpatriotic.

The tactic worked. Republicans re-took the Senate, and the president took the credit. Stunned Democrats acceded to the president's DHS bill soon after. The lame-duck Senate also confirmed a number of judicial nominees bottled up since earlier in the year.

Uniting the Party

Over the course of the 107th Congress, partisan polarization grew; both a result and cause of the president's style and his success. The president's claim to be a uniter had worked: Republicans and Democrats were united only in fervent opposition to each other. Republican discipline in the House—even on issues that many rank-and-file House members weren't enthused over, like fast-track trade authority, or a federal guarantee for terrorism insurance—held firm.[16] Democrats were able to use their control over the Senate to prevent the president's most conservative judicial nominees from receiving confirmation, and they were able to block the energy bill and modify some presidential measures. But they had little success in passing their own initiatives, though the president bowed to public opinion in some cases on issues he was not much vested in. He decided to avoid the criticism that would have come with vetoing a new campaign finance law, for example, and reversed course to endorse creation of a blue-panel commission to investigate the September 11 attacks.

As the 108th Congress began, the president again kept his legislative agenda short, but ambitious. It began, as in 2001, with tax cuts. Despite rising red ink (the 2001 surplus had become a US$185 billion deficit by the end of fiscal 2002) and the imminent expenses of war in Iraq, in January 2003 Bush proposed an additional US$726 billion in tax relief, centered on the elimination of the corporate dividends tax and the acceleration of some of the 2001 tax cuts. The House ultimately passed a budget resolution including the president's full request, in part because the start of the Iraq war made it difficult for Republicans to vote against the president in any area. (Indeed, Majority Leader Tom DeLay told holdouts their patriotism was in question.) A small band of Senate Republicans balked, and ultimately just US$330 billion of additional tax cuts were passed. However, the president rightly claimed victory for this half-a-loaf, given that he had now overseen cuts in taxes three years running—a streak that ran to four years when legislators approved additional extensions of the 2001 cuts, and a wide range of corporate tax breaks, in the fall of 2004. Other administration priorities were also attained in 2003–2004. The long-time Republican goal of banning late-term abortions was passed in the fall of 2003; and various bills funding the war on terror, especially the occupation of Iraq subsequent to the March 2003 invasion, generally received significant support. Most notable was the $87 billion request that so confused Democratic presidential nominee John Kerry (D-MA); his was one of just twelve Senate votes against it.

A measure for reorganizing the intelligence community in the wake of its pre- (and post-) 9/11 failures became law at the very end of 2004. The president sought first to forestall the bill by making some changes by executive order but was finally pressured during the election to pledge his support; he successfully used his clout both to weaken it and to overcome GOP resistance to the final product. The bill marked a rare case of legislative initiative in the national security arena, only possible because of the very public, unanimous efforts of the well-regarded 9/11 Commission and the families of the attacks' victims. As discussed below, most presidential defeats in the 108th Congress tended instead to be on roll calls requiring supermajorities, usually on Senate cloture votes that required bipartisan consent.

As the term progressed, then, unified government was the key variable. The GOP strategy was to govern less from the middle out than from the right wing in; as House Speaker Dennis Hastert put it, the Republican default position was to seek a "majority of the majority" rather than to pass bills that alienated much of his caucus.[17] The president would make large, bold proposals, and loudly "refuse to negotiate against [himself]." His legislative liaison staff would then blanket Capitol Hill, working closely with the party whip organizations.[18] The House—with its ability to quell dissent and amendment through restrictive rules governing debate—would find 218 votes (rarely many more) to pass his proposal.[19] The Senate (now in GOP hands, but with far more consensual rules, including the filibuster, to protect minority Democrats) would pass a more moderate variant—but then come down close to the House position in conference deliberations. In either chamber, party loyalty was closely held, as figure 5.2 suggests. The bars show the president's overall rate of success on roll call votes, while the line series suggest the breadth of the partisan divide. The average Republican House member voted with the president on roll call votes on which the president took a position almost 85 percent of the time—but the average Democratic congressman did so less than 30 percent of the time. In the

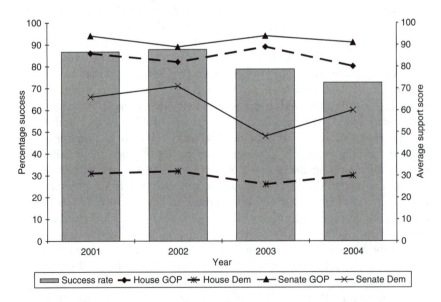

Figure 5.2   Presidential support in 107th–108th congresses, 2001–2004
Source: Congressional Quarterly (CQ) *Weekly Report* (December 11, 2004).

Senate the spread was somewhat less, but GOP loyalty topped an astonishing 90 percent on average, and 94 percent in both 2001 and 2003.

Because of bicameralism, the enhanced role of conference committees was an important asset to the Republican leadership. Conference committees, designed to compromise between different versions of legislation passed by House and Senate, exercised a good deal of independent authority: they felt free to add things that had not been adopted by either chamber, or to delete items that had been passed by both chambers (such as a prohibition on torture passed in the intelligence reform bill but deleted from the final conference report). Exacerbating polarization, Democratic conferees were sometimes refused entry to conference committee meetings.[20]

The Medicare restructuring and prescription drug bill of 2003 shows off many of these elements. After stressing the issue in the 2000 campaign and during 2001 and 2002, the president turned once more to Senator Ted Kennedy (D-MA) to craft a measure that could attract Democratic votes. But in the House, the president instead sought to build the bill he really wanted around a coalition of 218 Republicans. Because of conservative members' objections to the bill's cost (then publicly estimated at $400 billion) he barely managed this: when the fifteen-minute vote on passage was called at 3 a.m., the president's bill lost 215–219. Rather than close the vote, though, House leaders worked the floor and the president the phones, twisting arms and making offers. By 5 a.m. the tally was 216–218, and at 5:51 a.m. shifted to 218–217.

The conference committee, as appointed, contained ten Republicans and seven Democrats. But only two of the Democrats—moderates Baucus and John Breaux—were ever admitted to its deliberations. More than forty Republican representatives pledged not to support any compromise that tilted toward the Senate draft of the bill (which was far less generous to private health plans and drug companies). The conference committee report tilted heavily toward the House version, sprinkled with health care pork to attract Senate votes. Helped by Democrats wary of voting against what was, after all, a massive expansion of a public health care program, it was adopted in November.[21]

Between the Branches

A review of the Bush administration's relations with Congress would not be complete without examining areas where the administration hoped to avoid Congress altogether. Given the grueling gauntlet run even by successful legislation, unilateral action is a constant temptation for presidents; President Bush made it a mission. At a press conference in early 2002, he warned against "encroachment" on executive prerogatives. He argued that "I'm not going to let Congress erode the power of the executive branch. . . . I have an obligation to make sure that the Presidency remains robust and the legislative branch doesn't end up running the executive branch." Indeed, even before September 11, the Bush administration had asserted a wide range of unilateral claims aimed at rolling back the legislative claims of power developed after Watergate.[22] It refused to provide documents concerning the formulation of the administration's energy plan to the General Accounting Office (GAO), Congress's auditing agency. The president issued an executive order modifying the 1978 Presidential Records Act to make it easier for both incumbents and former presidents to block access to archived documents in the presidential library system. De-classification efforts were rolled back. Signing statements disclaimed the president's responsibility to implement portions of enacted legislation.

After September 11, not surprisingly, the pace picked up. The Justice Department rescinded the Ford-era restrictions on domestic spying by the FBI. Immigration hearings were routinely closed and many aliens held without bond. The president claimed the authority to set aside portions of the Geneva Conventions, removing prisoner-of-war protections from detainees in the war on terror; indeed, his Justice Department and White House counsel argued that statutes banning torture were unconstitutional when they interfered with the president's power as commander-in-chief. The president also argued he could create military tribunals outside the normal judicial system for some terrorism suspects and issued an executive order doing just that. Most dramatically, the administration claimed that defendants—even American citizens, arrested within the United States—could be held indefinitely without charge or lawyer if they were designated "enemy combatants." The determination of who qualified as an enemy combatant was, according to the president, entirely up to him, not the courts or legislature, and not even reviewable by those branches of government.

The Supreme Court rejected the last argument, at least in part, requiring minimal due process protections (though upholding the president's power under the September 2001 use-of-force resolution to designate and hold combatants).[23] Through 2004, though, Congressional response to presidential assertions of unilateral authority, whether to check or merely oversee, was minimal. It did not debate, for example, whether to suspend the right of *habeas corpus*, preferring to defer to the president's tribunal system. Even the power of the purse was dissipated by non-existent budget resolutions and appropriations processes capped by massive omnibus acts that enhanced leadership power as well as deference to presidential policy preferences. After all, as one appropriations aide admitted, with time running out, "If there's veto-bait, we've got to make sure that the administration is happy." This meant in fiscal 2005, for example, that riders aimed at limiting Bush administration outsourcing plans, relaxing trade restrictions with Cuba, and limiting new overtime pay regulations were discarded in conference.[24] The veto itself was not necessary.

Of course, Congress in recent years has spent less time doing anything at all, with two-day workweeks that dropped the average days spent in session by a third compared to the 1970s. In 2004, legislators allowed dozens of expiring authorization bills—most notably concerning highways and mass transit, early childhood and higher education programs, and even the much-vaunted 1996 welfare reforms—simply to roll over without substantive review. In some cases this gave the president power to reshape those programs by regulatory means without effective oversight.[25] No objection was heard from the White House.

Conclusions: Summing Up Success

"Responsible party government" was long a mantra of political scientists worried about Washington gridlock. Starting in 2001, they got what they said they wanted. Indeed, unlike in 1993–1994, the last period of unified government, aggressive efforts to harness party discipline usually succeeded to work substantive change. Recall Figure One: Bush's overall level of success on roll call votes on which he took a position was dramatically higher than any president in the last twenty years. The last president to come close was Jimmy Carter, who also had an extended period of unified government with which to work.[26]

Again, these scores should not be taken as exact measures in absolute terms, though they are useful in making comparisons. "Success" is hard to measure: roll call votes, for one, are limited since they include only what makes it to the floor and do not account for the substance of what actually becomes law. Votes can be gamed: holding all else constant, more ambitious presidents—because they ask for more—will have lower success rates, and presidents who ask for things that will pass anyway will boost their "batting average."

Still, in contrast to the Carter case, these complications tended to work in Bush's favor. It helped that he had a relatively narrow agenda of priorities. But most important measures actively opposed by the president never made it to a floor vote. Further, especially in 2003 and 2004, the "losses" attributed to Bush in figures 5.1 and 5.2 often reflected votes on amendments that never made it into statute but were, as in the fiscal 2005 omnibus appropriations act noted above, stripped in conference committee by the Republican leadership.[27] Other defeats came on supermajority votes, especially on cloture, where Democrats bonded in bitterness to filibuster ten judges or constitutional amendments, which require a two-thirds vote to pass. Yet these on the whole were not important substantive defeats. Fifteen votes in 2003 failed to close debate on the nominations of three judges: the three judges might be three losses, but not fifteen, and over two hundred others were confirmed. In 2004, while the president failed to gain the votes to approve an amendment banning gay marriage, winning the votes mattered little. It was enough to highlight the Massachusetts judicial decision providing for gay marriage in that state, revving up the conservative base across the Midwest and south, to provide the political victory Bush sought.[28]

Thus, President Bush's first term is best deemed a legislative success. Further, it was a political success. The president was reelected, despite lingering public doubts about the Iraq war and the administration's stewardship of the economy. The GOP picked up seats in both 2002 and 2004. Some of this was luck, of sorts—Democrats, for example, failed to provide either a unified alternative agenda or field a sufficiently credible alternative presidential candidate. And without September 11, the GOP legislative majority may well have been overturned in 2002, leading to, say, the first term of President Dick Gephardt in 2005. However, President Bush and his team proved an impressive ability to exploit opportunities ranging from the desire for public unity after the 2000 election, to the aftermath of the attacks, to the mantle of "war-time president" worn so proudly (if sometimes viciously) in 2004.[29] In general it is important to credit both the president and party with a cohesive message encompassing both hope and fear; extraordinary discipline in sticking to that message, and voting for it; and successful translation of that discipline to the electoral arena as well.

Legislative success, yes; political success, yes. However, whether all this could be considered successful *governance* remained open to question. That question would loom even larger as the second term began.

Looking Ahead: New Term, New Congress, New Problems

On November 4, 2004, the newly reelected president held a press conference. He used it to lay out four second-term priorities: tort reform to "confront the frivolous lawsuits" he argued drove up health care costs; education reform to expand the No Child Left Behind testing regime into high schools; reform and simplification of the tax code; and reform of the Social Security program to provide private investment accounts for younger workers, an idea revived from the 2000 campaign. Later he added "fighting and winning the war on terror" to the list. Bush's second inaugural address promised initiatives to spread freedom around the globe: "it is the policy of the United States," said the president, "to seek and support the growth of democratic movements and institutions in every nation and culture."[30]

As 2005 began—even as news from Iraq grew louder, and more dissonant—the president began touring the country in support of his domestic agenda. "I want you to think about a Social Security system that will be flat bust, bankrupt, unless the United States Congress has got the willingness to act now," he told one audience in January.[31] The day before, he spoke on tort reform; the day after, he visited a Virginia high school to tout expanded testing. Social Security occupied the bulk of his time through the spring, with a promise of "60 Stops in 60 Days" dedicated to convincing the public of the program's projected insolvency and the consequent desirability of funding private retirement accounts.

The 109th Congress was, on the face of it, likely to be receptive to this new set of presidential initiatives. The GOP had gained four seats in the Senate, even knocking off Minority Leader Tom Daschle in South Dakota. The remaking of the solid South as a Republican stronghold continued apace, with Republicans replacing long-time Democratic senators in Georgia, South Carolina, and Florida, plus vice presidential candidate John Edwards's seat in

North Carolina. In the House, Republicans gained four seats as well, expanding their majority to nearly thirty seats. By historical terms, these were not large margins, but by the standards of 2001 they seemed quite comfortable. Two early 2005 victories for the president came as Congress approved legislation removing class action legislation from state courts and making it harder for consumers to declare bankruptcy. And the fiscal 2006 budget resolution adopted many presidential preferences, including oil-drilling in the ANWR.

But of the priority issues noted above, only capping lawsuit awards, which came close to passage in the first term, seemed to be something like low-hanging fruit. Reform of the tax code involves closing loopholes dear to corporate interests that are in turn dear to legislative fundraising efforts on both sides of the aisle. Many Republicans are uneasy about further expansion of the federal role in education, and the Democrats who allied with the president in 2001 on the issue have expressed deep disappointment at the funding levels provided for education reform. Several states (including rock-ribbed Republican Utah) publicly chafed at NCLB's mandates and threatened to sue the federal government to avoid compliance. The Bush effort, it seemed, might wind up being directed largely at forestalling legislative attacks on NCLB rather than adding to it. Likewise, the idea of spinning private accounts off from Social Security is both contentious and expensive (transition costs are estimated at as much as $2 trillion); it faces near-unanimous Democratic opposition and a fractured GOP. Bush's road trip, featuring "conversations" with hand-picked locals, failed to gain much traction on public opinion through early 2005; a series of polls in late spring found 55 to 60 percent disapproval for the idea of private accounts and the president's leadership thereon. By the end of May, President Bush showed no signs of weariness, but admitted slow going: "it's like water cutting through a rock. . . . We're just going to keep working and working and working."[32]

A number of other issues will also compete with president's short list for limited legislative oxygen. Inspiring Iraqi elections in January 2005 lifted spirits there and abroad, but subsequent delays in forming a government, continued investigations into prisoner abuse—and a nihilistic insurgency that regularly continued to kill both American soldiers and Iraqi civilians—dampened hopes for peace and democracy there. An $80 billion supplemental spending request for Iraq and Afghanistan was approved in early 2005, even as military recruiting for the overstretched armed forces was showing signs of strain. Three months after the elections a solid majority of Americans believed that the war had not been worth fighting.[33]

Beyond Iraq, a host of global issues were on the horizon—and the Boxing Day tsunami of 2004 showed how quickly far-off events could surge onto the public stage. Likely flashpoints included the nuclear ambitions of Iran and North Korea, continuing efforts to bridge the Israeli-Palestinian conflict, humanitarian policies in Africa (from AIDS to genocide), and the economic expansion of southern Asia. Homeland security remained a key issue as well. The Patriot Act will sunset at the end of 2005 unless renewed; what balance between liberty and security will legislators choose? Opponents of the Act hoped to cut back FBI authority to act without judicial approval, while the administration sought to expand it.[34] The answer presumably depends in part on whether additional terrorist attacks target the United States.

All these choices were certain to require new policies and resources. Yet resources were increasingly constrained. The cost of the 2001–2004 tax cuts and Medicare prescription drugs will begin to rise sharply after 2006. Energy prices remain steep, and are likely to go higher. The individual Alternative Minimum Tax will hit more and more middle-income taxpayers and demands attention. So does the need to reauthorize federal highway spending (at $280+ billion), welfare reform (now two years late), and higher education (one year late). At the same time the fiscal 2005 deficit stands at $427 billion, the largest ever in nominal terms. Eight percent of the federal budget goes to pay interest on the national debt, which leapfrogged the $7.4 trillion mark in 2004: the $160 billion needed for annual debt service exceeded the amount spent by the federal government on education, homeland security, and law enforcement combined.[35]

Many of the members of Congress who left that body after the 108th Congress (nearly fifty in all) were centrists who served as what bridge there was between the parties.[36] The 109th Congress, then, may be even more polarized, especially in the Senate—which will be without a half dozen moderates of both parties, replaced by more ideologically extreme members. The fifty-five Senate seats now in Republican hands are not sufficient for cloture. Under current Senate rules, Democrats can still stage a filibuster, requiring sixty votes to cut off debate and move to a straight up-or-down vote. This makes action on various legislative fronts, especially Social Security, more difficult.

The filibuster itself will also be a point of contention. The president renewed his bid to win approval of seven controversial judicial nominees in the 109th Congress. In late May 2005, as the first of these reached the floor, Senate Majority Leader Bill Frist (R-TN) threatened to forge Senate rule changes that would prohibit filibusters on nominations and thus ease acceptance of presidential appointees. This so-called "nuclear option" was forestalled when a group of Senate moderates agreed to confirm some of the nominees and shelve others, while resisting rules changes. However, after a decade with no new vacancies on the Supreme Court, retirement rumors swirled about several of its members. It was unclear whether the filibuster détente would hold, especially once a showdown over a Court nomination began.[37] If the rules are changed, Senate routines premised on hundreds of unanimous consent agreements may come to a standstill. The symbolic fallout over the north wing of the Capitol may mean that *nothing* gets done in the second term.

Prospects: Ambition Rising?

In 2003, Congressman David Obey (D-WI) complained that "this administration thinks that Article I of the Constitution was a fundamental mistake."[38]

Presumably, though, Article I is fine with any president so long as its denizens do what he wants. And in his first term President Bush was able in the legislative arena to attain both his desired legislative outcomes and an expansion of executive prerogatives beyond their post-Watergate limits.

The second-term agenda reaches just as high. Bush argued in late 2004 that "I earned capital in the campaign, political capital, and now I intend to spend it."[39] Yet the history of enervated second terms noted at the outset suggests this might be an expensive proposition. The question comes, then: how much political capital does President Bush really have? One way to answer comes from reviewing the factors on presidential-congressional relations generally discussed above. On some, the president seems in good shape. He is coming off a successful re-election, if by a narrow margin; his party has control of both chambers of Congress; his party's leadership is powerful, unified, and disciplined. He has tended to keep his immediate wish-list short, and insisted only on achieving broad principles rather than micromanaging the devil in the details. His indefatigable bargaining style works with his partisans; he built a White House astute in managing the "permanent campaign"; and he has utilized the presidency's agenda-setting power to great effect, especially as regards education, economics, and foreign affairs. Further, President Bush is liberated in not having to gear his legislative energies toward setting up his vice president as heir to his agenda in the 2008 election.

Other fronts augur more ambivalently. The president's public approval ratings have hovered consistently at or below 50 percent since his re-election, and there is little evidence that he has reconstructed "political time" in a way to build a broad coalition of support that remakes the electoral landscape. As noted, his second-term initiatives are large, complex, potentially divisive, and expensive. Focusing events could, of course, go either way, depending on their nature—and foreign affairs could again rise to the fore, either through the administration's actions or others' decisions. But in the meantime, the support induced by September 11 does not readily translate to support for remaking Social Security.

In the American constitutional structure, too, ambition (as Madison told us long ago) is supposed to counteract ambition. President Bush has been nothing if not ambitious; but as yet Congress has rarely pushed back. More typical was the comment of Majority Whip Roy Blunt (R-MO) added: "the truth is that in time of war . . . there is not a whole lot for members of Congress to do."[40]

At least parts of that truth will likely change in the second term. Congress remains very much the first branch of government, should it choose to assert its extensive power over appointments, appropriations, and oversight. While members have sought sustenance in blame avoidance—if power is given to the president, then it is his fault when policy goes awry—legislative interests will not always coincide with the president's. If nothing else, the fact that congressmen must face re-election, while the president does not, should lead to friction in inter-branch relations. Republicans have already become edgy about aspects of the president's domestic agenda and about the way the war in Iraq has eroded military flexibility on other fronts. Polarization will likely increase further, given the centrist retirements noted above. By June 2005 the president had already issued two veto threats, of the transportation reauthorization bill and of a measure easing limits on stem-cell research.

President Bush nonetheless had to like his tactical chances. He retains a huge well of capital in the GOP caucus—and under a "majority of the majority" strategy, where measures that merely have a majority of the populace behind them are not allowed to the floor—that may be most of what matters. Thanks to aggressive gerrymandering, members of both parties are more beholden than ever to their constituencies' extreme voices; and unless something goes very wrong, Republican members want the president's campaign assistance in 2006. Party discipline generally remains tight, constricted by centralized leadership.[41]

It would be wrong, then, to discount the possibility of additional significant policy change in the second term. The nomination of John Bolton to be U.S. Ambassador to the United Nations in 2005 provides a likely template moving forward: Bush made an aggressive, provocative (arguably needlessly so) choice, and the battle over confirmation was tough, narrow, and loudly divisive. Yet it was successful, at least in the short term.

The problem is that tactical victories thusly achieved rarely accrete into a grand strategy that converts those gains into a lasting electoral coalition and policy regime. Polarization has delineated clear policy alternatives, and the president rightly pointed out to his critics that "we had an accountability moment, and that's called the 2004 elections." Yet the 2004 elections also served notice that within Three years of the extraordinary national unity wrought by the September 11 attacks, the 50–50 nation of 2000 had returned with a vengeance. The division was illustrated both in the president's overall approval ratings and public opinion across the issues that make up his agenda. One cannot cement governance, at least not on things that will lastingly matter—the deficit, entitlement programs, America's place in a globalized world—with fifty-one percent of the vote. Yet those who dissented from the administration's policies were termed unpatriotic, told that their position "aids terrorists," that vigorous debate, by undercutting the war effort, "erodes unity" and even verges on treason.[42]

As such, the president's legacy is very much an open question. His style of governance leads to short-term wins, but cannot build the coalition needed for long-term change. After all, democracy, as a wise political scientist once noted, "is a political system for people who are not too sure that they are right."[43]

Notes

1. Figures were adapted for contested votes by Jon R. Bond and Richard Fleisher, *The President in the Legislative Arena* (Chicago: University of Chicago Press, 1990), updated figures generously provided by Professor Bond.

2. Kenneth O'Donnell, oral history of July 23, 1969, Lyndon B. Johnson Library, p. 91.

3. Mitch Daniels to Dennis Thomas, memo of December 17, 1986, *'86 Planning Group Meetings (1 of 6)/ OA14157*, W. Dennis Thomas papers, Box 3, Ronald Reagan Library.

4. Miller Center Interviews, Carter Presidency Project, vol. XIII, January 1982, p. 105 [available at the Jimmy Carter Library].

5. George C. Edwards III, *At the Margins* (New Haven, CT: Yale University Press, 1989).

6. Rove quoted in Dan Balz and Michael Fletcher, "Looking to Apply Lessons Learned," *Washington Post*, January 20, 2005, p. A1. On "political time" see the introductory chapter to this volume or Stephen Skowronek, *The Politics Presidents Make* (Cambridge, MA: Harvard University Press, 1994); Mark A. Peterson, *Legislating Together* (Cambridge, MA: Harvard University Press, 1990), ch. 4, discusses the "pure" and "malleable" contexts presidents face, and shape.

7. John W. Kingdon, *Agendas, Alternatives, and Public Policies*, 2nd ed. (New York: HarperCollins, 1995). On the agenda, see Paul Light, *The President's Agenda*, 3rd ed. (Baltimore, MD: Johns Hopkins University Press, 1999); James P. Pfiffner, *The Strategic Presidency*, 2d rev. ed. (Lawrence: Kansas University Press, 1996). On legislative formulation, see Andrew Rudalevige, *Managing the President's Program: Presidential Leadership and Legislative Policy Formulation* (Princeton, NJ: Princeton University Press, 2002).

8. Gramm quoted in Barbara Sinclair, "Context, Strategy, and Chance: George W. Bush and the 107th Congress," in Colin Campbell and Bert A. Rockman, *The George W. Bush Presidency: Appraisals and Prospects* (Washington, DC: CQ Press, 2004), p. 109. Possibly Gramm's life began in 1982, when he left the Democratic Party. A summary of Bush's Texas experience is in John C. Fortier and Norman J. Ornstein, "President Bush: Legislative Strategist," in Fred I. Greenstein, ed., *The George W. Bush Presidency: An Early Assessment* (Baltimore, MD: Johns Hopkins University Press, 2003).

9. For detail on the NCLB process, see Paul E. Peterson and Martin West, eds., *No Child Left Behind?* (Washington, DC: Brookings, 2003).

10. Fortier and Ornstein, "President Bush: Legislative Strategist," pp. 147–151.

11. The energy bill returned to the agenda in 2005 and ANWR drilling won important test votes early that year.

12. Waters quoted in Carolyn Lochhead and Carla Marinucci, " 'Freedom and Fear are at War': Message to Americans, Warning to Taliban," *San Francisco Chronicle* (September 21, 2001), p. A1.

13. That this delegation was narrowed by Democratic intervention does not detract from the nature of the language approved. The language declared war but designated no opponent or timeframe—these were left to the president. Further, the Supreme Court ruled in June 2004 that the September 14 resolution was sufficient to give the president authority to designate even American citizens as "enemy combatants."

14. As a result the vote on the rule governing the bill was quite close—214 to 208—though the vote on final passage was not.

15. "The idea became his," note Fortier and Ornstein, "President Bush: Legislative Strategist," p. 164.

16. On terrorism insurance, see Alan Ota, "Calio's Assertive Style Moves Legislation, But Hill Republicans Have Paid the Price," *CQ Weekly* (December 14, 2002), p. 3251.

17. Charles Babington, "Hastert Launches a Partisan Policy," *Washington Post* (November 27, 2004), A1.

18. Ota, "Calio's Assertive Style." Calio was succeeded by his aide David Hobbs in 2003 and by Candida Wolff in 2005. Hobbs's background was in the House, Wolff's in the Senate. See Alexis Simendinger, "A Full Plate for Bush's New Hill Liaison," *National Journal* (March 5, 2005), pp. 685–686.

19. During the 108th Congress, only 28 percent of bills were open to amendment— only 15 percent in its second session, in 2004. The comparable figure in 1994 was 57 percent. Susan Milligan, "Back Room Dealing a Capitol Trend," *Boston Globe*, October 3, 2004, p. A1.

20. Carl Hulse and Robert Pear, "Feeling Left Out, Democrats Stall Bills," *New York Times*, May 3, 2004.

21. Mary Agnes Carey, "GOP Wins Battle, Not War," *CQ Weekly Report*, November 29, 2003, p. 2956. It turned out that Medicare analysts had not been allowed to pass along their final cost analysis of the bill, which was 25 percent higher (US$534 billion), for fear of losing additional conservative votes.

22. Presidential Press Conference, March 13, 2002, Office of the White House Press Secretary; also see Andrew Rudalevige, *The New Imperial Presidency: Renewing Presidential Power after Watergate* (Ann Arbor: University of Michigan Press, 2005), ch. 7.

23. See *Hamdi v. Rumsfeld* (03–6696), decided June 28, 2004.

24. Aide quoted in "Omnibus Negotiations Focus on Policy Riders, Debt Limit," *CQ Daily Update*, November 10, 2004; see also Joseph J. Schatz, "With a Deft and Light Touch, Bush Finds a Way to Win," *CQ Weekly Report* (December 11, 2004), pp. 2900–2904.

25. Alex Wayne and Bill Swindell, "Capitol Hill Gridlock Leaves Programs in Limbo," *CQ Weekly*, December 4, 2004, p. 2834; Helen Dewar, "Congress Leaves Some Priority Bills Unfinished," *Washington Post*, October 14, 2004, p. A29. Days in session are calculated from the calendar of the House of Representatives available at http://thomas.loc.gov/home/ds/index.html. For the sessions of 2002 and 2003, the House was in session just 126 and 138 days, respectively, and just 110 days in 2004.

26. "Presidential Success History," *CQ Weekly*, December 11, 2004, p. 2901.

27. Even *Congressional Quarterly*, which collected the data, admitted this—their 2003 Almanac entry, for example, was entitled "Score Belies Bush's Success," *CQ Almanac, 2003* (Washington, DC: CQ Press, 2004), p. B–7.

28. See Jim VandeHei and Michael A. Fletcher, "Bush Says Election Ratified Iraq Policy," *Washington Post*, January 16, 2005, p. A1.

29. A number of presidential surrogates suggested that those opposing the president were either unpatriotic, eager to provoke further terrorist attacks on the United States, or both. Republican National Chair Marc Racicot claimed that even Senator John Kerry, running against Bush, crossed "a grave line" because Kerry "dared to suggest the replacement of America's commander-in-chief at a time when America is at war."

30. President's Press Conference, November 4, 2004; "President Sworn In To Second Term," January 20, 2005—both from Office of the White House Press Secretary.

31. Michael A. Fletcher, "Bush Promotes Plan for Social Security," *Washington Post*, January 12, 2005, A4.

32. See the *Time* and NBC News/*Wall Street Journal* polls of May 10–12 and May 12–16, 2005, respectively, reported at www.pollingreport.com/social.htm

[accessed May 25, 2005]; President's Press Conference, May 31, 2005, Office of the White House Press Secretary.

33. See the CNN/*USA Today* poll reported in Bill Nichols and Mona Mahmoud, "Support for Iraq War at Lowest Levels," *USA Today*, May 4, 2005, p. A1.

34. Eric Lichtblau, "After Talk of Compromise, Panel is Again Split on Patriot Act," *New York Times*, May 25, 2005.

35. Jonathan Weisman, "The Tax-Cut Pendulum and the Pit," *Washington Post*, October 8, 2004, p. A1; Weisman, "Record '05 Deficit Forecast," *Washington Post*, January 26, 2005, p. A1.

36. Thanks to Matt Dickinson for making this point. See also Helen Dewar and Eric Pianin, "Congress is Losing Leaders and Unifiers," *Washington Post*, November 21, 2004, p. A12.

37. Ronald Brownstein and Janet Hook, "Senate Truce Faces Test of Bush's Next Nominations," *Los Angeles Times*, May 25, 2005, p. A1.

38. Lisa Caruso, "You've Got to Know When to Hold 'Em," *National Journal*, July 12, 2003, p. 2258.

39. President's Press Conference of November 4, 2004, Office of the White House Press Secretary.

40. Carl Hulse and David Firestone, "On the Hill, Budget Business as Usual," *New York Times*, March 23, 2003, p. A19; see also Rudalevige, *New Imperial Presidency*, ch. 1.

41. Helen Dewar and Eric Pianin, "Congress is Losing Leaders and Unifiers."

42. Rudalevige, *New Imperial Presidency*, pp. 245–256.

43. E.E. Schattschneider, *Two Hundred Million Americans in Search of a Government* (New York: Holt, Rinehart, and Winston, 1969), p. 53.

Chapter Six

Crusade: The Rhetorical Presidency of George Bush

John Robert Greene

If one was to mention the name Lenny Skutnik to a presidential speechwriter, no doubt they would be met with a smile and a sigh. On January 13, 1982, Skutnik, a government employee, dove into the freezing Potomac River to save a woman who had been ejected from the wreckage of Air Florida Flight 90, which had crashed into Washington's 14th Street Bridge. Some two weeks later, Ronald Reagan brought Skutnik as his guest to the State of the Union Address. Sitting in the balcony, Reagan referred to Skutnik as "the spirit of American heroism at its finest." Thus, Skutnik's name has became a part of the terminology of presidential rhetoric; used as a pronoun, it has come to refer in generic terms to those guests at the State of the Union Address to whom the president points to highlight a position—a human prop that now is *expected* to be included in each presidential address to a joint session of Congress.[1]

When speaking of the "rhetorical presidency," particularly as defined by Jeffrey Tulis in his seminal book on the subject,[2] and as refined by the recent work of Martin Medhurst and others,[3] one is referring to the appropriation and use of symbols—verbal, visual, and subliminal—by the presidency as a tool of both politics and policy. This concept is best known to the generalist as the "Bully Pulpit"—the relative ability of the president to use communications, usually his ability to speak, as an instrument of political power (since the contribution of Richard Neustadt, as an instrument of political persuasion).[4] A comprehensive study of the rhetorical presidency might well include analyses of the use of the White House Press Office to manage the Fourth Estate; to those operatives and advisors who craft the advertising message of a presidential campaign; or of the president's relative skill at one-on-one bargaining, particularly as that skill applies to the crafting of policy and law with representatives from Capitol Hill.

"Skutniks" serve to remind us that such communications devices are critical to the success or failure of the modern presidency. Indeed, the ability to recognize the need for rhetorical devices to augment the presidential message was key to the success of the Reagan presidency (if not the most durable part of the "Great Communicator's" historical legacy), and—perhaps—a key to the survival of Bill Clinton when faced with impeachment: the failure to utilize those devices was also one of the keys to the inability of George H.W. Bush to secure his re-election in 1992, even after successfully prosecuting a war. Thus it is important at the halfway point of the presidency of George W. Bush that a preliminary analysis of his rhetorical skills is offered—the strategizing of his overall message, his abilities as a speaker, and some amount of informed speculation as to where his rhetoric may or not take him for the balance of his second term. Indeed, as the "house historian" of this volume, it is appropriate that Bush II's[5] rhetorical development—which, I would argue, has been both significant and substantial—be seen in a historical perspective. This look at the rhetorical presidency of Bush II will concentrate on that part of the president's communication that showed the greatest growth and influence during the first term (particularly after the events of September 11, 2001), and has already shown itself to have had the greatest influence in his second term—the president as public speaker, and the influence over that role played by both his Director of Communications and his presidential speechwriters.

Background: Co-Opting the Message

Prior to the Nixon administration, the presidential speechwriting team was a relative autonomous idea shop. Nixon's team was deliberately constructed to offer the rhetorically challenged president input from different voices from across the ideological span of the Republican party. The consummate politician, Nixon also understood the difference between delivery and political message, as he created the Office of Communications, which would be in charge of developing the political message. Indeed, this office was of such importance to Nixon that he named as his Director of Communications Ronald Ziegler, who also served as his press secretary. Perhaps because he had chosen speechwriters from across the political spectrum; perhaps because he had chosen speechwriters whose political antennae were acute, the speechwriters held their own in the Nixon administration.[6] However, one could see a portent of the future in the Ford administration, when chief speechwriter Robert T. Hartmann began his tenure as a Counselor to the President. In 1976 he had the speechwriting team removed from his portfolio and turned over to those who ran Ford's unsuccessful reelection campaign.[7] In successive administrations, while the number of speechwriters actually increased (to a norm of eight), the Office of Communications drove the speechwriting unit.[8]

In many ways, the administration of George H.W. Bush was the apex of this trend. Holding a complete disdain for formal rhetoric, Bush did not even have a formal director of speechwriting until 1991 (Tony Snow). The speeches were generated in the Office of Communications, headed by David Demarest. Indeed, Peggy Noonan, the best known of the modern speechwriters, observed that during the term of Bush I, "in terms of the political pecking order, [the speechwriters] are just above the people who clean up after [presidential dog] Millie."[9]

This development has been institutionally solidified in the Bush II White House. Where, for example, his father's two communications directors were largely ineffectual, and where Clinton went through six communications directors, only one advisor has ever mattered in terms of the crafting of the message of Bush II. Karen Hughes has held a singular connection with Bush II for the entirety of his public career. Initially a television reporter, Hughes worked for the Texas RNC, and then became a communications consultant. After directing the communications team for his 1994 election to the governorship of Texas, Hughes became Governor Bush's communications director. During the 2000 campaign for the presidency, she applied the term "compassionate conservative," which had already been coined, to Bush.[10] She also ghosted his campaign biography, was the chief editor of his speeches, oversaw debate preparations, and ran the post-debate spin operation.[11]

When Bush II came to the White House, he rewarded Hughes—and showed the place that rhetoric and message would have in his administration—by conferring upon her a rather singular portfolio. Hughes initially held two titles simultaneously: Counselor to the President and Director of Communications. In this, she was not unique—in her memoirs, *Ten Minutes from Normal*, she gives Bush II's Chief of Staff Andrew Card the credit for suggesting her title and portfolio, and notes that it was a title given to Edwin Meese in the first Reagan administration.[12] Regardless, Hughes is unquestionably the most powerful woman to ever serve on a presidential staff (despite her entreaties otherwise in her memoir, observational evidence from the first term would suggest her to be more influential than Condoleezza Rice at the NSC); all press officers within the executive branch reported to her.[13] In her role as a director, Hughes kept the tradition of melding speechwriting with communications. She utilized the drafts of the speechwriters to craft her own draft, which then went to the president for his review and editing. In a thinly veiled insult to both principals, former Bush II speechwriter (and Hughes subordinate) David Frum encapsulated the view of both Hughes and political advisor Karl Rove to their boss: "Rove had ideas that no one else had—and that was his value to the president. Hughes had the same ideas that everyone else had—and that was hers."[14]

Giving voice to Hughes's direction was Michael Gerson, who began as Bush II's director of speechwriting. Gerson had worked as a Senate aide to Dan Coats in the 1990s. As one White House aide noted (with some amount of validity, with the important exception of Nixon), "Bush personally chose him. Most presidents don't personally choose their writers." Gerson was given a West Wing office, and attended the 7:30 a.m. staff briefing—a clear barometer of his influence within the administration.[15]Gerson chose as his deputies a group of young neo-conservatives who crafted a strident rhetoric that helped to position Bush in the mind of much of the public as much less compassionate than conservative. From the campaign came Matthew Scully, a former reporter for the *Washington Times*, editor for the *National*

Review, and speechwriter for Vice President Dan Quayle, and John McConnell, a graduate of Yale who had also written for Quayle, as well as for Bob Dole during the 1996 campaign. McConnell was ostensibly the chief speechwriter for Vice President Richard Cheney, but in effect worked for Gerson. After the election, Gerson added Peter Wehner, a libertarian and former aide to William Bennett, as his deputy. He also added David Frum, formerly of the *Weekly Standard*. In, perhaps, an attempt to add balance, the sixth speechwriter was John Gibson, a foreign policy specialist who was retained from the Clinton speechwriting team, and who was detailed to the NSC staff.[16]

A Comparison: Bush I and Bush II
as Communicators

When assessing the modern presidency in terms of public speaking, four men set the tone. Theodore Roosevelt created the "bully pulpit," and was the first president to use the force of his public character to convey his message; Franklin D. Roosevelt brought the word "charisma" into the political lexicon, and showed both physical dexterity at the podium (despite his need to be steadied while on his braces) and a soothing vocal delivery on the radio; John F. Kennedy added humor to the mix, showing an ease of public communications that would not be matched until 1980; Ronald Reagan brought his ability to play to the camera, as well as a comfort while speaking that soothed his audience—reminding one most closely of FDR.

No other modern president comes close in rhetorical skill to these four leaders; many observers have ranked both Bushes at or near the bottom of that list. The rhetorical presidency of Bush I was largely a failure because Bush didn't like doing it.[17] While Bush I was thoroughly comfortable in small groups and one-on-one communications (he was a master of the telephone), his formal speeches were stiff, pedestrian, and often elitist. Part of this, to be sure, was due to the fact that Bush I was poorly served by his speechwriters—hardly an inspired or inspiring lot. But, by his own admission, the lion's share of the blame rested with Bush I himself, who found public speaking a chore that needed to be endured. An informal, clubby man by nature, Bush I simply did not work hard at effecting the type of delivery that was necessary for him to be able to connect with the average American. Indeed, in most of his speeches, Bush I came across as wooden and detached; thus, he avoided speechmaking in favor of more informal settings. For example, Bush I installed a closed-circuit television hookup in the Old Executive Office Building that allowed him to communicate with distant audiences without actually having to face them. This technology—and this strategy—allowed Bush to face many more audiences than his schedule would probably have permitted, but it also permitted him to face fewer of them face-to-face.[18]

Bush II's understanding of the usefulness of the "Bully Pulpit" offers significant differences from that of the senior Bush. Unlike his father, Bush II is a formal man by nature (one Bush II speechwriter observed that "We learned not to insert idle compliments like a, I'm happy to be here with you' into his speeches. If he was not happy to be here with you, he would not pretend that he was.")[19] But also unlike his father, Bush II likes giving prepared speeches. By all accounts, he practices them with gusto, and understands the process of speechwriting. Unlike his father, he constantly questions his speechwriters, editing the speech for both syntax and style, challenging each word's right to be in the speech, and sends them notes on amendments to the message.[20] And, according to observers, Bush II truly wishes to improve himself as a communicator.[21] That being said, prior to September 11, 2001, Bush II's speaking delivery was often an exercise in the unexpected. He would often mangle what seemed later to be a well-crafted speech with a malapropism, or with hesitant vocal tics that marred his cadence, Despite his interest in the process, and despite his skill as an editor, Bush II seemed doomed to repeat the rhetorical performance of his father.

The Rhetoric of Evil

Bush II's first inaugural address, crafted largely by Gerson, was a rather uninspiring piece, delivered in classic Bush monotone. The speeches of the first eight months of his administration were little better. The issue of the moment was tax cuts (the law was passed in June 2001), and the monotony of the speeches on economic subjects did little to improve Bush's delivery. To be fair, the subject hardly created ringing rhetoric from the speechwriters—in a speech on an upcoming recession: "a warning light is flashing on the dashboards of our economy."[22] Bush was taking serious hits from the press.

As a result of his early difficulties with public communicating as president, Hughes and her communications shop began to more closely control the presidential message, using techniques to help the president. The most important, indeed groundbreaking idea in this regard came from Scott Sforza, Hughes's deputy communications director, who suggested the "message backdrop"—banners or signs that were strategically placed behind the president, labeling the main idea about which he was talking.[23] Sforza's concept helped the audience concentrate on the message of a president who could all-too-often go off message and ramble; the technique is now ubiquitous in politics, being used by most policymakers when they speak.

For her part, Hughes concentrated on helping the speaker's peace of mind. In summer 2001 she suggested he take a vacation. Bush II spent the month of August at the family ranch in Midland, Texas, using that time to symbolically reconnect with moderate America. He worked on a Habitat for Humanity home, rode his range, visited a Target store (thus breaking free of his father's stunned education in 1992 about how a department store scanner worked) and even visited a Harley Davidson factory.[24]

On September 11, 2001, events quickly conspired to focus and change Bush II as a rhetoritician. On the evening of that day, Bush was clearly at his rhetorical worst. One need not excuse or explain—the day's events, the stress, and the travel had clearly and understandably taken their toll. Nevertheless, when he spoke to the nation that evening, Bush was hesitant, disheveled (with a crooked tie and a loose fitting shirt), and unable to convey a feeling of either soothing or control. And yet the speech as crafted by Hughes gave an important hint as to what was to rhetorically follow:

> Today, our fellow citizens, our way of life, our very freedom came under attack in a series of deliberate and deadly terrorist acts. The victims were in airplanes or in their offices: secretaries, business men and women, military and federal workers, moms and dads, friends and neighbors. Thousands of lives were suddenly ended by evil, despicable acts of terror . . . Today, our nation saw evil— the very worst of human nature—and we responded with the best of America. . . . The search is underway for those who were behind these evil acts.[25]

The president's next major address, given on Friday, September 14 at the National Cathedral on a National Day of Prayer and Mourning continued to show Bush as awkward and hesitant, delivering his prepared text in a halting manner. However, the theme of evil was repeated—in defiant, militant language that many found inappropriate for the occasion or the religious setting:

> Just three days removed from these events, Americans do not yet have the distance of history. But our responsibility to history is already clear: to answer these attacks and rid the world of evil. War has been waged against us by stealth and deceit and murder. This nation is peaceful, but fierce when stirred to anger. This conflict was begun on the timing and terms of others. It will end in a way, and at an hour, of our choosing.[26]

Later that day, however, George W. Bush found his voice.

Standing on an obliterated fire truck at Ground Zero in Manhattan, Bush sounded the themes of defiance that would color his rhetoric from that point. This unscripted moment, three minutes in length, was the rhetorical turning point of his administration. It deserves to be read in its entirety; its brevity and clarity make it easy to do so:

> *Crowd:* U.S.A.! U.S.A.!
> *The President:* Thank you all. I want you all to know—
> *Q:* Can't hear you.
> *The President:* I can't talk any louder. (Laughter.)

I want you all to know that America today—that America today is on bended knee in prayer for the people whose lives were lost here, for the workers who work here, for the families who mourn. This nation stands with the good people of New York City, and New Jersey and Connecticut, as we mourn the loss of thousands of our citizens.

> *Q:* I can't hear you.
> *The President:* I can hear you. (Applause.) I can hear you. The rest of the world hears you. (Applause.) And the people who knocked these buildings down will hear all of us soon. (Applause.)

Crowd: U.S.A.! U.S.A.!
The President: The nation sends its love and compassion to everybody who
   is here. Thank you for your hard work. Thank you for making the nation
   proud. And may God bless America. (Applause.)
Crowd: U.S.A.! U.S.A.!
(The President waves small American flag.) (Applause)[27]

Following this appearance, one which affected Bush II in a raw, emotional
manner, a new, more strident Bush appeared. This was first seen in a formal
setting during his September 20, 2001 speech to a joint session of Congress.
In a February, 2002 article for the *Washington Post*, Bob Woodward labeled
the effort as "a presidency defined in one speech." More to the point, it was
Bush II's definition of his new presidency, shaped by the events of the previous week. As the speech developed, Bush was an insistent partner; even
before he had made the irreversible decision to speak to Congress (a course
of action which was not unanimously supported by his advisors), he
demanded an unheard-of 24 hour turnaround time for a first draft. Drafted
by Gerson, Scully, and McConnell, with input from Gipson at the NSC,
they completed the draft on time, but it hardly satisfied the president, who
felt it too lofty and high-minded. According to Woodward, "the speechwriters had rarely seen Bush so passionate." He wanted to bring the rhetoric down to the level of the common American, and to end the speech with
a pledge to the nation, "a personal commitment to see it through."[28] It can
be argued that this was accomplished. With a forcefulness of delivery that
took many observers by surprise, Bush II hammered the themes of the
Hughes-written address with a vigor that separated him distinctly from the
rhetoric of his father. He made it absolutely clear that there would, indeed,
be retribution:

> Tonight we are a country awakened to danger and called to defend freedom.
> Our grief has turned to anger, and anger to resolution. Whether we bring our
> enemies to justice, or bring justice to our enemies, justice will be done. . . .
> I have a message for our military: Be ready. I've called the Armed Forces to
> alert, and there is a reason. The hour is coming when America will act, and
> you will make us proud.[29]

He also kept alive, and expanded upon, what would continue to be the key
focus of his rhetoric throughout his campaign for re-election to the presidency
and into his second term. Bush II once again hammered the theme of good versus evil, this time to separate the motives of the terrorists from the religion
which they, and millions of others around the world, practice:

> I also want to speak tonight directly to Muslims throughout the world. We
> respect your faith. It's practiced freely by many millions of Americans, and by
> millions more in countries that America counts as friends. Its teachings are
> good and peaceful, and those who commit evil in the name of Allah blaspheme
> the name of Allah. The terrorists are traitors to their own faith, trying, in

effect, to hijack Islam itself. The enemy of America is not our many Muslim friends; it is not our many Arab friends. Our enemy is a radical network of terrorists, and every government that supports them.[30]

The duality of the "good-guy versus bad-guy" theme, so potently effective in modern political rhetoric, now permeated Bush II's post–9/11 speeches. It also led to the policy and rhetorical sound bite from his State of the Union Address of January 2002. Speechwriter David Frum is credited with coining the phrase that, for many, would label the foreign and national security policy of the United States for the rest of the Bush II administration:

Our second goal is to prevent regimes that sponsor terror from threatening America or our friends and allies with weapons of mass destruction.

Some of these regimes have been pretty quiet since September the 11th. But we know their true nature. North Korea is a regime arming with missiles and weapons of mass destruction, while starving its citizens.

Iran aggressively pursues these weapons and exports terror, while an unelected few repress the Iranian people's hope for freedom.

Iraq continues to flaunt its hostility toward America and to support terror. The Iraqi regime has plotted to develop anthrax, and nerve gas, and nuclear weapons for over a decade. This is a regime that has already used poison gas to murder thousands of its own citizens—leaving the bodies of mothers huddled over their dead children. This is a regime that agreed to international inspections—then kicked out the inspectors. This is a regime that has something to hide from the civilized world.

States like these, and their terrorist allies, constitute an axis of evil, arming to threaten the peace of the world. By seeking weapons of mass destruction, these regimes pose a grave and growing danger. They could provide these arms to terrorists, giving them the means to match their hatred. They could attack our allies or attempt to blackmail the United States. In any of these cases, the price of indifference would be catastrophic.

We will work closely with our coalition to deny terrorists and their state sponsors the materials, technology, and expertise to make and deliver weapons of mass destruction. We will develop and deploy effective missile defenses to protect America and our allies from sudden attack. And all nations should know: America will do what is necessary to ensure our nation's security.

We'll be deliberate, yet time is not on our side. I will not wait on events, while dangers gather. I will not stand by, as peril draws closer and closer. The United States of America will not permit the world's most dangerous regimes to threaten us with the world's most destructive weapons.[31]

It should be noted that for many, the "axis of evil" line went too far. The analogy was pilloried from all quarters, and editorials began to paint Bush II as a warmonger. Former Secretary of State William Christopher summarized the problem nicely: "It was a speechwriter's dream and a policy-maker's nightmare."[32]

In the planning of the State of the Union address for the following year, the phraseology of the "axis of evil" weighed heavily on the minds of both observers of the speech, and those who drafted the address. It may well have played a part in the mistake that was the colossal swing-and-miss claim that "The British government has learned that Saddam Hussein recently sought significant quantities of uranium from Africa. Our intelligence sources tell us that he has attempted to purchase high-strength aluminum tubes suitable for nuclear weapons production. Saddam Hussein has not credibly explained these activities. He clearly has much to hide." This claim, later challenged for both its source and its veracity, would create a political firestorm. Aside from that political gaffe, Bush II stayed on message, as he continued to talk about the duality between good and evil:

> The dictator who is assembling the world's most dangerous weapons has already used them on whole villages—leaving thousands of his own citizens dead, blind, or disfigured. Iraqi refugees tell us how forced confessions are obtained—by torturing children while their parents are made to watch. International human rights groups have catalogued other methods used in the torture chambers of Iraq: electric shock, burning with hot irons, dripping acid on the skin, mutilation with electric drills, cutting out tongues, and rape. If this is not evil, then evil has no meaning. And tonight I have a message for the brave and oppressed people of Iraq: Your enemy is not surrounding your country—your enemy is ruling your country. And the day he and his regime are removed from power will be the day of your liberation.[33]

Bush continued to hammer home this theme with a frequency and virulence that dismays many presidential watchers. Political analyst Stephen Hess, for example, grumbled early on that "I'm tired of it."[34] But Hess may well have been missing the point. More important than the fact that he was over-repeating a theme was the fact that Bush was now beginning to connect to average Americans with his speeches. As he railed against the enemy, his speeches became less elitist, more accessible, and more strident. He was becoming a *speaker*, rather than an average to below-average *speecher*. What would become one of the most important keys to his victory in 2004 had begun to take shape.

The Rhetoric of Faith

References to the role of God, both in his life and in his perception of public policy, have dotted Bush II's talks for the entirety of his public life. His own religious conversion, matched with the rather public statements of faith made by two of his speechwriters (Gerson and Hughes), seem to account for this rhetoric. But regardless of the motive, Bush II has utilized religious references in his speeches and messages more than any other modern president. The consistency of these references, even from before September 11, 2001, is noteworthy:

> Acceptance Speech to the 2000 Republican Convention: "I believe in a God who calls us, not to judge our neighbors, but to love them. I believe in grace,

because I have seen it; in peace, because I have felt it; in forgiveness, because I have needed it."[35]

May, 2001 Commencement Address at Yale University: "When I left here, I didn't have much in the way of a life plan. . . . Life takes its own turns, makes its own demands, writes its own story. And along the way, we start to realize that we are not the author."[36]

If anything, since September 11, Bush II's rhetoric has become even more overtly religious, both in its phraseology and its themes. It has joined with his defiant stance against evil to position him as a crusader, leading the United States in a worldwide conflict of almost biblical proportions. Note first the speech from the Oval Office on the evening of September 11:

> Tonight, I ask for your prayers for all those who grieve, for the children whose worlds have been shattered, for all whose sense of safety and security has been threatened. And I pray they will be comforted by a Power greater than any of us, spoken through the ages in Psalm 23: "Even though I walk through the valley of the shadow of death, I fear no evil for you are with me."[37]

Even more telling are the references made in the speech at the National Cathedral three days later:

> Our purpose as a nation is firm. Yet our wounds as a people are recent and unhealed, and lead us to pray. In many of our prayers this week, there is a searching, and an honesty. At St. Patrick's Cathedral in New York on Tuesday, a woman said, "I prayed to God to give us a sign that He is still here." Others have prayed for the same, searching hospital to hospital, carrying pictures of those still missing.
>
> God's signs are not always the ones we look for. We learn in tragedy that his purposes are not always our own. Yet the prayers of private suffering, whether in our homes or in this great cathedral, are known and heard, and understood.
>
> There are prayers that help us last through the day, or endure the night. There are prayers of friends and strangers that give us strength for the journey. And there are prayers that yield our will to a will greater than our own.
>
> This world He created is of moral design. Grief and tragedy and hatred are only for a time. Goodness, remembrance, and love have no end. And the Lord of life holds all who die, and all who mourn.[38]

The Second Term

I would be prepared to argue that the connection that Bush has made with "people"—on a defiant, religious level—were a key to his victory in the "red states" in 2004. Staying "on" this message was helped considerably by the return of Karen Hughes, who had left the White House in summer 2002 to spend more time with her family, to the campaign.

The second Inaugural Address, which Hughes helped to craft, kept alive the two rhetorical themes of defiance and faith. Indeed, the themes seem to have become so intertwined, as to present one seamless message to the world—that of a religious crusade:

> America's vital interests and our deepest beliefs are now one. From the day of our Founding, we have proclaimed that every man and woman on this earth has rights, and dignity, and matchless value, because they bear the image of the Maker of Heaven and earth. Across the generations we have proclaimed the imperative of self-government, because no one is fit to be a master, and no one deserves to be a slave. Advancing these ideals is the mission that created our Nation. It is the honorable achievement of our fathers. Now it is the urgent requirement of our nation's security, and the calling of our time. . . . We will persistently clarify the choice before every ruler and every nation: The moral choice between oppression, which is always wrong, and freedom, which is eternally right. America will not pretend that jailed dissidents prefer their chains, or that women welcome humiliation and servitude, or that any human being aspires to live at the mercy of bullies.[39]

However, as the second term progresses, that rhetorical edge has been dulled. While Bush II need not worry about electoral success or failure as he thinks through his rhetorical positions—perhaps the best thing about a second presidential term is the feeling in the White House that there is little to lose—it is clear that his wartime rhetoric has, at the very least, been put on hold. Challenges to the "crusade," most notably revelations of abuses to both prisoners of war and detainees at the hands of American soldiers, may well have played a role in the muting of Bush II's militant rhetoric. So too has been the policy direction—like speeches about the tax cut in the early months of 2001, Bush II's speeches on Social Security reform, laden with statistics and jargon, have hardly been spellbinders. And perhaps the burden of legacy—one of the most important foci of a second term—have served to soften the president's rhetoric (lest he "go down in history" as a warmonger, and little else). Whatever the reason, Bush II has proven to be a president who has grown as a speaker, and made effective usage of the "Bully Pulpit." When historians analyze his presidency, Bush II's rhetorical presidency may well turn out to be the most successful component of his tenure.

Notes

1. http://www.wordiq.com/definition/Lenny_Skutniks; http://www.reagan.utexas. edu/resourse/speeches/1982/12682c.htm.
2. Jeffrey Tulis, *The Rhetorical Presidency* (Princeton: Princeton University Press, 1998).
3. Martin Medhurst (ed.), Beyond the Rhetorical Presidency (College Station: Texas A&M University Press, 1996).
4. Richard Neustadt, Presidential Power (New York: The Free Press, 1960, 1990).
5. The Bush family kiddingly refers to the two presidents in their family by their number in presidential lineage—thus, the senior Bush is called "42," and the present president is "44." This numerical ID has never quite caught on with the

American people. This essay chooses to use "Bush I" and "Bush II," contending that this is the simplest way to distinguish between the two men.

6. John Robert Greene, *The Limits of Power: The Nixon and Ford Administrations* (Bloomington: Indiana University Press, 1992), p. 32.
7. John Robert Greene, *The Presidency of Gerald R. Ford* (Lawrence: Kansas University Press, 1995).
8. This development has also been enshrined—more or less accurately—into the pop culture poli-sci that is known as *The West Wing.* Toby Ziegler, played by Richard Shieff, carries both the title of Director of Communications and has been consistently scripted to be the primary drafter of all presidential speeches.
9. Ryan Lizza, "White House Watch: Write Hand," *The New Republic*, May 21, 2001, at http://www.tnr.com/052101/lizza052101.html.
10. Karen Hughes, *Ten Minutes from Normal* (New York: Viking, 2004), p. 111.
11. Hughes, *Ten Minutes from Normal*, p. 118.
12. Hughes, *Ten Minutes from Normal*, p. 184.
13. David Frum, *The Right Man: The Surprise Presidency of George W. Bush-An Inside Account* (New York: Random House, 2003), p. 40.
14. Frum, *The Right Man*, p. 35.
15. Lizza, "White House Watch."
16. Lizza, "White House Watch"; "Intercom," December, 2003 (at http://www.temple.edu/sct/intercom/index.htm); Hughes, *Ten Minutes from Normal*, p. 190; Frum, *The Right Man*, pp. 46–47; *Washington Post*, February 2, 2002.
17. John Robert Greene, *The Presidency of George Bush* (Lawrence,: University Press of Kansas, 2000), pp. 145–146, 185.
18. Comments in question-and-answer session, Bradley Patterson, January 21, 2004, "George Bush: Perils and Prospects," conference held at Villanova University.
19. Frum, *The Right Man*, p. 14.
20. Hughes, *Ten Minutes from Normal*, p. 81.
21. See, for example, Frum, *The Right Man*, p. 24.
22. Quoted in Frum, *The Right Man*, p. 32.
23. Hughes, *Ten Minutes from Normal*, p. 190.
24. Frum, *The Right Man*, pp. 104–106.
25. http://www.americanrhetoric.com/speeches/gwbush911addresstothenation.htm.
26. http://www.whitehouse.gov/news/releases/2001/09/20010914–2.html.
27. http://www.whitehouse.gov/news/releases/2001/09/20010914–9.html.
28. *Washington Post*, February 2, 2002.
29. http://www.whitehouse.gov/news/releases/2001/09/20010920–8.html.
30. Ibid.
31. http://www.whitehouse.gov/news/releases/2002/01/20020129–11.html.
32. http://www.commondreams.org/headlines03/0121–03.htm.
33. http://www.whitehouse.gov/news/releases/2003/01/20030128–19.html.
34. David L. Greene, "Bush Deems 'Evil' a Good Word to Use," *Baltimore Sun*, December 1, 2001.
35. http://www.vermontgop.org/bush_nom.htm.
36. Quoted in Frum, *The Right Man*, p. 30.
37. http://www.americanrhetoric.com/speeches/gwbush911addresstothenation.htm.
38. http://www.whitehouse.gov/news/releases/2001/09/20010914–2.html.
39. http://www.whitehouse.gov/news/releases/2005/01/20050120–1.html.

Part III

Domestic Policy

Chapter Seven

Judges, Courts, and Policy in President George W. Bush's Second Term

Amy Steigerwalt and Lori A. Johnson

The Role of Courts in the Policy Process

Students of American politics are taught that ours is a system of separation of powers and checks and balances. But, as presidential scholar Richard Neustadt observed, in actuality we have "separated institutions sharing power"[1] We typically assume that Congress is the most important branch that a president must deal with in effectuating his policy agenda. Nevertheless, the judicial branch plays a significant role in the policymaking process that must be considered by the president and his team. Even if George W. Bush succeeds in getting legislation enacted on key campaign issues like Social Security or tort reform, the federal courts will ultimately determine the long-term scope and impact of these policies either by evaluating the law's constitutionality or by interpreting and applying the laws in specific circumstances. Conversely, President Bush's power to appoint judges to the federal bench can directly impact the creation and implementation of policy for many decades to come.

Courts directly impact policy in two key ways. First, federal judges have the authority to determine the constitutionality, if challenged, of any federal legislation. For example, the appropriations act signed into law by Bush on December 8, 2004, included a provision in the Department of Health and Human Services budget known as the "federal refusal clause." This clause provides that a variety of "health care entities," including physicians, Health Maintenances Organizations (HMO's), and insurance providers, are allowed to refuse to perform, pay for, provide coverage of, or refer women for abortions regardless of federal, state, or local laws to the contrary. The constitutionality of this provision will undoubtedly be challenged in federal courts. If the Supreme Court ultimately determines that it violates the constitutional right to privacy of women, then the administration's policy success is meaningless. When it comes to the Constitution, the courts set the outer structural and policy parameters within which Congress and the President must operate, and if these other two branches exceed these parameters, their concrete policy objectives are doomed to fail.

Second, even if a law is constitutional, in our litigious times very few, if any, federal statutes escape litigation debating how the law should be interpreted and implemented. Indeed, as Congress has enacted more and more federal legislation in recent decades, the federal courts have played an ever-increasing role in directing national policy, as outside groups—usually those who either feel shut out of the normal legislative policymaking process or who simply lost in that arena—have increasingly turned to the courts as the mechanism through which to obtain their policy goals.[2] Environmental policy is a prominent example of this trend. Statutes such as the Clean Water Act and the Clean Air Act, first adopted in the 1970s, have been the subject of almost continual lawsuits by affected corporations and environmental interest groups. Since 1995, under the Clean Water and Clean Air acts alone 426 lawsuits have been filed, 315 of which resulted in judicial consent orders forcing compliance. In the same time period, over 4,500 notices of intent to sue were filed under all the different environmental statutes against federal agencies or regulated entities (May 2003). If a president cares about environmental issues, then clearly not only who he picks to head the Environmental Protection Agency but also which judges are sitting on the federal courts will play an important role in determining whether the goals of his administration are effectuated.

If courts are such a significant battleground for contentious social and political issues, what can a president do to influence what happens in the judicial branch? In one important respect, the judicial branch has much more independence and autonomy than the executive and legislative branches. Federal judges, because they have life tenure, are free from the electoral pressures that shape so much of the political interactions between the White House and Congress. Poll data showing strong support for the president's policy agenda is of little use to him if he wants to persuade the Supreme Court to affirm the constitutionality of his policies. Instead, the most important tool available to the president in influencing the courts is his ability to nominate like-minded judges he hopes will be favorably disposed to his own policy objectives. And, given federal judges' life tenure, by appointing like-minded judges to the federal bench, presidents can ensure that their policy legacy continues long after their term of office expires.

This chapter addresses the choices George W. Bush will face in making judicial nominations and getting those nominees confirmed by the Senate during his second term. The specific areas of discussion will be the structural and political factors Bush will confront and the strategic choices he must make that will affect his success in appointing his preferred judges.

The Changing Landscape of Judicial Appointments

Nowhere is the president's ability to influence the judicial branch clearer than in his power to appoint judges to the federal bench. While the president is charged with appointing a vast number of people to positions in the Executive Branch, such as Cabinet secretaries and their deputies, all of these appointees serve only during the president's term of office, and they can be removed at any point at the will of the president. Typically senators defer to the president's choices when it comes to appointing people to executive branch positions. While judges go through a similar appointment process, they are appointed for life; federal judges may only be removed from office on retirement, death, or impeachment, and senators therefore scrutinize these nominations much more closely.

Article II, Section 2 of the US Constitution stipulates that presidents will nominate judges to the Supreme Court and all lower courts with the "advice and consent" of the Senate. The fact that a majority of the Senate must vote to confirm a president's judicial nominees presents a significant potential hurdle to appointment, and senators have routinely exercised their right of "advise and consent" to vote against the confirmation of presidential nominees they do not support. In fact, the Senate made clear quite early in the country's history that its constitutional right to exercise "advice and consent" could—and would—be used to prevent objectionable nominees from being confirmed to the federal bench. Moreover, in recent years the Senate has expanded its right of refusal beyond Supreme Court judicial nominations to include lower court nominations as well.

The political reality of the Senate's role in the judicial confirmation process means that presidents must try not only to find like-minded nominees but also nominees who are likely to be confirmed by a majority of the Senate. Indeed, presidents consider a range of factors beyond the nominee's qualifications, including race, gender, religion, and prior political support. Presidents and their staff must also be attentive to the formal structure and stages of the confirmation process as well as the informal customs of the Senate that can often directly affect whether his nominees are in fact confirmed.

The confirmation process for judges and all other executive appointees consists of three main steps which nominees must successfully pass through. After a judicial nomination is formally sent to the Senate, the nomination is referred to the Senate Judiciary Committee.[3] The Judiciary Committee then holds a hearing at which the nominee responds to the questions of the Committee, after which the Committee votes on whether to send the nomination to the entire Senate for a vote. Importantly, if a majority of Judiciary Committee members vote against a judicial candidate, the nomination is defeated. If the nomination is favorably voted out of Committee, it is sent to the Senate floor where again a vote will be taken, this time by the entire Senate. If the nominee receives a majority of "yes" votes, the nominee is confirmed to the federal bench.

The Senate confirmation process thus presents a number of hurdles a judicial nominee must clear. As indicated, the confirmation process entails two major veto points whereby senators may defeat a judicial nomination, one at the Committee stage and one at the floor stage. Between 1987 and 2002, five Circuit Court nominees were actually defeated in Committee, while one

District Court nominee was defeated on the Senate floor.[4] Thus, while federal judges are *nominated* by the president, the ultimate fate of each nominee rests solely in the hands of the Senate as the Senate alone possesses the power to *confirm* each nominee to a seat on the federal bench.

Furthermore, while there are three main stages a nomination must pass through, the Senate has never guaranteed that all judicial nominees will be confirmed or even that all judicial nominees will get the *chance* to be confirmed. In particular, the Chair of the Senate Judiciary Committee and the Senate Majority Leader exert enormous control over the fate of judicial nominees. The Chair of the Judiciary Committee directly controls whether a nominee will receive either a confirmation hearing or a vote. If the Chair refuses to schedule either, the nomination is effectively dead, and there is no procedural mechanism opposing senators can use to force the Chair to give a nominee a hearing or a vote. For example, during Clinton's second term in office, seventeen of fifty-eight Courts of Appeals nominees (29.3 percent) never even received a Committee hearing, with some nominees languishing for two years or more.[5] Helene White, after being nominated to the sixth Circuit Court of Appeals, waited four years without any action ever being taken on her nomination.

The incoming Chair of the Senate Judiciary Committee, Arlen Specter (R-PA), made news shortly after both his and Bush's re-election when he was quoted as "warning" Bush that strong anti-abortion judges who might overturn *Roe v. Wade* were unlikely to be confirmed. Specter insisted his comments were not meant as a "warning," but merely a description of the political reality in the Senate.[6] Specter then promised to move quickly on all judicial nominees, including those who favor limiting abortion rights, after conservative groups waged a high-profile battle against his chairmanship.[7]

As with the Chair of the Judicial Committee, if Senate Majority Leader Bill Frist (R-TN) refuses to schedule a floor vote for a nominee, the nomination is effectively dead. Given Frist's strong loyalty to President Bush, this is unlikely to happen. For presidents faced with a Senate controlled by the opposing party, judicial confirmations are much more challenging. Between 1977 and 1998, over 90 percent of all judicial nominations made during unified government were confirmed, while on average only 76 percent of judicial nominations were confirmed during periods of divided government.[8] And, during Clinton's last two years in office (1999–2000), a period of divided government, only 61 percent of his nominees were confirmed.[9] Even more striking, in 1996, then-Senate Majority Leader Robert Dole only allowed 17 District Court nominees Clinton of (and no Circuit Court nominees) to be confirmed, the lowest number of judicial nominees ever confirmed in one year.[10] These numbers reflect not simply how many nominees failed to receive majority votes but also how many nominees the opposition party allowed to move through the confirmation process at all.[11] While presidents have routinely pushed for agreements that all nominees will at least receive hearings and votes, especially during periods when the Senate is controlled by the opposition party, the Senate usually rebukes such efforts.[12]

Informal aspects of the confirmation process also affect the likelihood of a president's success in judicial nominations. The Senate Judiciary Committee allows senators to block judicial nominations through the institutionalization of an informal custom known as "senatorial courtesy." Traditionally, senators who objected to a nominee from their home state would take to the Senate floor, declare the nominee "personally objectionable," and ask their fellow senators to have the courtesy to defer to their objections. In these instances, the norm of collegiality of the Senate trumped any deference senators felt they should accord to the president. Over time, this courtesy became institutionalized into what is known as the "blue-slip" procedure: the Chair of the Senate Judiciary Committee sends a blue slip of paper with the name of the nominee to each home-state senator. If one of the home-state senators objects to the nomination and returns a negative blue slip, the Chair of the Committee will refuse to move forward on the nomination. Obviously, the blue slip is only as powerful as the Judiciary Committee Chair allows it to be, and Chairs have differed on whether they view a negative blue slip as an absolute veto or whether home-state senators of the opposition party may exercise such a veto at all. Overall, however, Chairs usually do grant home-state senators a great deal of veto power, and this informal custom results in yet another hurdle presidents and their nominees must overcome.

In the past, "senatorial courtesy" also meant that presidents traditionally allowed senators the courtesy of selecting nominees for the district courts and courts of appeals from their home states, even if the home-state senator was of the opposition party. Senators often used these judgeships as a form of political patronage to reward faithful supporters or staff. However, presidents today are making more judicial appointments based on policy congruence and the nominees' ideological views on issues important to the president and his supporters.[13] Most strikingly, presidents beginning with Reagan have increasingly used judicial appointments, especially lower court appointments, as a mechanism to implement long-range policy goals.[14] As presidents have increasingly chosen nominees based on ideology rather than political patronage, they have also taken back the full prerogatives of their appointment powers and dramatically decreased the input of home-state senators.

In response, senators have made it harder and more politically costly for presidents to successfully appoint those nominees viewed as "outside the mainstream." While President George Washington's nominee to be the nation's third Chief Justice of the Supreme Court, John Rutledge, was defeated in 1795 due to his opposition to the Jay Treaty,[15] senators are much more likely in recent decades to question a nominee's fitness for office based on his or her ideological positions.[16] The most notable example is Senator Edward Kennedy's successful opposition to Robert Bork's 1986 Supreme Court nomination and his infamous "Robert Bork's America" speech which he gave on the Senate floor soon after Bork's nomination was formally announced.[17] Indeed, the blue-slip process is a direct result of the overall

Senate's ire of being left out of the nomination process, and it has been used even by senators of the president's own party. Senators are more willing to question judicial nominees about their views on key constitutional issues, and they increasingly acknowledge that a nominee's answers influence whether they will vote to confirm.

Senators are both pressured and emboldened in exercising such scrutiny by another significant change—the exponential increase in interest group participation in the judicial confirmation process. While outside groups have played an active role in Supreme Court nominations since the ninteenth century,[18] the amount and frequency of interest group participation in recent decades illuminates their heightened interest in who sits on the federal bench. Many have called the Bork nomination the "high-water mark" for interest group involvement in the judicial confirmation process,[19] and the level of interest group participation does not seem to be waning.[20]

Notably, the increased attention to ideology by presidents, scrutiny by senators, and interest group lobbying in judicial appointments process is now happening for all lower federal court nominations, not merely Supreme Court nominations. In today's political climate, judicial nominees at all levels of the federal courts are given significant attention. Especially during his second term of office, President Reagan began a concerted campaign to place young, bright conservatives on all levels of the federal bench as his administration realized the impact such appointments could have for decades to come. As Ronald Reagan's Attorney General, Edward Meese, explained, Reagan's judicial appointments were made in order to "institutionalize the Reagan revolution so that it can't be set aside, no matter what happens in further presidential elections."[21] Looking beyond just Supreme Court appointments, Reagan also focused on appointing like-minded justices to the Courts of Appeals (the federal appellate courts which are many times the final arbiters of important constitutional and statutory questions) and the District Courts (the federal trial courts). The Reagan administration recognized both the importance of the daily decisions made by the Courts of Appeals in particular and the fact that these judges many times become the so-called "farm team" for future Supreme Court appointments.

Senators and concerned interest groups feared this push by Reagan (and future presidents) to shape the federal bench and, as a consequence, they each began carefully scrutinizing lower court nominees. This heightened scrutiny has led to both the creation of a number of judicial watchdog groups on both sides of the aisle that continually monitor judicial appointments and the increased willingness of senators to oppose ideologically objectionable nominees to the lower courts and vote against their confirmations both in the Senate Judiciary Committee and on the Senate floor. These forces reached their apex during President George W. Bush's first term of office when outside interest groups opposed a record twenty-three Courts of Appeals nominees and Democratic senators filibustered a record ten nominees.[22]

The rules of the Senate favor the power of the one over the power of the many. This is especially significant given the increasing willingness of senators to use whatever mechanisms are available to defeat problematic nominees—including lower court nominees—since the second Reagan administration. According to the technical rules of the Senate, unanimous consent is required in order to bring a bill or nomination to a vote on the Senate floor. Thus, by definition, even one senator's objection can grind the progress of a nomination to a halt. By objecting and thereby refusing to limit debate, a senator commences a filibuster against a nomination. Once a filibuster begins, it now takes not a simple majority of fifty-one senators, but rather a super-majority of sixty senators, to end the filibuster and allow the nomination to come to a vote. Quite obviously, these rules are intended to—and do—favor the minority, and they clearly impact the likelihood of a president getting his nominees confirmed even during periods of unified party control of the presidency and the Senate. And, during the 108th Congress (2003–2004), Senate Democrats used these powers to successfully filibuster ten Circuit Court nominees. In the 2004 election, Republicans increased their majority in the Senate to 55 out of 100. This means that while Republicans do not have enough votes to defeat a filibuster attempt along party lines, they only need to convince five Democrats to defect in order to derail any potential filibusters, but such defections are difficult to acquire.

House Majority Leader Bill Frist threatened to push for a change in the rules of the Senate to eliminate filibusters of judicial nominees. Describing the Democrats as obstructionist and a "tyranny of the minority," at the very least Frist hoped to make the Democrats think about the political consequences of blocking nominations.[23]

The showdown over judicial nominees—or, at the very least, the first showdown of the 109th Congress—reached its apex on May 23, 2005. Frist devoted the entire week before to debate on the Fifth Circuit nomination of Texas Supreme Court Judge Priscilla Owen. Owen was actually defeated in the Senate Judiciary Committee during the 107th Congress, and then was filibustered during the 108th Congress. Frist scheduled a cloture vote on Owen to be held on the morning of Tuesday, May 24, with the implication that the so-called "nuclear option" would be invoked if the cloture vote failed. However, behind the scenes, a group of "mavericks, moderates, and old bulls"[24] worked to create a compromise that would, in the minds of many, save the Senate from a breakdown of longstanding traditions. And, at 7:30 p.m. on May 23, 2005 a group of 14 senators—seven Republicans and seven Democrats—announced that they had forged a compromise.[25]

The agreement of the 14 senators was significant: With the Senate split 55–45, seven defectors from each side was enough to tilt the balance of power away from each party's central goal and ensure that neither a filibuster, which needs 41 votes to be sustained, nor a change in the Senate rules, which needs at least 50 votes to force the Vice President to break a tie vote, could be achieved. The seven Democrats agreed to not filibuster judicial nominees except in "extraordinary circumstances," and the seven Republicans agreed not to vote for the "nuclear option" of taking away the right of senators to filibuster judicial nominees.[26] Strikingly, this compromise reinforces three central tenants about the Senate which are illuminated in the debate over the Senate's "advice and consent" function: First, each individual Senator wields tremendous power. Only 14 senators were needed to avert this showdown, and each senator in this "gentleman's agreement" will now exert tremendous power over all negotiations that take place during the rest of this Congress. Second, the power of individual senators can trump the power of even the Senate Majority Leader. To some, this deal reflects how, at least on this one day, "Republican Senate Majority Leader Bill Frist lost control of the Senate agenda."[27] As explained by the *Washington Post*, the leader of the compromise, Senator John McCain was able to "seize control of the debate" due to "Frist's inability or unwillingness to strike a deal."[28] Third, and most importantly, many are willing to step back from the partisan divide to reaffirm the institutional right of senators to engage in extended debate, and to protect the Senate as an institution. As one of the main architects of the brokered compromise, Senator Warner, stated, "What would happen to this Senate if the nuclear option were done?"[29] To this band of fourteen, that question was better left unanswered.

Given the structural realities of the confirmation process, presidents must clearly address the concerns of senators if they hope to get their judicial nominees confirmed. In making judicial nominations in his second term, and in working to get them confirmed, President George W. Bush and his staff must make several key strategic decisions that will in all likelihood impact his success.

Impediments to a Legacy: Strategic Choices that Affect a President's Ability to Shape the Federal Judiciary

As Bush (43) begins his second term in office, the partisan breakdown in the Senate and the willingness of Democrats to filibuster ten judicial nominations in his first term have enormous implications for Bush's second-term judicial appointments. Those managing judicial nominations for the President will have to make several crucial decisions concerning (a) what types of appointments Bush will make to the federal bench; (b) how much political capital he will expend in support of these nominees; and (c) whether he will re-appoint those nominees who were so bitterly opposed during his first administration. Examination of the record of judicial nominations under the Clinton administration and the first term of the Bush (43) administration provides important insights for Bush in making these strategic choices. The fate of judicial nominees during these twelve years also foreshadows what Bush (43) may expect during his second term in office.

Because Bush will have majority Republican control of the Senate, particularly instructive for consideration are Clinton's first two years as president, when he enjoyed Democratic control of the Senate and Bush's (43) last two years of his first term when the Republicans controlled the Senate. The other years of both the Clinton and Bush presidencies were marked by divided government—the opposition party to the president controlled a majority of the Senate.

One of the marked features of Clinton's presidency was the Republican Revolution of 1994, when Republicans gained control of both houses of Congress for the first time in decades. Though Clinton enjoyed unified government during his first two years in office (1993–1994), the Democratic Party he had to deal with was in considerable transition as Southern Democrats increasingly flocked to the Republican Party. To make matters more difficult, Clinton won with a mere plurality of the popularity vote in 1992 (caused in part by the strong third party run by Ross Perot who captured 19 percent of the popular vote), and his unsuccessful attempts to pass a national health care plan as well as to allow gays to openly serve in the military undermined his political strength. Nevertheless, most of Clinton's lower court nominees were successfully confirmed during his first two years (90.1 percent were confirmed), and he was able to successfully appoint two Supreme Court justices, Ruth Bader Ginsburg and Steven Breyer. However, these early judicial nominations are also noteworthy for the kinds of moderate, consensus-generating judicial nominees that Clinton put forward.

Not surprisingly, following the 1994 midterm elections, it was generally understood that the sizable Republican victory "limited the political capital Clinton could invest to get judges confirmed."[30] Clinton's judicial nominations thus continued to be rather moderate, and scholars have contended that Clinton focused more on increasing the diversity of the federal bench than forging a policy-based legacy.[31] Eleanor Acheson, Clinton's Assistant Attorney General for the Office of Policy Development during his two terms, admitted that a number of potentially controversial nominations were never submitted as a result of the Republican takeover and Clinton's fear that these nominations would be blocked.[32] Liberal groups roundly criticized Clinton for not supporting his judicial nominees strongly enough; for example, Nan Aron of the Alliance for Justice contended that "[Clinton] didn't fight for some nominees. He didn't fight for a vision of the courts."[33] Numerous reports also highlight the extent to which Clinton consulted with Republican Senators on nominations after 1994,[34] and examinations of the voting records of Clinton's nominees once on the bench showcase their moderate tendencies.[35]

However, even Clinton's consensus nominees occasionally ran into trouble during his next six years in office when Republicans controlled the Senate. Senate Republicans, led by then-Senate Majority Leader Bob Dole, refused to move forward on a number of judicial nominations in the hopes that Dole would win the 1996 presidential election, and only seventeen judges totaly were confirmed in all of 1996. Even after Dole lost the election, Senate Republicans felt emboldened enough to significantly slow down the judicial confirmation process during Clinton's second term. Between 1997 and 2000, only 60.3 percent of Clinton's Courts of Appeals nominees were confirmed, the lowest level of confirmations in history as of that date; additionally, the time between when a Circuit Court nomination was received in the Senate to when a confirmed nominee received a hearing grew from an average of seventy-nine days during the first Clinton administration to an average of 247 days in the 106th Congress (1999–2000).[36] Overall, at the end of 2000, 40 judicial nominees were left stranded in the Senate Judiciary Committee, and 36 of these nominees never even received a hearing.[37] Judicial nominations that were allowed to move, however, were usually confirmed easily and with little opposition, and only one Clinton nominee was defeated in either the Judiciary Committee or on the Senate floor during his eight years in office. A crucial component to this outcome was that, in the eyes of many, a key decision was made by Clinton and his administration to use its political capital on issues other than judicial nominations in order to avoid bruising confirmation battles. In the end, this decision meant that fewer nominees were confirmed overall and a large number of vacancies on the federal bench were left open when George W. Bush took office in 2001.

Bush (43) faced a somewhat similar landscape when he took office. Having won the presidency after a protracted legal fight that went all the way to the Supreme Court and having lost the popular vote, Bush (43) took office under extremely unusual circumstances to say the least. Then, in July of 2001, Senator Jim Jeffords of Vermont defected from the Republican Party, causing the Senate majority to switch to the Democrats. Bush (43), similar to Clinton's last six years, had to persuade Senate Democrats to confirm his nominees. In contrast to Clinton's consensus candidates, Bush put forward a crop of distinguished but ideologically conservative judicial nominees. Whereas Republicans in the Senate during the Clinton administration simply stalled problematic nominees and Clinton did little to fight them, Bush and the Senate Republicans pushed heavily for all of his nominees to be moved through the confirmation process. Thus, rather than moderating his judicial appointments in the face of opposition, as Clinton did, Bush used his bully pulpit to push for the confirmation of his admittedly conservative nominees.[38] The result was that two Circuit Court nominees, Charles Pickering and Priscilla Owen, were actually defeated by the Democrats in the Senate Judiciary Committee, while a number of other Circuit Court nominees faced bruising battles for confirmation.[39]

The climate for judicial nominations became even more heated following the 2002 midterm elections. Republicans regained a slight majority in the Senate, and Bush promptly renominated the controversial nominees still pending confirmation, as well as the two nominees who had been defeated during the previous Congress. Angered by Bush's actions, and his continuing refusal to nominate what they deemed consensus candidates, the minority Democrats fought back with a vengeance during the 108th Congress. Though they were unable to defeat any nominees in the Committee, a record ten Circuit Court nominees were filibustered by Senate Democrats on the Senate floor.[40, 41] Democrats effectively sustained each of these filibusters through multiple cloture votes, including seven failed cloture votes on the nomination of Miguel Estrada alone. The bitter partisan environment of the judicial confirmation process was reflected in the campaigns of the candidates in the 2004 presidential election.

The important pattern for judicial confirmations that emerged in Bush's first term was the continuing resolve of Senate Democrats to publicly fight—and thereby obstruct—the confirmation of judges perceived to be outside the mainstream, and the persistent decision by the Bush administration to fight these confirmation battles head on.

What do these two stories of recent judicial confirmation woes suggest for the second-term Bush (43) administration? Bush has already made his first crucial strategic decision, which will perhaps set the tone for the entire presidential term, when his administration announced that he would renominate those judicial candidates who were filibustered during his previous term, including especially controversial fifth Circuit nominee Priscilla Richman Owen and eleventh Circuit nominee William H. Pryor.[42] In terms of political strategies, Bush and his advisors may believe that he cannot lose in renominating these candidates, because he gains political points with right-wing conservatives whether they are confirmed or not; and, if his preferred candidates are not confirmed, he can blame the Democrats obstructionist tactics and accuse them of holding the federal judiciary hostage, as he and other Republicans seemingly successfully did in the 2004 election. Indeed, White House Press Secretary Scott McClellan's statement that Bush "looks forward to working with the new Senate to ensure a well-functioning and independent judiciary" foreshadows that tactic.[43] And, on May 23, 2005, Bush won one facet of this confrontation when the fourteen senators agreed to allow three of his previously blocked nominees, including Owen and Pryor, to come to a vote on the Senate floor.

An important question will be whether the increased majority margin of the Republicans will dilute the staying power of those Democrats who joined in the filibusters during the last Congress. Senate Democrats in the 108th Congress clearly demonstrated their resolve to fight objectionable nominees, and they did so across multiple nominees and on multiple cloture votes to end the filibusters. Not only was the use of filibusters on lower court nominees a surprising development, but so was the Democrats' decision (and ability) to filibuster so many nominees. Even more importantly, leading Democratic senators, such as Charles Schumer (D-NY), immediately voiced their intention after the 2004 presidential election to continue their vigorous fight against ideologically extreme judicial nominees.[44] As Schumer said, "In this opening shot, the White House is making it clear that they are not interested in bipartisanship when it comes to judicial nominees."[45] House Minority Leader Harry Reid echoed Schumer's sentiments, saying "Last Congress, Senate Democrats worked with the president to approve 204 judicial nominees, rejecting only ten of the most extreme. . . . It's a disservice to the American people to detract from the important work of the Senate to reconsider these failed nominees."[46] As this battle of rhetoric shows, the strategic choices of the Senate leadership will also impact how many of Bush's nominees will be confirmed during this term. What was most surprising during Bush's first term was Senate Majority Leader Bill Frist's willingness to "dual-track" judicial nomination filibusters. By placing the filibustered nominations on one "track" and all other pending legislation and nominations on another, Frist actually made it easier for the Senate Democrats to maintain their filibusters: Because Frist only brought the nominations up for cloture votes every few months, Democrats did not have to engage in a traditional filibuster where round-the-clock debate takes place, but rather they only had to occasionally ensure that they could produce forty-one votes against cloture. Democrats thus expended very little political capital in waging these filibusters, including those that lasted for well over a year. It should be noted that Frist's decision did allow the Senate to conduct its other business, and numerous Republican agenda items were successfully enacted. Since the presidential election, however, Frist has made strong statements to the Federalist Society on November 11, 2004, and on *Fox News Sunday* on November 14, 2004, in favor of ending Democratic opposition tactics quickly and forcefully.[47] A clear decision-point will arise if Democratic senators decide that "extraordinary circumstances" force them to filibuster a judicial nominee.[48]

In conclusion, Bush must decide how much of his own political capital he will expend to help his nominees be confirmed. The success of Bush's second-term nominees may depend on how badly he wants the Senate to focus on other legislative matters. During his first administration, he was quite willing to use his bully pulpit to help embattled nominees. Second-term presidents have much less clout available for influence in general. Bush has put forth an aggressive agenda of large, controversial issues such as Social Security reform and tax reform, and he will need to make a strategic assessment of how far his newly won political capital from the 2004 election extends. This is complicated by the fact that, in terms of his legislative agenda, he cannot even necessarily count on support from his own party. House Speaker Dennis Hastert (R-IL) recently declared that he would only bring to a vote on the House floor those bills supported by "a majority of the majority" or ones that had broad Republican support.[49] Judging by his decision to renominate filibustered judges and the political rhetoric of his administration, Bush shows no signs of backing down from nominating and supporting the kind of ideologically conservative, strict constructionist judges supported by his party base and the important evangelical constituency he courted in the 2004 election.[50]

Everyone interested in judicial nominations knows that the real battle will occur if and when a vacancy occurs on the Supreme Court, and Bush therefore has the opportunity to nominate a new Supreme Court justice. As the strong outpouring of concern by conservative groups over Arlen Specter assuming the chairmanship of the Judiciary Committee showed, these groups are already in "fighting mode." Similarly, leading liberal groups such as the Alliance for Justice and People for the American Way—who successfully convinced Democrats to stand strong against objectionable lower court nominees—have already begun positioning themselves to oppose a possible Bush (43) Supreme Court nominee. The abortion rights group NARAL Pro-Choice America circulated a petition immediately after Bush's re-election calling on its members to announce that they will "do everything possible to keep [Bush] from overturning *Roe v. Wade* by nominating an anti-choice justice to the Supreme Court."[51] In the current political climate of judicial nominations, there is virtually no doubt that a Bush nominee to the Supreme Court will face a heated partisan battle.

The importance of such a battle is heightened by the very real chance that the next vacancy on the Supreme Court may well be that of the Chief Justice. Bush will once again face some crucial decisions: Should he elevate some already on the Court to Chief Justice, thus opening up a second vacancy for which an appointment will have to be made? While this would allow Bush to nominate the conservative favorite Antonin Scalia for Chief Justice, it could also lead to not one but two costly confirmation battles. Similarly, should Bush nominate a person with a clear conservative record, or try to nominate a more consensus-based candidate? While appointing a clear conservative would appease his base, Democrats have already expressed their intention to filibuster such a nominee, and it is not clear that the compromise forged to stop the nuclear option would block the use of the filibuster in such a situation. Regardless of his decision, President Bush will have to weigh the impact of a protracted struggle on his administration's other key priorities for its second term, and on his ability to create a lasting policy legacy through his appointments to the federal courts.

Notes

1. Richard E. Neustadt, *Presidential Power* (New York: Wiley, 1964), p. 42.
2. Gregory A. Caldeira and John R. Wright, "Organized Interests and Agenda Setting in the U.S. Supreme Court," *American Political Science Review* 82 (1988), pp. 1109–1127; Susan Olson, "Interest Group Litigation in the Federal District Courts: Beyond the Political Disadvantage Theory," *Journal of Politics* 52 (1990), pp. 854–882; R. Shep Melnick, *Between the Lines: Interpreting Welfare Rights* (Washington, DC: Brookings, 1993).
3. Other executive branch nominations are sent to the Senate committee with jurisdiction over the nomination if the appointment is to an executive branch position. For example, while the nominee for Attorney General is referred to the Judiciary Committee, the nominee for Secretary of Commerce is referred to the Commerce, Science and Transportation Committee while the nominee for Secretary of Energy is referred to the Energy and Natural Resources Committee.
4. The Circuit Court nominees defeated in Committee were Susan Liebeler (100th Congress), Bernard Siegan (100th Congress), Kenneth Ryskamp (102nd Congress), Charles Pickering (107th Congress), and Priscilla Owen (107th Congress). Ronnie White was defeated on the Senate floor during the 106th Congress. President Bush (43) infuriated Senate Democrats by re-nominating both Charles Pickering and Priscilla Owen at the start of the 108th Congress, and he further fanned the flames by giving Pickering a recess appointment to the 5th Circuit Court in January of 2004.

5. Only 44 percent of Clinton's nominees were confirmed during his final two years in office.

6. Helen Dewar and Charles Lane, "Specter Denies Warning Over Bush Court Nominees," *Washington Post*, November 5, 2004, p. A5.

7. Robin Toner, 2004, "Political Memo: Changing Senate Looks Better for Abortion Foes," *New York Times*, December 2, 2004, p. A34.

8. Roger E. Hartley and Lisa M. Holmes, "The Increasing Senate Scrutiny of Lower Federal Court Nominees," *Political Science Quarterly* 117 (2002), pp. 259–278, 275.

9. Sheldon Goldman, Elliot Slotnick, Gerard Gryski, and Gary Zuk, "Clinton's Judges: Summing Up the Legacy," *Judicature* 84 (2001), pp. 228–252.

10. In comparison, 42 Reagan nominees were confirmed in 1988 and 66 Bush (41) nominees were confirmed in 1992 by Democratic Senates; Goldman et al., "Clinton's Judges," 2001; Hartley and Holmes, "The Increasing Senate Scrutiny," 2002.

11. To elaborate, of 201 nominations made to the Courts of Appeals between 1987 and 2002, only five of these nominees failed to receive majority votes and thus were actually defeated (2.5%) but 35 (17.4%) of these nominees were denied even a hearing, and 66 Bush nominees were confirmed in 1992 of which 41 were confirmed by Democratic Senates. This number was lowered considerably given that only two Bush (43) nominees out of fifty-two failed to receive hearings by the end of his first term, with thirty confirmation hearings held during the 108th Congress alone (as this was a period of unified government).

12. It should be noted, however, that while Specter publicly pledged to move judicial nominations swiftly through the Judiciary Committee, he did not enter any kind of binding agreement and neither the Senate nor the Judiciary Committee rules can prevent him from slowing down the nomination process if he so chooses.

13. Lauren Cohen Bell,. "Senatorial Discourtesy: The Senate's Use of Delay to Shape the Federal Judiciary," *Political Research Quarterly* 55-3 (2002), pp. 589–608; Nancy Scherer (forthcoming), *Scoring Points: Politicians, Political Activists, and the Lower Court Appointment Process* (Paolo AltoCA: Stanford University Press, 2005).

14. John Maltese, "Confirmation Gridlock: The Federal Judicial Appointments Process Under Bill Clinton and George W. Bush," *Journal of Appellate Practice and Procedure* 1 (2003); Amy Steigerwalt, *Cultivating Controversy: Senators, Interest Groups, and the Politics of Courts of Appeals Confirmations*. Ph.D. Dissertation, University of California, Berkeley (2004); Sheldon Goldman, "Reagan's Judicial Legacy: Completing the Puzzle and Summing Up," *Judicature* 72 (1989), pp. 318–329.

15. Henry J. Abraham, 4th ed, *Justices, Presidents, and Senators: A History of The U.S. Supreme Court Appointments from Washington to Clinton* (New York: Rowman & Littlefield Publishers, Inc., 1999); Michael J. Gerhardt, *The Federal Appointments Process: A Constitutional and Historical Analysis* (Durham: Duke University Press, 2003); John Anthony Maltese, *The Selling of Supreme Court Nominees*. (Baltimore, MD: Johns Hopkins University Press, 1995).

16. Jeffrey A. Segal, Albert D. Cover, and Charles M. Cameron, "The Role of Ideology in Senate Confirmation of Supreme Court Justices," *Kentucky Law Journal* 77 (1998), pp. 485–507; Mark Silverstein, *Judicious Choices: The New Politics of Supreme Court Confirmations* (New York: W. W. Norton, 1994); Norman Vieira,

and Leonard Gross, *Supreme Court Appointments: Judge Bork and the Politicization of Senate Confirmations* (Carbondale: Southern Illinois University Press, 1998).

17. Ethan Bronner, *"Battle for Justice: How the Bork Nomination Shook America"* (New York: Norton, 1989).

18. Maltese, *"The Selling of Supreme Court Nominees,"* 1995.

19. Gregory A. Caldeira, "Commentary on Senate Confirmation of Supreme Court Justices: The Roles of Organized and Unorganized Interests," *Kentucky Law Journal* 77 (1989), pp. 531–538; Abraham, "Justices, Presidents and Senators," 1999.

20. Amy Steigerwalt and Nancy Scherer, "Tracking Trouble: Do Interest Groups Influence the Lower Federal Court Confirmation Process?" Paper presented at the Southern Political Science Association Annual Meeting, New Orleans, January 8–10, 2004; Bell, "Senatorial Discourtesy," 2002; Steigerwalt, *Cultivating Controversy*, 2004.

21. David M. O'Brien, *Judicial Roulette: Report of the Twentieth Century Fund TaskForce on Judicial Selection* (New York: Priority Press, 1988), pp. 23–24.

22. Steigerwalt and Scherer, "Tracking Trouble," 2004.

23. Kathy Kiely, "GOP Sets Up Senate Collision on Judges," *USA Today*, December 27, 2004, p. A4.

24. Robin Toner and Richard W. Stevenson, "Justice Choice Could Rekindle Filibuster Fight in the Senate," *New York Times*, May 25, 2005.

25. Paul Kane and Mark Preston, "Deal Averts Showdown: Fourteen Senators Join to Keep Filibuster Intact," *Roll Call*, May 24, 2005, p. 1.

26. In addition, it was agreed that three previously filibustered nominees, Priscilla Owen, William Pryor, and Janice Rogers Brown, would receive floor votes. Two other previously filibustered nominees, Henry Saad and William Myers, were not included in the deal. It is likely that their nominations will remain stalled. Kane and Preston, "Deal Averts Showdown" (2005, at 21) included a copy of the "Memorandum of Understanding on Judicial Nominations" that the 14 senators all agreed to sign.

27. Editorial Board of the *Seattle-Post Intelligencer*, "Filibuster Deal: Judging from the Center," *Seattle Post Intelligencer*, May 24, 2005.

28. The article continued, "The body language of the two GOP senators—McCain ebullient in announcing the deal, and Frist taut and drawn in interpreting it moments later on the Senate floor—spoke volumes about the immediate reading of who won and who lost." Dan Balz, "For GOP, Deeper Fissures and a Looming Power Struggle," *Washington Post*, May 25, 2005, p. A 11.

29. CNN(2005), "Senators Compromise on Filibusters," CNN.com, available at http://premium.cnn.com/2005/POLITICS/05/23/filibuster.fight/

30. David Byrd, "Clinton's Untilting Federal Bench," *National Journal*, February 19, 2000.

31. Sheldon Goldman and Matthew D. Saronson, "Clinton's Nontraditional Judges: Creating a More Representative Bench," *Judicature* 78 (1994), pp. 28–34; Maltese, "Confirmation Gridlock," 2003.

32. Personal interview with the author, July 2002.

33. Byrd, "Clinton's Untilting Federal Beach," 2000.

34. Maltese, "Confirmation Gridlock," 2003; Goldman and Saronson, "Clinton's Nontraditional Judges," 1994.

35. Robert A. Carp and Donald Songer, "The Voting Behavior of President Clinton's Judicial Appointees," *Judicature* 80 (1996), pp. 16–20; Nancy Scherer, "Are Clinton's Judges 'Old' Democrats or 'New' Democrats?" *Judicature* 84 (2000), pp. 150–158; Robert A. Carp, Kenneth L. Manning, and Ronald Stidham, "President Clinton's District Judges: 'Extreme Liberals' or Just Plain Moderates?" *Judicature* 84 (2001), pp. 282–288; Susan B. Haire, Martha Anne Humphries, and Donald Songer, "The Voting Behavior of Clinton's Courts of Appeals Appointees," *Judicature* 84(2001), pp. 274–282.

36. It should be noted, however, that only one Clinton nominee, Ronnie White, was actually defeated; instead, Republicans just refused to allow nominees to move through the process; Goldman, et al., "Clinton's Judges," 2001.

37. Ibid.

38. Bush vowed to get "good conservative judges appointed to the bench and approved by the United States Senate." Reuters, "President Says 'Good, Conservative' Judges Needed," *San Diego Union-Tribune*, March 29, 2002, p. A6.

39. While only 53.1% of Bush's Circuit Court nominees were confirmed during the 107th Congress, it is interesting to note that all of the nominees who received confirmation hearings (other than the two defeated nominees) were eventually confirmed but one, including those who were objected to by liberal interest groups.

40. The filibustered nominees were: Henry Saad (6th Circuit); Janice Rogers Brown (DC Circuit); William Pryor, Jr. (11th Circuit); Charles Pickering, Sr. (5th Circuit); Priscilla Owen (5th Circuit); William Myers III (9th Circuit); David McKeague (6th Circuit); Carolyn Kuhl (9th Circuit); Richard Allen Griffin (6th Circuit); and Miguel Estrada (DC Circuit). Estrada eventually withdrew his nomination on September 4, 2003, following seven failed cloture votes.

41. However, it should be noted that 104 judicial nominees (82 percent) were confirmed during the 108th Congress, and another 100 nominees (76 percent) were confirmed by the Democratic Senate during the 107th Congress. Data on the outcomes of judicial nominations during Bush's first term (as well as information about current nominees) can be found at the US Department of Justice's Office of Legal Policy website, www.usdoj.gov/olp/judicialnominations.htm.

42. Michael A. Fletcher and Helen Dewar, "Bush Will Renominate 20 Judges; Fights in Senate Likely Over Blocked Choices," *Washington Post*, December 24, 2004, p. A1.

43. Richard B. Schmitt and Nick Anderson, "Bush to Revive Failed Judicial Nominations," *Los Angeles Times*, December 24, 2004, p. A1.

44. In fact, as of November 5, 2004, numerous articles reported Schumer's claim that "Everything stays the same, and the ball's in the president's court. I don't see the Democrats backing down this issue [of opposing extremist nominees]" (quoted in Jesse Holland, "Fight over Judicial Nominees Will Go On," *Associated Press*, November 5, 2004, available at www.cnn.com/2004/ALLPOLITICS/11/05/senate.judges.ap.

45. Schmitt and Anderson, "Bush to Revive Failed Judicial Nominations," 2004, p. A 1.

46. Ibid., p. A1.

47. The text of Frist's speech to the Federalist Society can be found at www.fedsoc.org/Publications/Transcripts/frist04.pdf; the text of Frist's appearance on *Fox News Sunday* can be found at www.foxnews.com/story/ 0,2933,138515,00.html.

48. The agreement reached by the fourteen senators on May 24, 2005, included the proviso that Democratic senators could filibuster a judicial nominee without breaking the agreement under "extraordinary circumstances." Kane and Preston, "Deal Averts Showdown," 2005.

49. Sheryl Gay Stolberg, "Quietly but Firmly, Hastert Asserts His Power," *New York Times*, January 3, 2005, p. A1.

50. Jeffrey Rosen, "Can Bush Deliver a Conservative Court?" "Week in Review," *New York* Times, November 14, 2002.

51. This petition can be found at http://prochoiceaction.org/campaign/ scotus_msg.

Part IV

The Policies

Chapter Eight

Domestic Policy in the Second Bush Term: The Un-Hidden Hand Leadership of a Conviction President

Michael A. Genovese

"I make foreign policy," said Harry S Truman, overstated but not far off the mark. But who—if anyone—"makes" domestic policy? The making of domestic policy is often likened to the making of sausage: if you knew what went into it, you wouldn't want to eat it!

In truth, the making of domestic policy often encompasses the best and the worst of American politics: A confused mish-mash of bargaining, compromise, deals and dirt, money and threats, high and low politics, pressure and power, intermediation and pleading, sleight-of-hand and gentle nudges, . . . a thing of beauty and a frightening cauldron of muck.

To be successful in the domestic arena, presidents must call upon the light and the dark, all their skill and power and even then, they often fail. There are just too many players who control too many veto points. Congress has most of the Constitutional authority; interest groups are organized and well funded; the public has its demands and expectations; the bureaucracy must be contended with; the media is always lurking; policy and partisan differences complicate matters; and then—always—lurking in the background is, depending on one's point of view, Madison's gift or Madison's curse: the separation-of-powers. Only through active and creative presidential leadership can this machine be made to move with any consistency.

George W. Bush enters term two with a level of political opportunity bolstered by the tragic events of 9/11, but moderated by the fairly close results of the 2004 election. How President Bush uses his opportunities, the level of skill and bravado he can muster, the type of agenda he pursues, and the team he builds around himself, will determine the extent to which he achieves his rather expansive domestic policy agenda in his second term.

Presidential Leadership

The President is at liberty, both in law and in conscience, to be as big a man as he can. . . . His capacity will set the limit.

Woodrow Wilson

In the social sciences, the words *leadership* and *power* are often used interchangeably. This is a mistake. Leadership suggests *influence*; power is *command*. Leaders inspire and persuade; power-wielders order compliance. Leaders induce followership; power-holders compel or force acceptance. Officeholders have (to some degree at least) power merely by virtue of occupying an office. Leaders, on the other hand, *earn* followership. The officeholder uses the powers granted to his official position. The leader tries to reshape the political environment; "he seeks to change the constellation of political forces about him in a direction closer to his own conception of the political good."[1]

On occasion, a president can act on his own authority, "independent" of other political actors. A president's pardoning power is a prime example of this form of command authority. But such unilateral acts as this are the exception, not the rule. In most cases, presidents share power. Therefore, leadership, the informal "powers" so eloquently elaborated upon by Richard Neustadt, becomes important to presidents who wish to wield the full range of power and to promote political change.

A president's formal power—for so long the focal point of presidential studies[2]—includes constitutional authority, statutes, delegated powers, and those areas in which others follow a president's command. But with the publication of Richard Neustadt's *Presidential Power* in 1960,[3] the more informal power to persuade took center stage in presidential studies. Rather than take an either-or approach to the debate over formal versus informal powers, we should see these two potential sources of strength as complementary, as presidential options in the pursuit of their goals. While presidents derive some of their powers from constitutional sources, they derive others from political and personal sources. Effective presidents use *all* the resources available to them. They assess the situation and determine where their best chances for success are, and they are flexible enough to make the adjustments necessary to optimize their power.

True leadership occurs when presidents are able to exploit the multifaceted nature of opportunities both to command *and* to influence. In his classic study, *Leadership*, James M. Burns suggests that leadership takes place when

> persons with certain motives and purposes mobilize, in competition or conflict with others, institutional, political, psychological, and other resources so as to arouse, engage, and satisfy the motives of followers. . . . Leadership is exercised in a condition of conflict or competition in which leaders contend in appealing to the motive bases of potential followers.[4]

For better or worse, only presidential leadership can regularly overcome the lethargy built into the American separation-of- power system and give focus to government. Congress can take the lead on a policy, as was the case when the Congress overcame presidential opposition from Ronald Reagan and imposed economic sanctions on the white minority government of South Africa or in the early days of Newt Gingrich's time as Speaker of the

House during the Clinton presidency. But such cases are infrequent and generally not long lasting: Congress simply is not well designed and cannot provide consistent national leadership over extended periods of time. In the second half of the twentieth century, citizens have most often looked to the White House for leadership and direction. If the president doesn't lead, gridlock usually results. In this sense, John F. Kennedy's view that "The presidential office is the vortex into which all the elements of national decision are irresistibly drawn"[5] rings true. Presidential leadership remains the key for moving the machinery of government. But, given all that is arrayed against presidents, how can they lead rather than merely preside?

The role of presidential leadership is even more significant when we focus on domestic policy. Presidents are accorded greater authority, more power, and more independent discretion in foreign affairs than in the domestic arena. Thus, for presidents to "get what they want" in domestic policy, they must exert forceful leadership. Others, most notably the Congress, compete with and are on more equal footing in the domestic realm. In fact, in domestic affairs, Congress has a more impressive list of constitutional powers than does the president.

Citizens expect their presidents to accomplish great things. They hold these officeholders responsible for the health of the economy, world peace, the overall state of the nation, even the weather (global warming). All occupants of the White House face a series of roadblocks, checks and balances that inhibit behavior and make governing difficult.[6] But all presidencies are not equal. Presidents vary in skill, experience, judgment, stamina, and in a variety of other ways. And all times are not created equal. President George W. Bush had a vastly different political context—and thus level of power, before 9/11, than after. To understand the opportunities and limits placed upon a president in the domestic arena we must calculate that president's "level of political opportunity."

Level of opportunity is measured by extrinsic factors such as public demand, pro- or antigovernment sentiments, issue ripeness, available resources, competing issues, and the strength of the president's party in Congress. Factors more centered on the presidency itself are the size of a president's election victory, the issues over which the presidential contest was fought, and the president's popularity. Opportunity levels set reasonable expectations—that is, high-opportunity presidents should achieve more than low-opportunity presidents. What determines whether presidents achieve the political results their opportunity levels permit? Skill.

If level of opportunity establishes a possible range of presidential performances, the leadership style employed by presidents helps determine the interaction and public face they present to the people, Congress, and other political actors. Presidents display tremendous differences in their leadership styles. Some seek to emulate the aggressive style of President Franklin Roosevelt (FDR); others choose less assertive approaches. Ronald Reagan, who admired Roosevelt's speaking style adopted a public style based in part on FDR's. George H. W. Bush's lack of action found some of his aides actually making lists of "speeches not given" because of his reluctance to engage in a strong public role. Jimmy Carter often pursued positions he judged to be in the long-run public interest, whether popular or not, whereas Bill Clinton relied heavily on opinion polls in developing policies and shaping his messages.

Leadership styles encompass *strategic choices*. Some presidents have sought to "hit the ground running"; others have been characterized as "hitting the ground stumbling," or even "marching in place."[7] In their public leadership, some presidents have effectively sought to "go public" to build support for legislation.[8] In fact, candidate Bill Clinton's enthusiasm for Theodore Roosevelt's use of the presidency as a "bully pulpit" to elicit public support for his programs led Clinton to take to the road in a continuation, as it were, of his election campaign. Other presidents have sought less-visible means of achieving their goals. That may explain why top-level negotiations (known as bipartisan summits) between administration leaders and congressional leaders have been used with increasing frequency. In another strategic choice, presidents frequently engage in policy shifts in the third year of their terms to reshape the direction of their administration—and their re-election prospects.

In choosing a leadership style, presidents are influenced by a variety of factors, including their own personalities and prior career experiences. Many presidents rely on their historical favorites for views of how the president should lead. Woodrow Wilson and Franklin Roosevelt are high on this list, but "silent" Calvin Coolidge rates only occasional mention. Some presidents have deliberately chosen a leadership style that contrasts with that of their predecessor. John Kennedy, for example, sought more assertive public leadership than that provided by Dwight Eisenhower. Carter strove to do away with the trappings of the "imperial presidency" and be a "man of the people." Reagan's short answer was to be the mirror image of Carter as he pursued a more optimistic persona and a more focused approach to his first-year agenda. George H. W. Bush showed an aversion to Reagan's limited attention to detail, and Clinton sought to have a more robust domestic agenda than Bush's. The combination of presidential wishes to be different and the public's tendency to seek leaders who compensate for the problems of their predecessors has contributed to sharp swings in leadership styles from president to president.

The readily observed differences in leadership styles have not produced agreement among political scientists on how much these differences affect public policy.[9] Those who believe individual skill has a limited impact on policy outcomes have emphasized the extent to which presidential actions are shaped by the opportunities produced by power relationships in Congress, economic conditions, and levels of public support for new policy initiatives, among other things. Indeed, as his second term began, Clinton lamented that his time in office thus far had not presented opportunities for achievements comparable to those experienced by presidents who had left large legacies.

Challenges and Opportunities

Some presidents face greater challenges than others in both the international and domestic arenas. Presidents Harry Truman and Richard Nixon began terms as the nation was waging unpopular wars.

Policy challenges often create opportunities because of a widespread desire for action. In 1981, public frustration over slow economic growth and high inflation created widespread sympathy for trying something new—in this instance, Reagan's supply-side tax cuts. Public frustration with existing conditions does not mean, however, that the policies proposed will address voter concerns or that policymakers will be able to build political support for any one specific option. Clinton, for example, found it extremely difficult to convert voter desires for reform of the health care system into support for one specific approach.

Public Mood

The public periodically displays a strong desire for government action, heightening presidential opportunities. President Kennedy, who was interested in these cycles, talked with historian and staff aide Arthur Schlesinger Jr. about their underlying patterns.[10] Over time, as problems grow and government action is seen as insufficient public sentiment builds for reform. At such times presidents can claim a mandate for change that often moves Congress to act. The desire for government action occurred in the first fifteen years of the twentieth century to the advantage of Presidents Theodore Roosevelt and Woodrow Wilson and again in the 1930s, the 1960s, and the 1980s. Likewise, presidents serving in between, such as Truman and Eisenhower, did not enjoy comparable desires for action.[11] Nor, for various reasons, including broader public skepticism about the scope and role of government, along with the constraints of budgetary deficits, did a comparable groundswell occur in the 1990s.

Levels of public trust in government also can have an enormous impact on a president's level of opportunity. During the 1960s presidents seeking to establish new programs were dealing with an electorate that, by today's standards, had a far higher degree of trust in the federal government. From the vantage point of the far more cynical era today, the 1960s appears to have been a stunningly different period: over 60 percent of the public agreed with the view that one can trust the government in Washington to do the right thing all of the time or most of the time, whereas when Bill Clinton entered the White House in 1993, the portion of the population with a similar view had fallen to only 22 percent.

Public Support

Differences in levels of public support are yet another factor in the opportunities open to presidents. Elections can produce several advantages. For example, a large winning margin can give presidents the opportunity to argue that they received a "mandate" for their policies. After the 2004 presidential election, President Bush claimed that, by gaining 51 percent of the popular vote, he had a mandate to govern. In addition, a large winning margin may give presidents the opportunity to claim that they pulled legislators into office on their "coattails." Leading students of voting behavior discredit the view that large segments of the electorate produce a mandate by understanding a president's policy goals and voting on that basis.[12] Nevertheless, in 1981 Reagan, who had campaigned hard on his economic program and won by 10 percent, plausibly asserted the existence of a mandate and gained an initial advantage with Congress.

Public support of the president's party also can make a difference (see table 8.1 for a review of President Bush's approval ratings). From the 1930s to the 1960s Democratic presidents such as Kennedy and Johnson benefited from belonging to a party that enjoyed a considerable advantage in party identification over the Republicans. This advantage has largely disappeared in recent years, as party identification figures have become more even and the number of independent identifiers has grown substantially. As a result, party identification is becoming less important in voter choices among presidential candidates. Party strength also may be reflected in the extent to which the party a president defeats becomes discredited in the eyes

Table 8.1   President George W. Bush's approval ratings: Gallup poll and *CNN/USA Today.* "Do you approve or disapprove of the way George W. Bush is handling his job as president?"

Dates	Approve (%)	Disapprove (%)	Unsure (%)
2/1–4/01	57	43	10
3/5–7/01	63	22	15
4/20–22/01	62	29	9
6/11–17/01	55	33	12
9/7–10/01	51	39	10
9/14–15/01	86	10	4
9/21–22/01	90	6	4
11/26–27/01	87	8	5
3/8–9/02	80	14	6
7/26–28/02	69	26	5
11/8–10/02	66	26	8
3/22–23/03	71	25	4
8/4–6/03	60	36	4
12/5–7/03	55	43	3
3/5–7/04	49	48	3
9/24–26/04	54	44	2
12/5–8/04	53	44	3
2/21–24/05	51	45	4
3/21–23/05	45	49	6
4/29–5/05	48	49	3

of the voters. Discredited opposition parties worked to the advantage of Roosevelt in 1933, Johnson in 1965, and Reagan in 1981.[13] A discredited party serves as a weak opposition, thereby allowing the president more political latitude.

The Legislative Setting

The size of the president's party in Congress is one very important indicator of the opportunities available to presidents to shape policy, but ideological orientations within the party may work against the president. For Democratic presidents, at least until the 1980s, conservative voting tendencies among southern Democrats frequently derailed new domestic policy initiatives and negated any advantages produced by the size of the party's delegation in Congress.

Although control of Congress by the president's party can be an advantage to the White House on some issues, David Mayhew found that some policy opportunities also may arise when presidents form coalitions with members of a Congress controlled by the opposition party (known as divided government). In 1996, for example, Republicans in Congress and a Democratic president concluded that each had a better chance in the fall elections if Congress enacted and the president signed major legislation than if they had to face voter dissatisfaction with continued stalemate on issues such as welfare reform. Thus, surprisingly, Mayhew's study of the period 1946–1990 revealed that the amount of major legislation passed with divided government was comparable to the results obtained when one party controlled both branches of government.[14]

Related to the strength of a president's party in Congress is the length of the president's coattails on election to office for the first time.[15] Newly elected Republican president Ronald Reagan enjoyed an increase of thirty-five seats in the House and a Republican recapture of the Senate by adding twelve new Republican members. By contrast, more recent elections suggest that the coattail phenomenon may be a thing of the past.

A president's success in the legislative arena owes something as well to Congress's organizational characteristics and the policy preferences and political skills of those in powerful leadership positions.[16] In the two decades after World War II, southerners' dominance of congressional committees was a major issue. In fact, when Kennedy moved into the Oval Office in 1961, ten of the fifteen top committee chairmen were from the South and in most instances were decidedly conservative. The political skills of party leaders and the Speaker of the House also can make an important difference. For example, Kennedy's opportunities were reduced in early 1962 when the death of House Speaker Sam Rayburn (D-Texas), brought to power John McCormack (D-MA)., a less skillful Speaker.

More recently, efforts by the Speaker of the 104th Congress, Newt Gingrich (R-GA)., to capitalize on Republican gains in the 1994 midterm elections and pass the legislative proposals contained in the Republicans' "Contract with America" succeeded for a time in pushing President Clinton's agenda to the sidelines. Yet by 1996 Gingrich's stunning fall in popularity and a widespread public perception that House Republicans had strayed too far to the right moved the ball back into Clinton's court, providing him with considerable opportunity for centrist strategies.

Promising Issues

John Kingdon, who applies the label "windows of opportunity" to promising issues, has identified situations favorable to government action on a given policy.[17] According to Kingdon, a "window of opportunity" exists when three influences converge: recognition that a problem needing a solution exists, the availability of a policy proposal around which support can be built, and the presence of a "political stream" of forces able to instigate change such as a popular president with considerable support in Congress (considered earlier).

For problem awareness, Kingdon argues that social and economic conditions that might seem to warrant a high level of attention by presidents, members of Congress, and the press may actually generate little comment. This tendency to overlook problems is most likely to occur when no acceptable solution seems to be available. The deafening silence in the face of mounting budget deficits at points during the 1980s and again in the runup to the 2004 presidential race, and the postponement until after the 1988 election of any attempt to cap the surging costs of the savings and loan debacle illustrate this tendency.

Economic Conditions and Budget Deficits

Economic conditions and budget deficits also play a key role in shaping a president's level of opportunity. In 1997, for example, the impact of a strong economy was central to Clinton's ability to negotiate a balanced budget proposal with Republicans. As negotiations proceeded, each Congressional Budget Office projection of the amount of money needed to be found in spending cuts, or the amount needed to absorb tax cuts, was lower than the last. This congressional sleight of hand helped each side avoid having to sign off on some of the more painful decisions they had been discussing.

Other impacts of the controversy have been at least as dramatic. A sense that the economy was performing badly helped to create opportunities for promoting new policies in 1933 and 1981. Conversely, in the mid-1960s, a rapidly growing economy helped to create opportunities as Congress actually lowered taxes while also instigating landmark Great Society programs.

Deficits have had an enormous impact on presidential opportunities as well. Periodically, large deficits and the concern they generate have given presidents an opportunity to promote deficit-reduction packages. More frequently, however, deficits have reduced opportunities for presidents to establish new programs. In 1993 Clinton found it necessary to move away from new spending initiatives as he complained that his budget package was beginning to make him look like an "Eisenhower Republican."

Foreign Policy Influences

The demands of foreign policy, especially those involving the deployment of U.S. troops to trouble spots, often have strong yet unpredictable impacts on opportunities for domestic action. The success with which George H. W. Bush executed the 1990–1991 Persian Gulf War produced a surge in popularity that seemed to give him some additional basis for promoting domestic policy initiatives. Clinton's first term saw quite a different outcome despite his desire to be primarily a domestic president. In October 1993 eighteen American soldiers were killed in Somalia, and in a chilling scene viewed worldwide on television, the body of one was dragged through the streets of Mogadishu, the Somali capital. Suddenly, strategies for effecting the withdrawal of American forces were placed at the top of Clinton's agenda rather than strategies for promoting his health care reforms.

Foreign entanglements, then, may generate public support, but quite frequently they weaken a president's opportunities for domestic policy initiatives, as President George W. Bush discovered with Iraq in 2003–2004. Other important examples include the impact of the Vietnam War on Lyndon Johnson's Great Society programs and Jimmy Carter's involvement in unpopular foreign policy issues, among them the attempt to free U.S. embassy personnel taken hostage in Iran in 1979.

The Second Term

Presidents generally have less opportunity for effective leadership in their second term. Limitations begin with their reelection efforts. Sometimes presidents have won landslide victories, but their campaigns revolved around slogans like "Four More Years" rather than efforts to develop support for new initiatives. The departure of staff and cabinet may be a problem as well. A president's key aides, weary after four years of very long hours and tempted by financially lucrative opportunities, may leave the administration. In dealing with Congress, presidents can anticipate a decline in their party's strength in the midterm elections during their sixth year in office. A president's lame duck status is yet another reason a member of Congress would doubt that there are advantages in being "on the president's team." Finally, on occasion, presidents have contributed to their own difficulties. Perhaps actions taken in their first term come "home to roost" in the second—the Watergate scandal in the early 1970s, Reagan's Iran-Contra scandal in

1986, and Clinton's fund-raising and sexual escapades in 1997–1998 are examples. Or presidents may take politically unwise actions in the flush of victory such as FDR's Court-packing scheme in 1937.

Declining Opportunities?

Any study of presidential performance over several decades must heed changes in the potential for presidential leadership. Ryan Barilleaux and Richard Rose have argued that presidents are now immersed in a "post-modern" presidency that makes their job more difficult than the one held by their predecessors between about 1933 and 1973.[18] Presidents, they conclude, face political obstacles with fewer resources and greater external demands than ever before. The perspectives of Barilleaux and Rose include several dimensions mentioned in the preceding review of the factors that determine a president's opportunity level. They are: changes in the public's confidence in the federal government, changes in legislative settings, and the impact of federal deficits. Several other factors, however, warrant attention such as the dramatic proliferation of interest groups. In the 1960s the number of consumer, environmental, and civil rights groups grew sharply. The business community, feeling increasingly beleaguered, responded with its own surge of organization activity, in part through the new opportunity to organize as political action committees and later 527s. And since the mid-1970s, many new groups have organized for and against the agenda being promoted by the Christian right.

Building Power On a Vision

Beyond question, the most important "power" a president can have is the ability to present to the public a clear and compelling vision. A well-articulated, meaningful, positive vision that builds upon the building blocks of the past, addresses needs and hopes of the present, and portrays a hopeful, optimistic image of a possible future opens more doors to presidential leadership than all the skills and other resources combined. A moving vision can transform a political system, recreate the regime of power, can chart a course for change. Vision energizes and empowers, inspires and moves people and organizations. A president with a compelling vision can be a powerful president.

Few presidents fully use what Theodore Roosevelt referred to as "the bully pulpit" to develop a public philosophy for governing. Rather than attempting to educate and lead the public, most presidents seem content to serve as managers of public business. But if presidents wish to craft change, and not merely preside, they must use the bully pulpit to promote a moral and political vision in support of change.

A visionary leader, akin to what James M. Burns calls a transforming leader,[19] gives direction to an organization, gives purpose to action. Visionary leadership charts a course for action. Such leaders are both instrumental for change and catalysts of change.[20]

When asked how he worked, Albert Einstein replied, "I grope." Groping may be acceptable for a genius of Einstein's caliber, but presidents must do more than grope; they must lead. Of course, the reality is that most presidents grope and are thus mere officeholders. But groping is not enough; holding office is not enough. And one of the essential differences between a leader and a mere officeholder is that leaders have a vision, communicate that vision, and animate the public and Congress through expressions of that vision. Effective leaders, in government, business, and public organizations, share a common trait: they are visionaries. Nanus writes:

> There is no mystery about this. Effective leaders have agendas; they are totally results oriented. They adopt challenging new visions of what is both possible and desirable, communicate their visions, and persuade others to become so committed to these new directions that they are eager to lend their resources and energies to make them happen. In this way, effective leaders build lasting institutions that change the world.[21]

Visions do not spring full blown from the belly of the leader. Developing a vision involves the ability to consider "existing realities as transformed possibilities."[22] Visions are enabling and empowering. They are derived from the core values of community, flow from the past, and are about the future. Visions inspire, give meaning and direction to a community, and are road maps. Visions are about achieving excellence.

Bennis and Nanus offer this description of leaders:

> Leaders articulate and define what has previously remained implicit or unsaid; then they invent images, metaphors, and models that provide a focus for new attention. By so doing they consolidate, or challenge prevailing wisdom. In short, an essential factor in leadership is the capacity to influence and organize meaning for members of the organization. . . . Communication creates meaning for people. Or should. It's the only way any group, small or large, can become aligned behind the overarching goals of an organization.[23]

Visionary leaders are remembered and continue to have an impact long after they leave office. For example, it has been over forty years since John Kennedy was killed, and over thirty-five since the death of Martin Luther King, Jr., and yet the memories of their leadership—the power of their ideas and the impact of their words—remain influential forces in the contemporary political arena.

On a smaller and decidedly opposite political scale, Ronald Reagan was able to mobilize and inspire his followers because he was skilled at presenting his vision to the public. In contrast, George H. W. Bush, who admitted he wasn't big on "that vision thing," was a singularly uninspiring officeholder, and weeks after his leaving office, he had all but faded from political memory. Why is Reagan's presence still felt while Bush has become invisible? Vision.

No other actor on the political scene is better positioned to present a vision to the public than a president. Already the focus of much media and public attention, presidents can become "highlighters" of important issues to be addressed as a part of the president's vision. While presenting a somewhat more limited role, political scientist Lester Salamon has written that presidents need to develop

> a more strategic approach to the office, one that conceives of the president not as the ultimate decision maker but as the preeminent "national highlighter," whose most important task is not to settle all issues, but to identify a handful of issues of truly national importance and focus on them the attention, visibility, and support that only a president can provide. Such a role is far more consistent with the unique advantages of the office. . . . And far more compatible with the capabilities of the institution and demands of the job.[24]

Categorizing and comparing presidents

As defined by the categories discussed above, the modern presidents who enjoyed the greatest opportunities to shape domestic policy were Franklin Roosevelt, Lyndon Johnson, Ronald Reagan, and the post–9/11 George W. Bush. Presidents with moderate opportunity levels were Harry Truman, Dwight Eisenhower, and John Kennedy. The low-opportunity presidents were Richard Nixon, Jimmy Carter, George H.W. Bush, and Bill Clinton.

President George W. Bush started off a low opportunity president. Elected by a slim margin in a disputed election, with only a few issues placed on his domestic campaign agenda, in a country split down the middle; his prospects for success seemed slim. But to his credit President Bush got a huge tax cut (usually an easy thing to do), education reform (more difficult) through Congress, and seemed to get more than his level of opportunity might have suggested.

Bush's level of political opportunity changed dramatically and quickly. September 11, 2001 changed that. He became a high opportunity president overnight. Bush used the opportunity to focus on a war against terror and building homeland security. He had the power, he used that power, he got a lot out of this opportunity.[25]

Political timing

The "when" of politics matters greatly: when major legislation is introduced, when the public is ready to accept change, when the Congress can be pressured to act, when the president leads and when he follows, when he pushes and when he pauses. A sense of political timing, part of the overall "power sense" all great leaders have, helps a president know when to move, when to retreat; when to push, when to compromise. Primarily, there are two elements of political time most germane to the domestic leadership dilemma of a president: the *transition* and the *honeymoon* period.

The Transition

Getting a good start is a key element of political success, and during the transition—the eleven-week period between the November election and the January inauguration—some of the most important work of an administration is done.[26] In this preparation stage before taking office, the president-elect lays the groundwork for much that is to follow, and he sets the tone that shapes the way others see the new administration. During the transition, the president-elect must, in essence, make all of the following key decisions: who will be the top advisers, who will fill important cabinet positions, and how will the staff be structured; what decision-making (management) style will he employ; will he pursue a partisan strategy or try to woo the opposition; how will he mobilize the public; and what issues will the administration push during the first year. Much like the journalist's key questions, these five *w's* (*who, what, when, where and why*) and an *h* (*how*) of politics set the stage not only for how the administration will operate but also for the way the public, Congress, and media will view and respond to the new administration. The Clinton transition—slow, awkward, drifting—was seen as an opening by the Republicans and the press to jump on the new president earlier than is customary. Thus Senator Bob Dole (R-Kansas) led a highly orchestrated series of early attacks on the new president, designed to undermine his leadership. Likewise, the press, sensing disarray (and wishing to show bipartisanship after Republican attacks on the media), jumped all over themselves in an effort to find negative things to say about Clinton.[27]

Of Honeymoons and (Un) Happy Marriages

Gerald Ford, upon taking office in the midst of the Watergate scandal, said he wanted a happy marriage, not just a honeymoon. He got neither. The marriage between a president and Congress is a mixed marriage that rarely turns out to be a happy one over the long haul. Therefore, presidents need to get all they can as early as they can before the marriage slips into bickering and sniping. To do this, a strategic president does all he can to take advantage of the honeymoon period. The honeymoon is a brief period of time, lasting anywhere from roughly three to ten months (or, for Clinton, three to ten minutes), immediately following a presidential election, when the public, press, Congress, and others begin to give the president the benefit of the doubt, go soft on him, refrain somewhat from criticism, and are most likely to vote for measures proposed by the president. The president 'claims" an electoral mandate; the opposition, uncertain of how strong the new president will be, usually goes easy on him; and everyone is waiting to see if indeed the new guy will seize power. In short, the vultures are not yet circling the president's carcass. Thus the president is often at the peak of his power in his honeymoon period.

As Lyndon Johnson said, "You've got to give it all you can, that first year. Doesn't matter what kind of a majority you come in with. You've got just one year when they treat you right."[28] And the best way to get as much as you can, early, is to have a short, disciplined agenda, focus exclusively on that agenda, and push, push, push.

Presidents are more likely to propose new programs in their first year in office than at any other time. Their success rate with Congress in the first year is usually the highest of their term. The irony here, as Paul Light points out, is that presidents are at their strongest when they are least knowledgeable.[29]

To take advantage of this potential to exercise power during the honeymoon, a president must strategically approach his transition and early weeks of the new administration with a clear game plan, a focused mode of presentation, a short, disciplined agenda, and an unceasing sense of political pressure on the system.

It is considered wise to select a few big issues in the early going and to focus all attention on attaining those goals. The difference here, between Ronald Reagan on the one hand, and Jimmy Carter and Bill Clinton on the other, is striking. When Reagan took office, his administration very self-consciously chose to focus on a select few big-ticket items: a tax cut, for example. All other issues, including important foreign policy matters, were put on the back burner (which infuriated Alexander Haig, the new and short-lived secretary of state).[30] This allowed the Reagan administration to devote all its energies to hitting a select few legislative home runs, and it also conveyed an image that this president could succeed, could get his way, could win. He appeared to be, and for a time was, powerful.

By contrast, both Carter and Clinton had large, unwieldly legislative agendas. What did they want? Everything, it seemed, and nothing. They could not decide what was most and what was least important. President Clinton, when he should have been focusing attention on his economic stimulus package in early 1993, instead got sidetracked by the issue of gay rights in the military. This issue may have been important, but in the big scheme, it ranked well behind the economic stimulus package. When Carter and Clinton seemed sprawling and unfocused, Reagan maintained a short, disciplined issue focus.

Overall, Clinton had a very shaky start. In the early going he suffered defeat on his economic stimulus package, fumbled the Haitian refugee issue, backed away from his middle-class tax pledge, blundered on several early cabinet appointees, and was indecisive on Bosnia-Herzegovina and Somalia. At the time when Clinton was supposed to be at his strongest, he kept shooting himself in the foot. And the Democrats in Congress, unaccustomed to having a compatriot in the White House, at the first smell of presidential blood seemed instinctively to form a circle for a firing squad. It was not a pretty sight. It is amazing that, in spite of his shaky start, President Clinton was able, time and again, to recover and even to snare a few wins. While he missed opportunities in the honeymoon, he recovered and was able to win significant victories later.

In the honeymoon period, a president must "hit the ground running"[31] by concentrating on a few key policy issues, working hard to cooperate with (even co-opt) Congress, focusing public attention on his agenda, promoting himself and his program, seizing center stage, controlling the agenda, and setting the terms of debate. That's all. But that is the time when the president's window of political opportunity is often open fairly wide, and a skilled president can drive his legislative program through the system. In the United States, and in other systems, the early part of a new leader's term often finds the most significant political changes occurring.[32]

Finally, where timing is concerned, Machiavelli reminds us that *fortuna* also guides our fates. Luck, good and bad, plays a role in presidential leadership. For example, Jimmy Carter had the bad luck of being president at a time when the oil-producing nations (OPEC) clamped a stranglehold on the West by sending the price of oil through the roof. This caused the economies of the developed nations to plunge into a tailspin of low productivity and high inflation.

By, contrast, Ronald Reagan had the good fortune to become president at a time when OPEC was breaking up and oil prices shot downward. This picked up the economies of the developed nations and cooled inflationary pressures. Thus, through no effort of his own, Carter's popularity suffered (Carter reminded us of the old blues song, "If it wasn't for bad luck, I wouldn't have no luck at all") and Reagan's was aided by events beyond his control.

Controlling the Agenda

The president's top job, as stated earlier, is to articulate and promote a vision for the nation's future. Presidents must identify the national purpose, then move the machinery of government in support of that vision.

Goal-oriented presidents sometimes control the political agenda; they take charge, are masters and not victims of their fate. To have a chance to control the agenda, a president must (1) develop and articulate a compelling vision; (2) present a series of policy proposals designed to achieve that vision; (3) sell it to the public and Congress; and (4) place emphasis on the presentation of self and programs. If accomplished with skill and time, this program *may* allow the president to control the political agenda and thereby make the rest of the political system dance to his music.

While opportunity often shapes the parameters of permissible presidential actions, presidents do have some control over their fates. But in setting the agenda, every president must remember that other officials and interest groups have their own priorities, and that they compete with the president for control of the agenda. While the president may be the center of attention, he is only one of many actors vying for attention.

Think of the presidents who had an impact, who dominated the political landscape. They may not have been the "best" presidents (e.g., Reagan), but they were the ones who mattered, who won, who got their way. Of course, one thinks of FDR and Reagan. Both dominated the issue agenda, refashioned the debate, and forced the rest of the system to respond to their initiatives.

Reagan presents an interesting case in agenda control because he was probably the most ideological president of the last century. And Reagan's extreme conservatism helped him develop a clear vision, a policy agenda, and an action program. There is a good and bad side to being an ideologue. On the plus side, a strong ideology can simplify complex problems; on the bad side, some problems (most problems) do not lend themselves to simple solutions. On the good side, ideology gets the administration marching in the same direction; on the bad side, they may be marching like lemmings, over a cliff. Ideology highlights certain variables in problem solving; at the same time, it hides or obscures other equally important variables. Finally, ideology gives passion to purpose; it can also degenerate into crusading extremism.

In contrast with the ideologues, Bill Clinton, a political moderate, attempted to re-create himself on every issue. Being more moderate and pragmatic helped him avoid the mistakes of either extreme, but it created problems of its own. It is difficult to develop a vision and generate a committed following around a moderate position. While it may be easier for political moderates to *get* elected, it may be harder for them to set visions and govern.

Because power in the American system is floating, a policy entrepreneur can, on certain issues, capture control of the policy agenda. If this can be done, a president may be able to force an otherwise reluctant Congress to at least meet him partway on his policy goals. And no one is better positioned to attract attention than the president. If he is to lead and not merely preside, the president must control the agenda. If the agenda escapes him—as it did after the 1994 midterm election for Clinton—a president appears weak and distracted, which may force him into a reactive, not a proactive, mode.

Coalition *and* Consensus Building

The model on which the American system of government was founded is based on consensus and coalition building. Consensus means agreements about *ends*; coalitions are the *means* by which the ends are achieved. Since power in our system is fragmented and dispersed by design, something (usually a crisis) or someone (usually the president) has to pull the disparate parts of the system together.

In other words, power can be formed *if* the president has a clear, focused agenda and can forcefully and compellingly articulate a vision, and *if* the public is ready to embrace that vision. If a president can develop a consensus around his vision, he can then muster the power to form the coalitions necessary to bring that vision to fruition. Simply placing a legislative package at the doorstep of Congress is not enough, as President Carter so painfully learned: presidents must work to build support within and outside Congress.

To govern in the United States is to build coalitions, to form alliances and power networks. There are relatively few areas in which a president can act unilaterally and not face at least a few challengers to his authority. Custom and the design of the U.S. system necessitate coalition building by political leaders.

Of course, this is easier said than done. The centrifugal force of American politics pulls the system apart, encourages independent entrepreneurship. Power is not fused as it is in parliamentary democracies; instead, the president and the Congress are elected in campaigns that are relatively independent of one another, and political parties do not develop a great deal of cohesion among the branches. Political scientists Benjamin Ginsberg and Martin Shefter argue that since elections fail to provide clear governing coalitions, the president and Congress end up resorting to "politics by other means" in order to influence policy.[33] Institutional combat, not power sharing, characterizes this relationship because both branches attempt to unsurp power and govern autonomously. Of course, this usually leads to conflict and/or gridlock.

George W. Bush's Un-Hidden Hand
Conviction Leadership: A Radical President
In a Conservative Age

In the second Bush term, is the domestic cupboard bare? Is the president's team out of ideas? Or are bold new initiations in the making? The early hints point to the latter view.

George W. Bush is as stated earlier, a high opportunity *and* a high risk president. In spite of the fact that the 2004 election did not grant him a clear domestic mandate, the aftermath of the 9/11 tragedy has opened a door to power that the president clearly intends to exploit.

While much of the Bush agenda in the first term focused necessarily on fighting terrorism, he was nonetheless able to build on his popularity to begin a transformation of domestic policy as well. And while much of the president's time and attention will remain fixated on foreign affairs, especially with the ongoing war on terrorism; plus the issues that—for political reasons—had to wait until a second term (e.g., what to do about North Korea, Iran, and of course trying to regain and reinvestigate the traditional alliances so severely damaged in term one), Bush nonetheless has an ambitious plan for term two domestic policy.

His model is not his father, George H. W. Bush, but Ronald Reagan. Bush hopes to implement and even go beyond the domestic hopes of Ronald Reagan. In this he hopes—and because of the opportunity granted as a result of 9/11—believes he can implement a radical agenda for America, challenging some of the core programs of the New Deal.

President Bush hopes to create what he calls a "culture of ownership" by which he means the following:

> One of the most important parts of a reform agenda is to encourage people to own something. Own their home, own their business, own their health-care plan, or own a piece of their retirement. Because I understand if you own something, you have a vital stake in the future of America.[34]

To create this culture of ownership, Bush wants to pursue a radical restructuring of the federal role in economic and domestic policy, one calling for smaller government, smaller taxes, and a smaller safety net.

Is it sound policy to stir the embers of class warfare? A conservative would protect the states quo. But President Bush is no mere conservative. He is a *conviction* politician who wants to dramatically change the system, not conserve or protect it. A conviction politician, like, for example, Margaret Thatcher, wants to transform, recast, and fundamentally change the status quo. This drive for change comes from a strong ideological sense of conviction, not from the pragmatic transactional view of politics as practiced by Bush's father. What is President Bush's domestic level of political opportunity as he enters his second term? Mixed, but with some premise.

He won the 2004 Presidency in a narrow and bitterly divisive contest. He is himself a polarizing figure. His popularity early in the second term hovers around the 50 percent mark, quite low for a second term president at this stage of the game. His opposition is angry, reasonably well funded, and spoiling for a fight. He did not run for re-election on the basis of a clear domestic agenda, he brought into the Congress only a few members of his party, and the budget deficit is immense.

Looking towards term two, President Bush can go in one of two directions. First, he might look to Mount Rushmore and focus on attaining a strong historical legacy. Or second, not having to go to the voters again he might feel liberated to be himself and pursue a more conservative domestic policy that his base expects—especially the fundamentalist religious right. It looks like a little of both.

More tax cuts? Tort reform? Privitization of Social Security? A ban on same-sex marriage? Stop stem-cell research? Open federal land to development? Cut government regulations? Promote prayer in school? Reduce gun controls? Stack the Supreme Court with conservatives? Ban abortion? Stem the flow of immigrants into the United States? With the weak dollar, Bush may have to cut the massive budget deficit. Will he slash popular programs such as Medicare and Medicaid?

Even a smattering of such proposal would make this a radical, transformative agenda, promoted by a politician of strong principle, emboldened by a deep and obvious set of religious beliefs. Bush is a high-risk president, willing to take chances because he sees himself as God's agent. Armed with religious and political conviction, Bush's unilateral style of foreign policymaking has extended into the domestic arena as well.

In the immediate aftermath of the 2004 election victory, Bush moved quickly to transform his Cabinet. Out were the moderates and internationalists; in were the Bush loyalists. This would not be an independent thinking Cabinet but a Cabinet of Bush clones. Dissent, not prized in any administration, was loathed in the Bush administration.

Employing high levels of secrecy, independent executive authority, willingness to bypass Congress where possible, and a propensity to use executive orders aggressively, President Bush is an opportunity-driven, highly ideological president freed in his second term of electoral constraints, and thus freed to pursue a transformative domestic agenda.

But soon after the election, a spate of bad news (an escalation of fighting in Iraq) and self inflicted political blunders (the improperly vetted nomination of Bernard Kerik as secretary of Homeland Security) interrupted the transition to the second term and undermined Bush's hoped-for honeymoon. His popularity dropped below the 50 percent mark (the first such drop in the past fifty years, and the lowest popularity rating of any president in half-a-century).

However, the President had three opportunities to recover: his Inaugural address (January 20), his State of the Union speech thirteen days later, and the January 30 elections in Iraq.

The administration is well aware of the "second term curse" where few second terms in the past hundred years have been good for the incumbent. Hubris strikes, arrogance sets in, as does the threat of overreaching, there is sometimes a lack of energy or ideas (not a problem in the Bush agenda) scandals come to the surface, the president becomes a bit of a lame duck (if not a dead duck) politically, the six-year itch of the midterm congressional elections usually cut into the president's numbers in Congress, and with a spate of presidential candidates coming out of the Senate, sometimes the president's agenda is not on the top of the political hit parade. Second terms have been unkind to most presidents, with pitfalls easy to recognize but hard to avoid.

Conclusion: The Un-Hidden-Hand Leadership of George W. Bush

American elections determine who will hold office, but they rarely determine who will exercise power. Thus, calculations of the level of political opportunity are essential if one is to get a handle on the parameters of power a president might have. President Bush enters term two with a moderate level of opportunity. But the president has been bold in asserting presidential authority in domestic affairs under the cloak of "national security." It remains to be seen whether the president can continue to exert bold leadership abroad as he pursues an aggressive agenda at home. The command model of leadership, so evident in the foreign policy realm, may not play out quite as smoothly in the domestic arena, as the difficulties President Bush has had with his Social Security Reform agenda would attest. A leader must "style-flex," that is, fit his political dance to the music being played. When the President has wide ranging authority, as Bush had in the aftermath of the 9/11 tragedy, he could exert a command model; but now, in domestic politics, he must practice a different style of leadership. In the early days of his second term he has not displayed great adeptness in doing so.

Immediately following his 2004 electoral victory, President Bush held a press conference in which he announced that he interpreted his victory as an endorsement of his first term and as a mandate for the second. He claimed that the election gave him "political capital" and promised to use it aggressively.

George W. Bush is a conviction leader who believes and believes strongly. His is a "faith based presidency"[35] in which evidence takes a back seat to belief.[36] Mount Rushmore or the conviction base? While President Bush's level of political opportunity may dictate moderation, his certainty and deep convictions point to heated and divisive political battles on the domestic front. As the great American philosopher Bette Davis said, "Hold on boys, we're in for a bumpy ride."

Notes

1. James MacGregor Burns, *Roosevelt: The Lion and the Fox* (San Diego, CA: Harvest/HBI, 1984), p. 197.
2. Edward S. Cronin, *The President: Office and Powers* (New York: New York University Press, 1957).
3. Neustadt, *Presidential Power.* (New York: Wiley, 1960).
4. Burns, James M.*Leadership*, Pt. 3 (New York: Harper, 1982).
5. John F. Kennedy, Foreword to Theodore C. Sorenson, *Decision-Making in the White House* (New York: Columbia University Press, 1963), p. xi.
6. Michael A. Genovese, *The Presidential Dilemma: Leadership in the American System* (New York: HarperCollins, 1995), ch. 2.
7. James P. Pfiffner, *The Strategic Presidency: Hitting the Ground Running*, 2d ed. (Lawrence: University Press of Kansas, 1996).
8. Samuel Kernell, *Going Public: New Strategies of Presidential Leadership*, 3d ed. (Washington, DC: CQ Press, 1997).
9. Robert J. Spitzer, *The Presidency and Public Policy: The Four Arenas of Presidential Power* (Alabama: University of Alabama Press, 1983).
10. Arthur M. Schlesinger Jr., *The Cycles of American History* (Boston: Houghton Mifflin, 1986).
11. Erwin C. Hargrove and Michael Nelson, *Presidents, Politics, and Policy* (Baltimore, MD: Johns Hopkins University Press, 1984), ch. 3.
12. On the ability of presidents to literally create a mandate, see Edwards, *At the Margins*, ch. 8. George Edwards *At the Margins* (New Haven, CT: Yale University Press, 1989).
13. Stephen Skowronek *The Politics Presidents Make: Leadership from John Adams to George Bush* (New Haven, CT: Yale University Press, 1993).
14. David R. Mayhew, *Divided We Govern: Party Control, Lawmaking, and Investigations, 1946–1990* (New Haven, CT: Yale University Press, 1991), ch. 7.

15. The importance of surge as an aspect of a president's opportunity level is discussed in Charles O. Jones, "Campaigning to Govern: The Clinton Style," in *The Clinton Presidency: First Appraisal*, ed. Colin Campbell and Bert A. Rockman (Chatham, NJ: Chatham House, 1995), ch. 1.

16. Roger Davidson, "The Presidency and Presidential Time," in *Rivals for Power: Presidential—Congressional Relations* 2d ed., James A. Thurber, ed. (Washington, DC: CQ Press, 1996), ch. 2.

17. John Kingdon, *Issues, Agendas, and Alternatives*, 2d ed. (Boston, MA: Little, Brown, 1994).

18. Richard Rose, *The Postmodern President: George Bush Meets the World* (Chatham, NJ: Chatham House, 1991); Ryan J. Barilleaux, *The Post-Modern Presidency: The Office After Ronald Reagan* (Westport, CT.: Greenwood Press, 1988); Michael A. Genovese, *The Presidency in an Age of Limits* (Westport, CT.: Greenwood Press, 1993).

19. Burns, *Leadership*, Pt. 3; William W. Lammers and Michael A. Genovese, *The Presidency and Domestic Policy* (Washington DC: CQ Press, 2000).

20. Donald T. Phillips, *Lincoln on Leadership* (New York: Warner, 1992), p. 137.

21. Ibid., p. 4.

22. Sheldon Wolin, *Politics and Vision* (Boston, MA: Little, Brown, 1960), p. 436.

23. Warren Bennis and Burt Nanus, *Leaders: Strategies for Taking Charge* (New York: HarperCollins, 1985), pp. 39, 42.

24. Lester Salamon, *The Illusion of Presidential Government* (Boulder, CO: Westview Press, 1981), p. 292.

25. For an explanation of opportunity and domestic policy leadership, see: William W. Lammers and Michael A. Genovese, *The Presidency and Domestic Policy: Leadership from FDR to Clinton*, (Washington, DC: CQ Press, 2001).

26. Pfiffner, *The Strategic Presidency*.

27. For an excellent review of how the press treated President Clinton, see David Shaw, *Los Angeles Times*, September 15–17, 1993.

28. Quoted in Hedrick Smith, *The Power Game*, (New York: Ballantine Books, 1988), p. 331.

29. Paul Light, *The President's Agenda*, (Baltimore, MD: Johns Hopkins University Press, 1983), pp. 41–45.

30. Alexander Haig, *Caveat: Realism, Reagan, and Foreign Policy* (New York: Macmillan, 1984).

31. James P. Pfiffner, "The Carter-Reagan Transition: Hitting the Ground Running," *Presidential Studies Quarterly*, (Fall 1983): pp. 522–544.

32. Valerie Bunce, *Do New Leaders Make a Difference?* (Princeton, NJ: Princeton University Press, 1981).

33. Benjamin Ginsberg and Martin Shefter, *Politics by Other Means* (New York: Basic Books, 1990), pp. 164–165.

34. Quoted in John Cassidy, "Tax Code," *The New Yorker*, September 6, 2004, p. 70.

35. Ron Suskind, *New York Times Magazine*.

36. See: Ron Suskind and Paul O'Neill, *The Prince of Loyalty*, (New York: Simon & Schuster, 2004).

Chapter Nine

Economic Policy: Responsibility but with Limited Authority

Jeffrey E. Cohen

Aside from matters of war and peace, no policy area commands as much presidential effort or is as important to the president as the economy. From the earliest days of the republic, the quality of the economy affected the fortunes and careers of presidents. Martin Van Buren, for example, lost his re-election bid in 1840 in part because of the economic panic of 1837. Other presidents, and their parties, who presided over bad economic times have been turned out of office, while those in office during good times tended to be returned to office.[1]

Although the impact of the economy on the presidency has been enduring, presidential policy, as opposed to political, responsibility for the state economy is a more recent phenomenon, dating to the mid-1900s. In 1921, Congress passed the Budget and Accounting Act, which gave the president the responsibility to prepare a budget and submit it to Congress. Presidential policy responsibility for the economy grew during the Depression of the 1930s, as government in Washington started becoming more important than state and local governments, and as the federal government assumed increased authority to regulate, manage, and oversee the economy. This transformation in economic policy responsibility was capped in 1946, with the passage of the Full Employment Act, which made it the formal or legal responsibility of the federal government to insure the health of the economy.

The presidency, more than most other branches of the national government, benefited from this transformation in economic policy responsibility and authority. The public began to hold the president responsible not only for the state of the economy, but for doing something about the economy.[2] As a consequence, presidents now spend considerable time and effort on economic policy.

But presidents do not control all of the economic policy tools at hand. The Federal Reserve (Fed) controls monetary policy, while the president shares fiscal and budgetary authority with Congress. Finally, market forces, technological change, and globalization of the economy may have weakened the ability of government during the past quarter century to steer the economy and deal with important economic problems. Thus, while presidents are held to account, they do not always possess the authority to act in the way that they would like when it comes to making economic policy.

George W. Bush is no different from other presidents in this regard. Economic policy has been one of his top priorities. As he entered his second term of office, President Bush staked out two major economic policy initiatives; reform of Social Security and the tax code. During the transition from his first to second term, no other domestic policies have occupied as much time or energy as these economic policy proposals.

Yet his ability to deliver on these policy thrusts is constrained. First, legislation will be required for each reform effort, which will require cooperation with Congress. Despite the Republicans gaining or having enhanced their control of Congress in the 2004 election, Democrats may impede Bush's policy initiatives by resorting to filibusters in the Senate. Moreover, the public is not yet behind the president in either policy front and congressional Republicans may balk if the president can not rally the public behind his efforts.

Other factors also might hinder the president's efforts on Social Security and tax code reform. As happened so often in his first term, international politics, especially the war on terrorism and the situation in Iraq, has pulled the president and the public's attention away from economic policy.[3] The huge costs of these international relations policies have also cut off any economic policy thrust that might increase the federal deficit, which has mounted impressively since 2001.

Finally, the international economy may divert presidential attention away from his reform efforts and potentially undermine these economic policies priorities. Here the major issue is the increasing trade imbalance and high value of the dollar compared to other currencies. Reducing the trade deficit might require deficit reduction, which could imperil the Social Security reform, because such a reform will in all likelihood require some increased expenditure, at least in its initial years. The Fed, too, will likely take on a major role here, due to the Fed's ability to set currency rates.

In this chapter, I discuss George W. Bush's economic policies during the transition period form his first to his second term. I begin by placing this discussion within the context of the 2004 election results, which set the stage of opportunities and constraints on the president. The recession of 2001 and weak job growth as the nation pulled out of recession were the most important economic factors affecting the 2004 election. But factors other than the economy probably helped Bush most as he sought re-election, and he emerged not only personally victorious, but also possessing majority control of both houses of Congress. Unified government probably stimulated the ambition of Bush's economic policy proposals for his second term,[4] but the ambition of those proposals, lack of public support, and the narrowness of his party's control of Congress all present hurdles to overcome if the president is to see his policy initiatives enacted into law.

The Economic Context Entering Campaign 2004

As the 2004 election approached, the economy showed signs of both strength and weakness. On the plus side, the recession of 2001 had officially ended long before the election and the equities markets began to show signs of recovery from the bubble burst of 2000. On the negative side, labor markets remained soft and the trade and federal deficits were ballooning. Not surprisingly, the Democrats tried to claim that not all was well in the economy, while the Bush administration counter-argued that the economy was on the mend and that the future looked bright. The public mirrored this dual-sided picture, being split relatively evenly over whether the economy was in good shape or not.

The 2001 Recession and Its Aftermath

Early in George W. Bush's term the nation slipped into recession. The National Bureau of Economic Research (NBER) the formal arbiter of the economic cycle, marked March 2001 as the onset of the recession, just two months after George W. Bush assumed office. According to some economists, the stock market dive that began in 2000 set off the recession. Notably this predated the terrorist attack on September 11.

Figure 9.1 plots the S&P 500 stock index from 1995 through 2004. The figure displays the unmistakable growth in the stock market in the late 1990s. For instance, in early 1995 the S&P index stood at about 4000. By 1999 it stood at about 11,000, nearly a tripling in value in half a decade. After peaking at nearly 12,000 in 2000, the index fell to 8,000 by 2003, wiping out approximately one-third of the index's value, an enormous amount of wealth. The Internal Revenue Service estimated that American's average income fell in both 2001 and 2002, the first back-to-back income declines since the end of World War Two, when the modern income tax system was invented.[5]

Yet, as figure 9.1 shows, the market rebounded in 2003, gaining back nearly 20 percent of what it lost in the two previous years. The market, however, sputtered throughout much of 2004, and while the stock market in 2004 displayed some gains by the end of the year, it remaining essentially flat until after the election. A whopping amount of wealth was destroyed during 2001–2002 and had not been rebuilt by the end of 2004. At the end of 2004 the stock market was still 15 percent lower than its peak four years earlier.

On many counts, the recession of 2001 looks remarkably like the recession of 1990–1991, which so greatly affected George H. W. Bush's re-election prospects. Both recessions, according to the NBER, lasted for the same duration, eight months (July 1990–March 1991 and March 2001–November 2001).

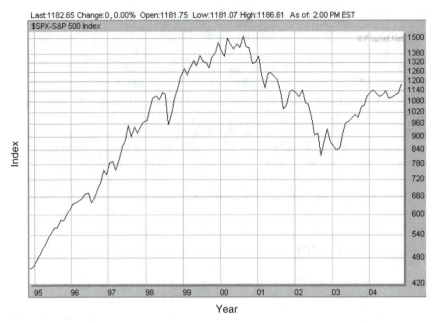

Figure 9.1   S&P 500 index, 1995–2004

In both cases, job growth lagged long after the end of the recessions. In both cases, critics charged that the slow pace of job recovery was due to each administration's insensitivity to American workers, who, critics argued, bore the brunt of the effects of the recession.

Figure 9.2 plots the unemployment levels of both recessions, beginning in the first month of each recession and continuing for three years after the official end date. Unemployment in the 2001 recession never reached the level of its predecessor, but the two economies started at different places, with unemployment higher by about one percent in 1990 than in 2001. Still, the two trends track each other quite closely, correlating at 0.89 (p = .000), despite some minor differences.

Unemployment peaked 16 months after the official end of the first recession, in June 1992, when it hit 7.8 percent compared to 5.5 percent, the value of the first month of that recession, a rise of 2.3 percent. In the next 12 months, unemployment dropped to 7 percent, a 0.8 percent point decline. In contrast, for the 2001 recession, unemployment peaked 20 months later (June 2003) at 6.3 percent, compared to an unemployment rate of 4.3 percent in the first month of the 2001 recession. Thus, the 2001 recession, which produced slightly less unemployment than the 1990–1991 recession, also prolonged for slightly longer than the earlier recession. Twenty-eight months after the end of the 2001 recession, unemployment stood at 5.6 percent, a 0.7 percent decline, which is comparable to the rate of unemployment decline for the earlier recession.

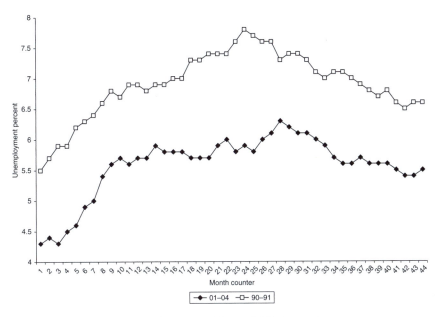

Figure 9.2   Unemployment, the 1990–1991 and 2001 recessions

The major difference between the two recessions, at least a difference with major political implications, however, lay in their timing. The elder Bush saw his recession begin a year closer to his re-election than the younger Bush. For the 1990–1991 recession, unemployment only began to recede about five months before the presidential election. In contrast, for the 2001 recession, the unemployment peak began a full year earlier. However, in late spring and summer of 2004, although job production surged, the unemployment rate hardly budged.[6]

Budget Deficits

After several years of budget surpluses, the federal budget returned to deficits. Although the deficit did not become a major issue in the 2004 presidential election campaign, its magnitude will probably severely affect economic policies during George W. Bush's second term. Figure 9.3 plots the deficit (surplus) as a percentage of GDP from the mid-1970s through 2003. After progressively mounting deficits in the early 1980s, figure 9.3 shows that the size of the deficit relative to the economy began to shrink in the late 1980s. It widened in the early 1990s, a function of the 1990–1991 recession, but progress on dwindling the deficit continued thereafter. By 1999 the federal budget showed a small relative surplus, which grew impressively to 1.1 percent of GDP in 2000 and 2001.

Several factors account for the deficit of 2002 and thereafter. The stock market decline stemmed the flow of revenues that the government realized

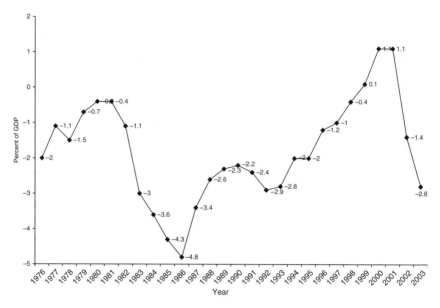

Figure 9.3   Federal deficit/surplus as a percentage of GDP, 1976–2003

from capital gains. The recession that followed the decline in the stock market depressed incomes across all economic classes, which in turn squeezed federal tax receipts at the same time that they also increased automatic stabilizers outlays, like unemployment insurance. Declining revenues and increased expenditures naturally added to the deficit.

But the recession was not the only source of the deficit problem. The Bush tax cuts of 2001 also had their effect on the deficit, while the post–9/11 international climate forced increases in defense spending. And the aging population put financial pressures on government entitlement programs, such as Medicaid, Medicare, and Social Security. The magnitude of these new federal deficits, plus projections that they would last for years, would foreclose any possibility of more tax cuts and would send chills throughout international financial markets as Bush entered his second term.

The Economy in the 2004
Presidential Election

In 2004, George W. Bush won a decisive, if not resounding, re-election victory over John Kerry. Economic issues played a major role in that election, although the economic factor did not always cut to the president's benefit, and other issues, especially the war on terrorism and the war in Iraq may have been more important in accounting for the Bush win than the economy.

The Most Important Problem

That economic issues should rank among the public's most important concerns should not be surprising. Such was the case in the 2004 presidential election campaign. The recession of 2001 cast a large shadow in the 2004 campaign. The economy seemed slow to pull out of the recession, economic recovery was uneven, most apparent with the tardiness and unsteadiness of job growth.

Figure 9.4 plots results of Gallup polls from January through September 2004, asking people to name the most important problem facing the nation. Across 2004, along with the economy, the war in Iraq and terrorism, stood apart from all other issues, garnering significant public attention. As the figure shows, across the year, the economy clearly outranked either the war in Iraq or terrorism as the most important problem facing the nation with about 40–50 percent so naming the economy. In contrast from 10–30 percent cited either the war in Iraq or terrorism as the nation's most important problem.

Figure 9.4 also shows that across 2004 the economy dwindled in importance. From a high of 52 percent citing the economy in February, the percentage citing the economy as the most important problem declined to 35 percent in July, but rebounded to 45 percent in August and 41 percent in September. Two factors likely account for this overtime movement. First, reports in late spring indicated huge numbers of jobs being created. With the economy looking like it was on the road to full recovery, public concern

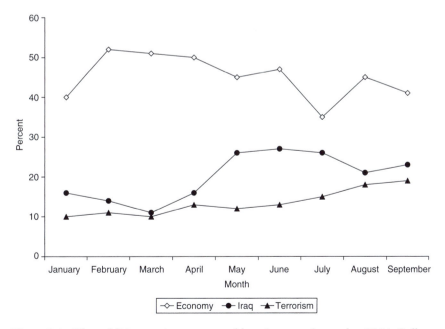

Figure 9.4   The public's most important problem, January–September 2004, Gallup polls

Table 9.1   Most important issue and the 2004 vote

Problem (% citing)	Bush (%)	Kerry (%)
Taxes (5)	57	43
Education (4)	26	73
Iraq (15)	26	73
Terrorism (19)	86	14
Economy/Jobs (20)	18	80
Moral values (22)	80	18
Health care (8)	23	77

Source: 2004 Exit Poll, downloaded from CNN.com; http://www.cnn.
com/ELECTION/2004/pages/results/ states/US/P/00/epolls.0.html

would be expected to ebb. But weak jobs reports in summer 2004 reignited public concern.

Second, as the election campaign progressed, and President Bush realized his vulnerability on the jobs issue, his campaign turned its emphasis to the war on terror and to linking the war in Iraq to the war on terror. We see in figure 9.4 the apparent pay off of this campaign strategy. From March to May, public concern with the war in Iraq grew, perhaps not entirely to the president's advantage. The continuation of violence in Iraq and accumulating U.S. fatalities and causalities may have led many to question the president's leadership on that issue. But at the same time, the percentage citing the war on terror as their most important concern doubled across the year, from 10 percent in January to 19 percent in September.

Finally, exit polls on election day asked people to identify the most important problem facing the nation from a list of seven issue—taxes, education, Iraq, terrorism, the economy and jobs, moral values, and health care. Together the economy and taxes, the economic issues, garnered 25 percent of responses, compared to 34 percent for Iraq and terrorism, the foreign policy issues (see table 9.1).

Voters and the Economy in Election 2004

As the results for elections 1992–2004 detail (see table 9.2), the parties find their support in different economic classes. Where Bush scored solid majorities of 10–17 percent with those in the upper half of the income scale (US$50,000 and above), in the lower economic categories (under US$30,000) lopsided majorities of 15–27 percent did not support him. But there is little evidence of increased economic polarization for most income categories from the early 1990s on. In fact, the poorest group (under US$15,000) showed even greater Democratic support in 1992 and 1996 than in 2004, perhaps a reflection of a populist Democratic candidate in Bill Clinton. But those in the solidly middle to upper middle class (US$50,000–99,999) seemed to have moved more strongly into the Republican camp in 2004 compared to the previous three elections. The

Table **9.2** Republican minus Democratic vote by income category, 1992–2004 presidential elections

Income category	1992	1996	2000	2004
Under $15,000	−35	−31	−20	−27
$15,000–29,999	−10	−17	−13	−15
$30,000–49,999	−3	−8	−1	−1
$50,000–74,999	1	2	5	13
$75,000–99,999		4	7	10
$100, 000 and over		16	11	17

Source: New York Times, "Portrait of the Electorate, Week in Review," November 7, 2004, downloaded from http://www.nytimes.com/2004/11/07/weekinreview/07conn.html

marginal middle class, those in the US$30,000–49,999 have become the major battle ground for the parties. While slightly tilted in the Democratic direction in 1992 and 1996, this group split evenly in the two Bush elections. The economic fortunes of this group will clearly have major implications for the electoral fate of the two parties.

The economic cycle figures importantly in whether the middle class will sit with the Democrats or Republicans in an election. As noted above, the economy presented a mixed picture, which should lead us to expect the broad middle class to be divided in its partisan presidential preferences.

For instance, in March and April 2004, jobs registered impressive gains of about 300,000 per month, only to fade throughout the summer and early fall. As a consequence, the emerging economic optimism in the public in early spring began to show signs of erosion as the election neared. By election day, Bush could not say that the public was in an optimistic mood, nor could his opponents claim that the public had rejected his economic leadership. The Edison-Mitofsky exit poll showed that while 32 percent felt better off financially today, 28 percent felt worse off, and 39 percent saw no change in their family's finances. As expected, Bush drew heavily from those who felt better off, 80 percent to Kerry's 19 percent. Kerry's support came disproportionately from those who felt worse off, 79 percent to Bush's 20 percent. The middle group, those who saw no change, split evenly down the middle, 50–49 for Kerry-Bush, respectively.

We see much the same pattern in assessments of the national economy. Here, according to the exit polls, 47 percent felt that the national economy was in excellent or good shape, while 52 percent saw it in either not good or poor shape. Of those who saw the economy in excellent or good shape, 89 percent and 87 percent cast their ballots for Bush. In contrast, of those who saw the economy in either not good or poor shape, 72 percent and 92 percent respectively voted for Kerry.

This pattern clearly reflects the ambiguous impact of the economy and Bush's economic policies. One chunk of the nation fared well under Bush, a tribute to his tax cuts and the performance of the stock market in 2003. But another segment of the nation did not fare as well. Jobs were slow to rebuild, and many lost manufacturing jobs were unlikely to ever return within the United States. Without wanting to sound like a partisan, John Edwards' assessment that there were two Americas is partially on point—but only one of those Americas responded to the Kerry-Edward's theme. The other America responded favorably to the President's economic themes and stewardship, having prospered under Bush's tenure.

Second Terms: Opportunities and Constraints

Since Jimmy Carter tried for a second term in 1980, only George H. B. Bush failed to be reelected. Ronald Reagan, Bill Clinton, and now George W. Bush, among late twentieth-century and early twenty-first-century presidents have been reelected. The Reagan and Clinton second terms present a model or set of expectations for the second Bush term. Both Reagan and Clinton increased their electoral margins over their first election, but neither saw much improvement in their party's position in Congress. In this sense, both the Reagan and Clinton re-elections were mostly personal triumphs. Moreover, neither Reagan nor Clinton offered any expansive new policy ideas for their second term, instead focusing more on consolidating the policies of their first term.

In contrast to the consolidation theme of the Reagan-Clinton examples, other presidents have sometimes staked out bold new policy departures for their second terms. Here Franklin Roosevelt is probably the paradigmatic case. Roosevelt's Second New Deal was composed of more radical and expansive programs than his First New Deal, which focused more on stabilizing the economy and restoring public confidence in government.[7]

George W. Bush seems to be following the FDR model, at least with regard to economic policy. He offered several major economic policy proposals coming off of his electoral victory, such as privatization of Social Security and tax code reform. In part Bush's policy boldness derives from his reading the 2004 election as not merely a personal victory, but one for his party. Although holding both houses in the 2003–2004 Congress, the 2004 election increased the Republican margin in both chambers, impressively so in the Senate. Like FDR after the 1936 elections, Bush and the Republicans viewed the 2004 results as a public reaffirmation of support, but at higher levels than in 2000, and as an opportunity to implement some major policies. Thus the Bush second term, at least in economic policy, will likely depart from the consolidation model of Reagan and Clinton.

Social Security Reform

Social security reform was on the president's agenda during his first term. How can we then argue that its appearance as a major second term policy theme presents Bush as a bold and innovative versus a consolidating second-term president? Despite the fact that privatizing Social Security appeared on the first-term agenda, it was relegated to second-level priority status, behind tax cuts. The terrorist attacks of 9/11, the reshaping of the policy agenda and government priorities that followed, and the recession of 2001 pushed Social Security reform off the president's and the public's agenda. Strong resistance among Democrats and entrenched groups, like the American Association of Retired Persons (AARP), limited any opportunity to push for Social Security reform, and the president lacked the political capital or congressional support to make much headway either.

Despite the fact that Social Security reform has languished on the agenda for years, and that the president has spoken about it on occasion during his first term, it represents a bold departure in economic policymaking for several reasons. First, reforming Social Security was the first major policy pronouncement that the president issued, merely days after his election victory. Doing so on the heels of his election victory breathed new life into the president's hope of reforming Social Security. Second, Social Security is the largest federal domestic program, with massive support for it among the public. Third, the president's plan for reform proposes not a mere tinkering, but a full scale reformulation of the retirement program.

Part of the impetus for Social Security reform is the feeling among Republicans, including the president, that the financial foundation of the program must be restructured to insure adequate resources for retirees by mid-twenty-first century. But perhaps more important is Bush's vision of restructuring the relationship between citizens and government. His proposal's aim to privatize some fraction of Social Security is well in line with the "ownership" society theme that pervades most of his economic policies. Not merely aiming to hem in the power of the federal government, especially with respect to the economy, Bush hopes to instill a greater degree of personal responsibility among citizens and materially benefit them as well.

An unstated spillover of privatizing Social Security would be to lessen the power of strong private interests, like the AARP, over government, which Bush and others believe have frustrated government attempts at reform on many fronts and policies. Thus, despite the fact that the idea of privatizing Social Security is far from fresh, it represents a radical departure for a massive and hugely popular program. In this sense, we must think of this proposal as bold and innovative, and not merely one that consolidates the first term's successes and initiatives.

Tax Reform and Other Issues

George W. Bush has taken much from Reagan's presidential play book. Like Reagan, Bush presents a public face of optimism and hope. Bush's economic policies also owe much to the supply side policies that Reagan introduced some twenty years ago. And Bush's tax cuts, while broad based, offered more tax relief to the upper than middle or working classes, like Reagan's. Bush's call for tax code reform again echoes Reagan, who did the same in his second term.

Bush has been less vocal about the nature of his tax reform proposal than his Social Security reform initiative. He appears to be aiming for tax simplification, revenue neutral reform of the tax code. Revenue neutrality will fend off members of his own party who want to reduce taxes and mollify Democrats who fear tax simplification as a backdoor approach to tax cuts.

Some proponents of tax simplification might view this as an opportunity to implement a flat-tax. The Regan tax cuts of 1981–1982 certainly moved in such a direction by drastically lowering marginal tax rates, but were not able to abolish progressivity in the tax code, where higher marginal incomes are taxed as higher marginal tax rates. If Bush proposes that tax simplification move in the flat-tax direction, he may be opening a radical shift in the tax structure that matches the degree of restructuring of his Social Security reform proposal. There are few recent polls that measure the public's willingness to do away with progressive principles in taxation. Certainly the Democrats will oppose such a reform as vigorously as they appear intent on stopping privatization of Social Security.

The international economic scene may interpose itself into these and other policy debates, and stymie the president's reform efforts. As the U.S. economy has become more exposed to international economic conditions, these factors have a larger effect on the performance of the U.S. economy and may call for policy attention. Of these factors, the U.S. trade imbalance and the declining value of the dollar present the gravest threats at the time of this writing.

The trade imbalance has been growing as U.S. consumers import more than they sell overseas. A highly valued dollar contributes to this situation, making U.S. goods relatively more expensive than foreign goods, even within the U.S. economy. The mounting federal government deficit further contributes to the trade imbalance and affects the value of the dollar. Thus, a falling dollar may help ease the trade imbalance, but too steep a decline may upset international markets and erode the ability of the United States to pay for its trade imbalance with dollars as the credibility of the dollar fades in the eyes of international investors.

A crisis in the dollar and U.S. trade may undermine the president's domestic economic agenda in two ways. First, it may slow the economy, as policymakers find ways to stem the tide of a too swiftly falling dollar and the ballooning trade imbalance. It is often hard to implement economic reforms that aim at the future, such as the Social Security proposal, in the face of crises of the present. The Fed will have more say over these international economic issues than the administration and/or Congress, since these issues are primarily monetary. Thus, the Fed may implement policies that make it less possible for the administration to follow the reform path for which it is aiming.

Second, an international monetary crisis may divert attention away from domestic economic issues. Windows of opportunity to pass new reform initiatives are fragile and tend not to last long. With the president a lame duck, he has little time to enact his reform package before everyone starts to spend more time talking about the 2008 election than the president. A lame duck president who appears unable to move his policies through the thickets of the legislative process quickly may turn into a political and policy dead duck. The more Bush weakens, the more readily the Democrats will attack him and the more likely that his party will distance itself from him.

Transitions Processes and Economic Policy

Besides identifying policy priorities, re-election transitions are also opportunities for presidents to establish a strategy to realize those priorities into actual policies. To develop such strategies requires building a team and selling the policy proposals to the public.

Building a Team for the Second Term

Besides identifying policy priorities, the most important substantive decision that presidents make is appointing people to important posts in the White House, the cabinet departments, and the other agencies of government. Presidents rely on these appointees for a variety of reasons—to help manage the government, to promote the president's policies, and to provide the president with advice and information about matters under their jurisdiction.

Presidents possess two ways to build an administrative team for their second terms. They can replace appointees by asking them to leave or presidents can wait until those appointees leave office. Commonly many first term appointees leave office shortly after the president has won re-election. High level government service imposes hefty costs on those who serve. Days are long and often tension filled, which take a toll on families and perhaps the health of these public servants. Financial costs are burdensome too—government pay can hardly match what these high level appointees could earn in the private sector. Some even see such public service as a stepping stone into a financially lucrative job in the private sector, typically law firms, political consulting agencies, and corporate offices.[8]

A heavy exodus of first term appointees shortly after his re-election allowed President Bush to fill vacancies without having to remove anyone from office, and pay the public costs of such action, although rumors circulated that some sitting appointees were being pressured to leave, like John Snow at the Treasury Department. The first term appointees who remain and the types of people appointed to office in the second term give a sense of how the president envisions his second term administration to operate.

Many journalists and observers commented that the new appointees tended to be loyal Bush people, already possessing some Washington experience. These commentators saw this as a sign that the president would not brook as much debate, dissension, and disagreement in the second term as the first, when outside of foreign policy, little dissent actually existed or was made public. However, another rationale may underpin these second-term appointees.

Incoming presidents need to repay voters for their support and tie those supporters to his administration. They often do this by naming to appointive positions people who can be thought of as representatives of certain groups that supported the president in his first election. Such people come to office, naturally, with independent bases of power and sometimes their own agendas, which might deviate from the presidents. While such an appointment strategy has political benefits for the president, it also imposes costs. Commentators focus on the costs of administration discord, but another cost is that these types of "political" appointees may not make very good managers of large cabinet departments and other agencies with important policy implementation responsibilities. The Washington experience of many of Bush's second-term appointees, while they may indicate a desire on the part of the president to minimize discord within his administrative team, may also represent an attempt by the president to place in office people with strong management skills.

Unlike much of the rest of the cabinet, little personnel reshuffling among the president's economic policy team for the second term took place, in part because so much personnel replacement took place during the first term. Secretary of the Treasury John Snow survived attacks, some made by important Republicans. This is likely a sign that economic policy will be run out of the White House and that economic policy will be a high presidential priority. The president does not need strong aides, who may possess their own agendas, if he is to engage economic policy and commit much of his time and energy to securing his economic policy aims. A danger of this approach is that if his agenda steers away from economic policy, perhaps because of international policy needs, like Iraq, the Middle East, or international economic problems, then the president's economic policy reforms may get lost.

Selling the Agenda

The ambition of the president's economic policy proposals will require that he alter public sentiment about privatizing Social Security and reforming the tax code. Recent research suggests that presidents have a difficult time shifting public attitudes on policies, especially when the public already holds relatively well-developed opinions,[9] as seems to be the case for Social Security, a long standing program that is quite popular with the public.

The president's reform proposal does not seem to command much public support either, which presents another hurdle for the president. In a Democracy Corps/Institute for America's Future Poll of November 5, 2004, 57 percent supported or strongly supported preserving "the Social Security system and guarantee current benefit levels," compared to 40 percent who supported or strongly supported allowing "individuals to invest a portion of their Social Security funds in private retirement accounts," the president's alternative. Moreover, few lacked an opinion (3 percent), perhaps an indication of reasonably well-formed attitudes about Social Security that might be resistant to change.[10]

Realigning public opinion behind the president's proposal is critical to the president's efforts to gain congressional approval. Although Republicans control both chambers, the GOP may not have enough votes to stop a Democratic filibuster in the Senate. Republicans may be able to peel off just enough Democrats to quell any filibuster, but such a strategy has its costs. A reform that looks too partisan to voters may not gain public support, which may lead Democrats to dig in their heels and also lead some Republicans to defect. The high degree of animosity between the parties in Congress also bodes poorly for bipartisanship on Social Security.[11]

The president has already begun his efforts to generate public support on his economic policies. On December 16–17, 2004, the president convened an economic summit at the White House, but the summit, whose attendees consisted mostly of like-minded economists and corporate leaders, did not generate front page coverage.[12] At a time when security concerns rank so high for the public, and which were instrumental in the president's re-election, the president may have a hard time keeping public attention focused on Social Security reform, something that is necessary if he is to see that proposal enacted. Still, the president possesses two major public ceremonies where he can highlight his economic reform packages, the Inauguration and the State of the Union Address. How he prioritizes among the many issues that he is confronting may give us a sense of the likelihood of success.

The Inauguration

Presidents tend not to use the inauguration to present detailed or concrete policy proposals to the nation. Rather, Inaugural addresses and their attendant ceremonies aim at healing the divisions that election contests induce. Further, presidents have used the inaugural occasion as an opportunity to instruct the nation on democracy, especially on the peaceful transfer of power and the collective nature of democratic polities. Third, presidents may refer to policy in their inaugural, but often do so in idealistic, general, and vague terms, in language upon which all citizens can agree.[13]

On January 20, 2005, George W. Bush was no different as he was sworn in for the second time. If a theme suffused the text of his Inaugural address, it was freedom and liberty, values important to most Americans. And while his address rarely mentioned concrete policies to reach these lofty goals, most of his address focused on spreading freedom and liberty around the globe; rarely did Bush discuss the freedom and liberty from a domestic consequence. If an inaugural suggests or hints at the president's policy priorities for the next term, then this inaugural placed international affairs above domestic.

In the run-up to the inaugural, the president's Social Security reform package already hit rocky shoals. During the period from the election to the inaugural, in several public appearances, the administration began to outline what the reform package would look like. At this early stage, it would contain two major provisions, the privatization of Social Security and reductions in benefits to pay the estimated two trillion dollar cost over ten years.

Democrats in the House stood steadfast against the privatization provision, as expected, with the implication that support for the president's proposal would have to be built almost entirely on the slim Republican majority. But Republican members of Congress, home for the holidays after the 2004 election began to hear from constituents, who opposed benefit reductions. As a result, when Congress reconvened in early January 2005, indications of dissension in the party over the reform proposal were already evident. During the week of the inaugural, the chair of the Ways and Means Committee in the House, Bill Thomas, declared the president's proposal, in the form that the president was talking about it, dead. A supporter of the President, Thomas suggested melding other features into the reform package to gain support; some Republicans suggested raising taxes on social security to cover the cost of transition to private accounts.[14]

While trouble brewed on Capitol Hill, the president seemed to be making headway in steering the public to his side on the social security issue. First, the public was paying attention to the debate. At this early stage 47 percent claimed that they have a lot of knowledge or some information about the president's plan to privatize the retirement program, based on a January 14–18, 2005 *New York Times* poll. Yet, to the public, social security is not yet a highly important issue. Only 3 percent in the same *New York Times* poll cited it as the most important problem. In contrast, the combination of the war in Iraq, Osama bin Laden, and terrorism, garnered 29 percent.

The president has painted Social Security as a system in financial crisis, one that will not be able to meet its obligations to future retirees without drastic overhauling. This message seems to have affected public thinking. First, a January 14–18 *New York Times* poll found that 54 percent of the public does not think that the "Social Security system will have the money available to provide" benefits that respondents expect when it is their time to retire, compared to 34 percent who think that such money will be available. Also, 50 percent from the same poll think that the Social Security crisis is real compared to 40 percent who think that the crisis is being invented so that political leaders can make the reforms that they want. Another indication of public discomfort with the financial underpinnings of the retirement program is that 51 percent think that fundamental changes in Social Security are needed and another 24 percent think that a complete overhaul of the system is required. Only 23 percent see a need for minor changes.

While the public generally believed the message of a crisis looming in Social Security, less support existed for the president's solution in January 2005. For example, although 45 percent supported privatization, 49 percent opposed such an approach from the same *New York Times* poll. This is a modest decline from mid-late November 2004, when the *New York Times* poll reported 49 percent support and 45 percent opposition. This public ambivalence to the president's solution is reflected within Congress, as noted above. As of the inaugural period, the president may have moved Social Security reform onto the agenda and created a demand for reform. But the public, at this juncture, was not ready to support his radical new vision.

From the Inaugural to the State of the Union Address

In his study of agenda setting, John W. Kingdon argues that advocates must soften up the public and Congress, prepare them for new agenda problems and solutions.[15] In a sense, President Bush has been engaged in softening up since his 2000 presidential election campaign when he first broached the topic. The 2004 presidential election results have provided the president with a window of opportunity to couple together the problem and solution streams, to use Kindgon's terminology. Thus since the 2004 election, President Bush and his administration have engaged in numerous public appearances to curry attention to Social Security and support the president's privatization solution. In the period from the Inaugural to the State of the Union the serious work of building support begins. If the president can not show strong movement by then, prospects for building support will dim. This is because the State of the Union is the last major occasion for which the President can expect widespread public attention in a ceremony that emphasizes the head of state, rather than the chief executive, role of the presidency.

On February 2, the president issued his State of the Union Address, barely two weeks after the Inaugural. The close timing of the two events signals that the president wanted to move quickly on establishing his second term administration and in pushing his agenda through Congress before whatever political capital he thinks he gained from the election dissipates.

After the State of the Union

In retrospect, the President used the State of the Union to initiate a more extensive publicity campaign to build public support for the Social Security reform. Beginning in February and extending until late April, the president began 60 days of travel around the nation to sell his idea to the public.

Despite his efforts, the president's public campaign for Social Security reform seems not to have paid off. Instead, by heightening public concern for the issue and stimulating the activity of opponents, the public support for Bush's reform proposal seemed to dwindle, just the opposite of what he expected. For instance, a late April *Washington Post/ABC News* poll found that 64 percent disapproved of the president's handling of Social Security, compared to 31 percent who approved. The same organization's poll of mid-March found 56 percent disapproving and 35 percent supportive. Similarly, an April 1, 2005 *Gallup-CNN* poll showed that only 35 percent approved "of the way George W. Bush was handling Social Security" compared to 57 percent who disapproved. Using the *Post-ABC* poll as a baseline, the president's public campaign, while not markedly generating support led to the mobilization of opposition, from 56 to 64 percent. Perhaps as damaging, a mid-March 2005 *Pew* survey found that 44 percent trusted the Democrats on Social Security, while only 33 percent trusted the President. Despite his campaign to build support for his proposal to reform Social Security, the president's efforts seemed to have backfired.

As a result of the failure of this campaign, in late April, as the president's travels around the nation for his reform wound down, the president shifted strategies, going national. On April 28, 2005 the president offered a prime-time press conference, something not only rare for him, but for presidents over the past three decades. Supposedly, invoking a rarely used forum would generate national public attention for the president. The 60-day national tour, in contrast, generated little national coverage. The press conference forum would also allow the president to present an image to the public that he was well informed on the topic, among others, and that he was reasonable and open to compromise, and thus, defuse criticisms.

Lastly, the president used the press conference and the days after to offer another compromise; to cut Social Security benefits to the upper income tiers but maintain benefit levels to the lower income groups. The president argued that such a move would help rescue the system financially, and allow the transition to private or personal accounts. His new proposal came under sharp Democratic attack, fearing that the conversion of Social Security into a means tested program would undermine long-term public support for the program and spell its eventual demise. From another perspective, this proposal may also indicate the trouble that the program reform is in and its dim prospects for passage.

Conclusions

Throughout the transition period, journalists, commentators, and other prognosticators gazed into their crystal balls and tried to foretell whether George W. Bush would, like many other two-term presidents, suffer some great failure or scandal that would mar his presidency. These seers would recall the Lewinsky scandal and impeachment during Clinton's second term, Iran-Contra under Reagan, Watergate and Nixon, and FDR's Court-packing plan as examples of the second term jinx.

None of these political clairvoyants has a theory or explanation for the second-term jinx, nor do political scientists. Some suggest that the two-term limitation uncouples presidents from the constraints that public opinion imposes, leading them into adventures that they would not take if they were concerned about their re-election. This idea fails to account for FDR's Court-packing plan; FDR was not constrained by formal term limits. Nor does this second-term jinx theory explain that many of these "adventures" had their roots in the president's first term. Finally, a second-term jinx notion can not explain why so many first-term presidencies end in failures, often because of either being too mindful or not mindful enough of public opinion.

George W. Bush is not destined to failure in his second term. Over each election cycle his party's margin in Congress has grown, almost unprecedented in American history. Moreover, Bush governed in his first term mostly without strong public popularity and without trying to curry public favor. Instead his policy initiatives were grounded more upon what he thought was appropriate policy, not public popularity.[16] And he won re-election despite this governing style, an ambiguous economic record, a growing deficit, and increasing public skepticism that the venture into Iraq was well advised.

Bush's re-election in which both he and Congressional Republicans increased their margins with the public provides Bush, as a second-term president, with a political opportunity unlike most re-elected presidents. Neither Reagan nor Clinton nor Nixon nor Eisenhower, who all won mighty and impressive re-election victories, could point to their party's fortunes also improving in Congress as Bush could. While the 2004 election was a personal triumph for Bush, it was also a victory for the Republican Party more generally. This context, along with Bush's ideological orientation towards policymaking, explains Bush's boldness in offering new economic policies for his second term.

Whether Bush succeeds in seeing Social Security and tax reform enacted will depend in part on his skills as president in leading the public and in forging a working majority in Congress. But his success will also depend upon economic circumstances that are for the most part beyond his control, especially the international economy.

Yet even if Bush is unable to see his dreams fulfilled in his second term, he is likely to have set the terms of debate between the parties for years to come. Even if Republicans in the future decide to distance themselves from Bush's radical vision of an ownership society for something milder and more moderate, he may have also provided the Democrats with a road to redefining themselves. George W. Bush may bequeath us a lasting legacy no matter the success or lack thereof that he achieves in his second term.

Notes

1. On the impact of the economy on presidential elections into the nineteenth century see Patrick G. Lynch, "Presidential Elections and the Economy 1872 to 1996: The Times They Are A 'changin' or the Song Remains the Same?" *Political Research Quarterly* 52 (December 1999), pp. 825–844.
2. See Jeffrey E. Cohen, *Politics and Economic Policy in the United States.* 2d ed. (Boston, MA: Houghton Mifflin. 2000), pp. 145–156; and John Frendreis and Raymond Tatalovich, *The Modern Presidency and Economic Policy* (Itasca, IL: Peacock, 1994); For an account from both an insider and an economist see Herbert Stein, *Presidential Economics: The Making of Economic Policy from Roosevelt to Reagan and Beyond* (Washington, DC: American Enterprise Institute, 1988).

3. Richard W. Stevenson, "News Analysis: Bush's New Problem: Iraq Could Eclipse Big Domestic Agenda," *New York Times*, December 22, 2004. This and all other articles from the *New York Times* were downloaded from the *Times* web cite, nytimes.com

4. Bush has been characterized as policy ambitious throughout his presidency. See Steven L. Schier, ed., *High Risk and Big Ambition: The Presidency of George W. Bush* (Pittsburgh: University of Pittsburgh Press, 2004).

5. David Cay Johnson, "I.R.S. Says Americans Income Shrank for 2 Consecutive Years," *New York Times*, July 29, 2004.

6. One of the ironies of the job situation in the aftermath of the 2001 recession was that even in months of increased job growth unemployment remained essentially flat. This happened in part because of the long duration of weak employment picture; during the long wait for job growth many of the unemployed had not only exhausted their unemployment benefits, but had stopped seeking work. When the job markets improved they re-entered the ranks of those seeking jobs, swelling those numbers.

7. On Roosevelt see James MacGregor Burns, *Roosevelt: The Lion and the Fox* (New York: Harcourt and Brace, 1956).

8. On the decisions of cabinet secretaries to stay or leave, see Jeffrey E. Cohen, *Politics of the U.S. Cabinet: Representation in the Executive Branch, 1789–1984* (Pittsburgh: University of Pittsburgh Press, 1988).

9. George C. Edwards III, *On Deaf Ears: The Limits of the Bully Pulpit* (New Haven, CT: Yale University Press, 2003).

10. In contrast, in a search of the Roper Polls database, I have been unable to find a question on tax reform posed to voters in November and December 2004, despite the president having raised the issue.

11. Robin Toner, "Political Memo: Good-Will Reserves Run Low for Social Security Talks," *New York Times*, December 19, 2004.

12. Edmund L. Andrews, "Clamor Grows in the Privatization Debate," *New York Times*, December 17, 2004 and Richard W. Stevenson, "Bush Says Social Security Plan Would Reassure Markets," *New York Times*, December 17, 2004.

13. Karlyn Kohrs Campbell and Kathleen Hall Jamieson, *Deeds Done in Words: Presidential Rhetoric and the Genres of Governance* (Chicago, IL: University of Chicago Press, 1990).

14. Edmund L. Andrews, "Lawmaker Links Overhauls on Social Security and Taxes," *New York Times*, January 19, 2005 and Edmund L. Andrews, "Republicans Urge the White House to Consider Tax Increases for Social Security," *New York Times*, January 20, 2005.

15. John W. Kingdon, *Agendas, Alternatives, and Public Policies* 2d ed. (New York: Longman, 1995).

16. Such a governing style seems common among recent presidents. See Lawrence R. Jacobs and Robert Y. Shapiro, *Politicians Don't Pander: Political Manipulation and the Loss of Democratic Responsiveness* (Chicago, IL: University of Chicago Press, 2000).

Part V

Foreign and Security Policy

Chapter Ten

Homeland (In) Security

Anne M. Khademian

Introduction

Three broad approaches define the second term of the Bush Administration's effort to fight terrorism. First, and most prominent is to fight terrorism overseas before it reaches the shores of America. In the words of President Bush, the wars in Afghanistan and Iraq are one part of a broader strategy "to break terror networks, to deny them refuge, and to find their leaders."[1]

Second are efforts to "connect the dots" across federal government agencies and with state and local governments to make the country more capable in preventing and responding to terrorism.[2] In some instances, the Administration has supported the effort to coordinate across agencies and levels of government, such as the release of the *National Response Plan* in December of 2004 by the Department of Homeland Security (DHS) "to establish a comprehensive, national, all hazards approach to domestic incident management." The plan sets out a blue print for coordinating the efforts, resources, and authorities of federal, state, local, and tribal governments as well as nonprofit and private sector organizations to prevent, prepare for, respond to, and recover from disasters from floods and hurricanes to electrical blackouts to biological and chemical terrorist attacks.[3] In other instances, the Administration has initially opposed and then supported connecting the dots through structural changes. For example, after strong opposition to changes in the structure of the intelligence community, President Bush signed the Intelligence Reform and Terrorism Prevention Act in December of 2004.[4] The Act established a Director of National Intelligence (DNI) to oversee and coordinate the work of agencies such as the CIA, the FBI, the National Security Agency, the Defense Intelligence Agency, and a host of other agencies that together make up the National Intelligence Program.[5] The capacity of the DNI, a post now held by John Negroponte,[6] to connect the dots rests with the exercise of significant budget authority over national intelligence program activities, for example, and responsibility for editing and presenting the daily intelligence briefing for the president.[7] The other major structural effort to connect the dots was of course the creation of DHS to build a coherent, centralized approach to combating terrorism among 22 agencies with missions related to homeland security. As in the case of intelligence reform, the administration initially opposed the consolidation and favored an office of homeland security within the Executive Office of the President; as congressional support for a new department grew, and revelations about the mistakes made in the intelligence community prior to 9/11 emerged, the administration rallied to the new department.[8]

Finally, in an effort to make the homeland more secure, existing systems of enforcement and security have been expanded primarily through increases in personnel and technological innovations. In some cases, the changes have been called "exponential", such as passage of the Patriot Act which enhances the investigative capacities of law enforcement officials to investigate and prevent terrorism.[9] While the Act removed information barriers between intelligence gathering and criminal prosecutions, the dramatic change is primarily one of scale, not approach. The focus is on making more arrests, prosecuting more suspected terrorists, gathering more information, and building more data bases through expanded venues. Other forms of prevention represent the same trend; monuments and critical buildings have more concrete barriers, more agents conduct inspections and patrol the borders, airports have more passenger screeners and all luggage is now screened, cities have hired more police, more equipment has been purchased for first responders, more containers are examined before and after arriving in U.S. ports, and a greater effort has been made to better record and monitor individuals upon entering the United States.[10] In dollar terms, the government is spending approximately $25 billion more today on homeland security than before 9/11.[11]

This third approach builds upon the capacities of existing agencies rather than building possible alternative systems for securing the homeland. The current approach is similar, as two experts have written, to "big bumper America" in reference to the big bumpers that were put on cars in the past to protect passengers in a collision.[12] If we knew what the next terrorist attack would be and where it would be carried out, we could fortify the communities, buildings, and infrastructures with bigger bumpers designed for that particular threat. But we don't know when the next terrorist attack will occur, how or where it will occur. We could spend billions to protect the nation against anticipated threats that might never occur, and not be ready for the one type of terrorist attack that does occur. We risk, in short, a false sense of security by building bigger bumpers rather than considering the overall design of the system, the training of personnel, and the assumptions underlying safety.

While all three approaches to the fight against terrorism pose tremendous challenges for the president and his administration in this second term, improving upon this third dimension of the war on terror is perhaps the most essential. American vulnerabilities to terrorist attack are vast. The country has 7,500 miles of land borders and 12,000 miles of coastal borders through which terrorists may enter with weapons of mass destruction; critical infrastructures in communication, finance, transportation and energy spread across the country, 85 percent of which is in private hands in various stages of security;[13] in the busiest ports on the east and west coasts, more than 1.8 million containers per year are imported from around the world and off loaded;[14] over the past two decades approximately 15 million immigrants entered the United States legally, while an estimated 8 to 12 million illegal immigrants live and work in the United States;[15] and more than 87,000 local governments across 50 states face the challenge of preparing for and paying for homeland security.[16]

But how should the homeland be secured in a country that places high value on freedom of travel, the privacy of its residents, economic opportunity, and freedom of speech and participation in the politics and ideologies of choice? What approach should we take to secure the homeland against terrorists whose method of attack, timing, and location as well as the consequences may be completely unknown until the attack occurs? What level of risk, if any, is politically acceptable, and what constraints on liberties are feasible or desirable? Most critically, how can the president sustain the urgency of homeland security to make essential changes as the immediacy of 9/11 wanes and public and political interest turns to other agenda items?[17] The president must attend to these challenges in the midst of rivalries between congressional committees, battles over turf between federal agencies, limited organizational capacity, constraints on communication and coordination across fifty states and 87,000 local governments, and the big basic political questions of how much money to spend, where to spend it, and what to spend the money on.

The State of Homeland Security

What is the state of homeland security at the start of President Bush's second term? To put the challenges facing President Bush in context, it is useful to examine the progress of the new Department of Homeland Security (DHS), the efforts to build state and local government preparedness, the status of immigration, border and transportation security, and organizational progress in the collection, analysis, and use of intelligence data.

The Department of Homeland Security (DHS)

In November of 2002 President Bush signed legislation that merged 22 federal agencies with more than 170,000 employees to create the DHS. Despite early opposition to a new cabinet department following 9/11, President Bush introduced DHS as "a single agency with the full-time duty of protecting our people against attack" that would "significantly improve our ability to protect our borders, our coasts, and our communities."[18] More than two years later, DHS faces strong criticism from Congress, state and local governments, first responders, businesses and analysts.[19] Ports and borders remain vulnerable,[20] immigration backlogs remain high,[21] secure travel remains problematic, coordination with state and local governments is spotty and confused, the integration of 22 different agencies and personnel systems is progressing slowly, and the public remains disengaged from the challenge.[22]

The problem is easy to define but very difficult to fix: The expectations for what DHS might do to secure the homeland are high, while the resources, authority, and clout of DHS to meet the high expectations are simply not there. At one level the department is limited by the basic capacities of its internal agencies to accomplish this mission. While some agencies came to DHS with reputations for high performance,[23] others faced difficulties before they were made part of the DHS umbrella. The difficulties of patrolling the borders, enforcing immigration and customs laws, and securing ports are not made easier for the new bureaus of Immigration and Customs and Enforcement (ICE) and Customs and Border Protection (CPB) by consolidation in a new department. The Transportation Security Administration (TSA) in particular, created shortly after 9/11 to strengthen airport security, is continually challenged by the management of over 60,000 new airport screeners requiring essential training and development,[24] and others, such as the Coast Guard, are challenged by the need to maintain old responsibilities while taking on new missions set by homeland security—and doing so with limited budget increases.[25]

At another level, the ability of DHS to meet expectations is limited by the need to coordinate with other departments and agencies as well as the private and nonprofit sectors to accomplish its mission. The CIA, Department of Justice, Department of Defense, Health and Human Services, the Environmental Protection Agency, the Centers for Disease Control, and the Department of Energy, to name a few, have authority in the homeland security effort. Any effort to coordinate across agencies requires clout to navigate the turf wars of federal agencies.[26] Without vigorous presidential attention to the efforts of DHS, strong and clear congressional support, and a leader of DHS with a clear vision of the homeland security effort, such clout will likely not materialize. In addition, the DHS is highly dependent upon cooperation of the private sector where much of the nation's transportation, communication, and energy capacities rest, and many of the resources for technological advances in homeland security are lodged within the research and development departments of corporations and the laboratories of academia; DHS must rely on contracts and partnerships to develop these technical capacities. The work of the Red Cross and other nonprofit organizations play a prominent role in education and preparedness, and recovery from disasters; DHS must secure the cooperation of these organizations, as well. Finally, but perhaps most critically, DHS must secure the cooperation of 50 states and 87,000 local governments to build a federal system of prevention, preparation, recovery and response.[27]

State and Local Governments: Spending the Money to Build Capacity

The tool kit available to DHS to accomplish these vast levels of coordination is limited. This is most evident in its challenge to help state, local, and tribal governments to plan and prepare for homeland security and to integrate these governments into a federal approach to homeland security. The primary tool available to DHS is grant money, and since the attacks of September 11, 2001, DHS has distributed billions of dollars to states and local governments to develop plans, train responders, buy equipment, inventory critical infrastructure, and conduct exercises to respond to a terrorist attack.[28] The effectiveness of these billions of dollars, however, is limited by the formulas mandated by Congress for spending the money, and a lack of a clear understanding of what it means for a state or local government to be *prepared* and hence what the money should be spent on.[29]

At one level, DHS has limited control over where the money goes because a significant portion of the spending is mandated by formula. In FY 2004, $1.7 billion of the grants allocated by DHS was spent on formulas or "fair shares" for individual states as mandated by Congress.[30] Every state, regardless of its population or risk of a terrorist attack, received a fair share of the funding from the State Homeland Security Grant program; the result was homeland security spending skewed heavily toward states with low populations.[31] For FY 2005, Congress approved $1.5 billion for the formula-based grants, and half the amount ($885 million) for grants targeted at high density urban areas[32]—viewed by most observers as more likely to be the target of a terrorist attack.[33]

In addition to congressional constraints on where the money is allocated, DHS must rely upon the strategies of state governments to distribute the money in a strategic manner.[34] Yet the needs and priorities of every state and locality differ. The challenge is to define a national strategy to guide the planning and preparation for each state. Should, for example, local governments spend money to upgrade their 9/11 systems and to equip fire fighters with basic gear that might be lacking, or should the money be spent on state-of-the-art biochemical suits and decontamination tents for a possible chemical or bio-terror attack? Whether the community is in South Dakota, southern Florida, or New York, what do a prepared community and state look like? Does every community need state-of-the-art equipment for a potential terrorist attack, or is money better spent on basic response capabilities for any disaster?[35] Clearly, some communities are better prepared than others, and some communities and metropolitan regions are perceived to be at greater risk of a terrorist attack because of population and critical infrastructures. Just how these differences ought to be addressed in terms of grant spending, however, remains problematic without a clear articulation of what constitutes a prepared community.

Immigration, Border and Transportation Security

The Bush Administration faces challenges in clearly defining policies for immigration, border and transportation security, as well, in part because of the dual pressures and the resulting politics that have always defined these policy areas. Consider immigration—an issue that divides the President's own political party.[36] Political and economic pressures for easy immigration are strong. Immigrants make up a key portion of the work force in industries from agriculture to construction, and increasingly in high tech regions such as Silicon Valley.[37] Yet a lower wage work force competes directly with American workers, and organized groups across the country target the costs to schools, social services, and other government services associated with serving populations that do not speak English.[38] Defining an immigration policy that enhances security to eliminate the entry of potential terrorists and to fight the war on drugs further complicates the articulation of a clear immigration policy. Similarly, the pressures for high security in transportation systems and at ports of entry to prevent terrorist attacks are countered by expectations for easy travel, open and inexpensive commerce, and low tariffs on goods.

These dual pressures are manifest in political battles that don't necessarily produce logical policies for homeland security. Instead, policies in these areas are often defined by gaping holes and idiosyncrasies. For example, approximately 11,000 DHS agents patrol the nation's borders. Along the American border with Canada, approximately 1,000 border patrol agents monitor more than 5,500 miles;[39] along the American border with Mexico, nearly 10,000 agents patrol approximately 2,000 miles—a number that increased by 500 in 2005 to help strengthen patrols along the Mexico-Arizona border.[40] As of March 2003, not a single border patrol agent was stationed on the border of Alaska and Canada.[41] Of the approximately 500,000 undocumented immigrants who enter the country each year, half arrive from Mexico, heightening the demand for more border agents in the southwest. Yet, while the flow of illegal immigrants from Canada is less than from Mexico, the sheer volume of people crossing into the United States from Canada through 132 legal points of entry is significant—more than 250,000 people each day. The Mexican border with the United States has 43 ports of entry.[42] A similarly awkward distribution of resources related to immigration is reflected in the number of illegal immigrants residing in the United States—8 to 12 million.[43] But the Bureau of Immigration and Customs Enforcement (ICE) focuses primarily on the 400,000 absconders, who have been ordered to leave the country but don't, and felons with little attention to the millions of other illegal immigrants.[44]

Presidential leadership is required to find a balance between the need for an open immigration policy that supports economic growth, with concerns for low-wage competition for U.S. workers and stress on government services, and with concerns for security. President Bush's proposal for "fair and secure" immigration reform would have offered temporary worker status to undocumented men and women currently employed in the United States, and to others outside of the United States with an offer of employment.[45] The proposal facilitated immigration for purposes of temporary labor, but was less clear as to how the new policy would work in conjunction with increased security concerns.

Similar idiosyncrasies exist in efforts to secure ports and transportation. U.S. ports are visited by approximately 8,000 ships that make 50,000 stops each year,[46] with more than 7 million cargo containers that are unloaded in the US each year.[47] The Coast Guard estimates billions more are needed over the several years to develop and implement port security plans mandated by Congress.[48] Yet, as of 2004, only $500 million had been allocated, and only 5 percent of cargo containers shipped through U.S. ports each year inspected.[49] More troublesome, small pleasure boats and fishing vessels are left outside of the mandated regulations established by the Maritime Transportation Security Act of 2002, despite the potential dangers posed by small watercraft that could be used to commit terrorism.[50] The situation is similar in aviation security. While billions have been spent to make ticketed jet travel more secure, the cargo and private aircraft flights remain unregulated. As Marla Felcher writes in her examination of airline safety, "Two important but largely neglected sectors of the aviation industry, air cargo and general aviation (private planes), remain as vulnerable to terrorist attack today as they were on September 11, 2001."[51]

Intelligence

In the immediate wake of 9/11, analysts pointed to the communication gaps between the efforts of intelligence agencies across the federal government as a key failure in preventing the attacks.[52] Finding ways to connect and integrate information available to the Central Intelligence Agency (CIA), the Federal Bureau of Investigation (FBI), the National Security Agency (NSA), the Defense Intelligence Agency (DIA), and others, it was argued, was essential for preventing future terrorist attacks. When Congress passed the Intelligence Reform and Terrorism Prevention Act in December of 2004,[53] coordination was to be achieved by creating a new Director of National Intelligence (DNI) with budget and personnel authority over what is now called the National Intelligence Program (NIP). The new DNI has more authority over the intelligence community than the position of Director of

Central Intelligence that the legislation replaces. Specifically, the legislation provides authority to develop an annual consolidated budget for the National Intelligence Program, to transfer and reprogram funds across the intelligence community with the approval of OMB and consultation with affected agencies, and to transfer personnel in the community.[54] Nevertheless, the power is not real until successfully exercised by a DNI and there are many obstacles to this effective use of authority. The challenge for the Bush Administration is to provide support and clarity for the efforts of the new DNI—John Negroponte—to bring collaboration in the intelligence community to fruition—a difficult challenge, to say the least.

The primary limitation is the competing power of the Department of Defense (DOD). The DNI has budget authority over those programs involved in the National Intelligence Program (NIP),[55] or those programs involved in "foreign intelligence and counterintelligence activities of the government that respond to national needs as opposed to the needs of a single department or agency."[56] This includes intelligence gathering and analysis by agencies such as the CIA, the FBI, and intelligence offices within the Departments of State, Treasury and Energy. The NIP, however, also includes agencies based inside the Department of Defense such as the National Security Agency (NSA), the National Reconnaissance Office (NRO), the National Geospatial-Intelligence Agency (NGA) and the Defense Intelligence Agency (DIA). As in the real estate business, location is everything, or at least *something* in determining the primary focus for the efforts of these DOD agencies. Intelligence activities conducted under another program, the Joint Military Intelligence Program, will continue to be coordinated by the (DOD) to provide defense-wide intelligence needs, and tactical military intelligence programs will continue to be managed by the individual services in Defense.[57]

The significance of this distribution between the (DOD) and other agencies is highlighted by the budgets for intelligence programs. Of the approximately $40 billion spent annually on intelligence, approximately US$20 to 27 billion is spent on activities within the NIP, while US$5 to 7 billion is spent on the Joint Military Intelligence Program, and US$12 to 15 billion is spent on tactical intelligence. Of the US$20 to 27 billion spent on the NIP, however, approximately US$15 to 20 billion is spent on agencies within DOD—such as NSA, NRO, DIA, and NGA.[58]

This breakdown in funding has two big implications for efforts to coordinate intelligence activities across the federal government. First, despite the DNI's authority to "participate" in the development of the tactical and military-wide budgets,[59] these budgets and intelligence activities remain outside of the NIP venue of the DNI. Second, among the NIP activities that do fall under the jurisdiction of the DNI budget authority, three quarters of the funding will be spent within the DOD-based agencies. This shared authority with DOD will require cooperation and coordination in practice. In short, if the new DNI is to exert leadership over NIP, the White House needs to provide strong support.

A Presidential Vision? Defining and Debating Homeland Security

Since the attacks of September 11, 2001, much of the effort to secure the country against terrorism has taken three approaches. The first, as noted in the introduction, has been to fight the war against terror over seas. The second, consolidating and centralizing activities related to homeland security as a means to connect the dots or close the gaps that became evident in post 9/11 analyses. The creation of DHS as the 15th cabinet department, the newly created Director of National Intelligence, and the completion of a National Response Plan to integrate the work of federal, state, and local governments in responding to an emergency, illustrate this approach. The third approach has been to accelerate the security approaches of the past. While legislative change in the form of the Patriot Act has blurred boundaries between intelligence gathering and criminal investigations, the overall approach to preventing terrorism and working to respond has not changed. More police officers patrol U.S. cities—particularly when DHS heightens the alert for possible terrorist attacks—more barriers have been built around public buildings and monuments, more suspects have been arrested and prosecuted for possible links to terrorist activities, more information about potential terrorists is maintained in data bases, and more grant money has been spent to purchase additional emergency response equipment and to train more first responders. The analogy noted in the introduction is appropriate;[60] at some point, no matter how strong the bumper, passengers in a collision will still be injured. The challenge for making automobile travel safer has since been to improve the design of cars, the engineering of highways, and the training of drivers to enhance safety on the roads. The challenge for the Bush Administration in this second term is similar. No matter the thickness of the security system, a terrorist attack will likely occur. Rather than rely primarily on thicker dimensions of security such as more border patrol agents, police, and barriers, for example, the focus could be on considering the design of security systems, the role of communities, and the components of training of professionals involved in prevention, preparation, and response to terrorist attacks.

Part of the challenge for the Bush Administration is deliberative and exploratory. What do communities around the country expect in terms of homeland security? What are the basic needs in terms of building capacities for responding to an emergency? And what kind of public policy approaches could we engages to build a homeland security system that has the capacity to improvise—to respond to a terrorist attack with the necessary capacities, whatever form that attack might take? Part of the challenge is also definitional, or setting out the basic concept of what is meant by homeland security—what is it we are doing when we prepare for homeland security? On this last point, the Bush Administration has important choices to make. Specifically, should the articulation and development of homeland security policy take place within a framework built upon the capacities for "all hazards?" Or should the framework be focused primarily on preventing, preparing for, and responding to a terrorist attack—with capacities and emphasis that might be distinct from all hazards capacities? The Administration has used the language of "all hazards" but has developed and implemented policies focused specifically on acts of terror. Important implications for preparedness flow from each perspective.

"All Hazards" Versus a Focus on Terrorism

For the past two decades emergency professionals across the country have focused on developing an "all hazards" capacity. Rather than focus on different types of emergencies—from hurricanes and tornadoes to toxic chemical spills, fires, or terrorist attacks—emergency professionals focus on the functions of emergency management: *mitigation* (reducing the impact of future disasters), *preparedness* (training, technical assistance, and exercises), and *response and recovery* (immediate action following a disaster followed by restoration of the community). States and communities have gradually moved toward this all-hazards approach over the past decade with the support of the Federal Emergency Management Agency (FEMA)—now the DHS Directorate of Emergency Preparedness and Response—and state emergency managers. FEMA's efforts to establish uniform standards of all-hazards emergency management capabilities have provided state governments with a means to benchmark their progress and to identify the gaps in emergency preparedness to respond to earthquakes, fires, floods, hurricanes and tornados as well as other disasters.

Homeland security adds two dimensions to this all-hazards approach: (1) an emphasis on terrorist attacks as a type of disaster, and (2) an emphasis on preventing and mitigating terrorism, and building a general awareness of potential terrorism. This is where the Administration must provide guidance for federal, state and local agencies working to meet the demands of homeland security: should we build preparedness through an all-hazards approach to emergency management with one element of that broad approach being homeland security, or should the primary framework be the war on terror, with an all-hazards capacity as part of that focused effort? There are important differences between the two. One is the emphasis upon law enforcement if preparedness is framed primarily in terms of preventing and responding to terrorist attacks, rather than all-hazards. Specifically, law enforcement officials must be focused on counterterrorism activities like identifying threats and building interagency and cross-government relationships for information sharing and investigation. The efforts by city and county police departments of major metropolitan regions to build intelligence gathering and analysis capabilities are a manifestation of this approach. New York City now has a deputy commissioner of intelligence, a post created after 9/11 and filled by a former CIA veteran with thirty-five years of experience who was also a former director of operations.[61] The New York Police Department (NYPD) spends 20 times more man hours on counterterrorism than before 9/11, with more than 130 officers posted to a joint terrorism task force directly involved with federal agencies investigating terrorism internationally and often posted to cities such as Tel Aviv and London to learn counterterrorism techniques.[62] While not as extensive, county and city police departments outside of New York are pursuing similar counterterrorism strategies—an extension of the focused emphasis on preventing and preparing for terrorism as a national strategy.

If the primary focus were on an all-hazards form of preparedness, however, with preparing for and responding to terrorism one aspect of that framework, the work of law enforcement across the country would be less focused on prevention and counterterrorism and perhaps more focused on responses to terrorism—working with other first responders to rescue, secure roads, evacuate, prevent looting, and investigate the attack. The issue is not whether it is wise to try to prevent terrorism—of course this is a critical dimension of the effort. The issue is how resources are best allocated. Should the bulk of homeland security funds go toward counterterrorism, or toward building capacities to respond? It's not an easy trade off to make.

Historically presidents have struggled to structure programs aimed at responding primarily to natural disasters and those focused on national security (or civil emergency) preparedness.[63] President Carter created FEMA in 1978 to integrate separate functions aimed at preparing for and responding to natural disasters, war time emergencies, and what was considered an "intermediate category of civil emergency preparedness and response measures" related to acts of terror, or disruptions in the supply of essential electricity, transportation, or oil.[64] Yet the criticism of FEMA in its first fourteen years was its inability to integrate "the personnel dedicated to the national security mission of the agency and those tasked with natural disaster preparedness and response."[65] Indeed, rather than work to integrate the tasks more explicitly when he was appointed in 1993, FEMA director James Lee Witt built FEMA as a coordinator and planner of the emergency deployment of resources by separating the agency's all-hazards capability from its long-time civil emergency capacity.[66]

Witt's opposition to the merger of FEMA within DHS represents the concern that FEMA's all-hazards capacity would be diminished by the greater emphasis on preventing and responding to a terrorist attack.[67] The reaction of state emergency managers to the first draft of the National Response Plan as "slanted toward terrorism-specific incidents" revealed a similar concern about the need to maintain a strong all-hazards approach: "We know that the possibility for natural disasters and emergencies to occur far exceeds the possibility for terrorist events.[68]

Despite the emphasis in the *National Strategy for Homeland Security* on an "all hazards" approach to avoid creating "boutique response entities",[69] the current emphasis in DHS upon terrorism as the primary concern—in contrast to all hazards—has the potential to do just that. In addition to the emphasis upon terrorism as a distinct hazard or disaster, differentiation in training, equipment, and planning is emerging around different types of potential terrorist attacks—biological, chemical, nuclear, and the like. It is, ironically, the similar situation in which FEMA floundered in its first fourteen years when one of its emphases was on responding to natural disasters, but those response efforts were differentiated according to the type of natural disaster—hurricane, flood, earthquake, and so on.[70]

These are complex issues, with no easy answers for the Bush Administration in its second term. Yet without clarity about what approach the nation is taking and hence what frameworks the nation will utilize to build a secure homeland, billions of dollars will be spent on training, equipment, fortification, and police overtime, without a clear policy blue print for the effort.

The Rhetoric and Reality of Homeland Security

The nation needs to discuss the risks that are present, the resources needed, the resources the nation is willing to commit, and the role of citizens and communities in the homeland security effort. In his insightful book, *System Under Stress*, Donald Kettl poses the question, how much risk will the nation accept? No program can be designed that will guarantee the prevention of any terrorism. More importantly, the cost of any system aimed at eliminating the risk of terrorism would be phenomenal—both in terms of dollars spent and the quality of life. So how much security is enough, and what form should security take?

Much of the answer depends upon the way in which the debate is framed and the options that are put forth. Should the discussion be framed as a series of tradeoffs that must be made between the rights to privacy, speech, travel and association, and the need for security? In other words, we would weigh the cost and demands of a more secure country against the strains upon valued rights. The current approach pursued by the Administration encourages this type of approach. The fundamental manifestation of homeland security policy is to fortify the national bumper—more arrests, more information gathered through a variety of means, more barriers, more border patrol agents, more airport screeners, more data bases with personal information, and more monitoring of individuals upon entering the United States. Yet, as critics of the Patriot Act and policies related to homeland security point out, each increase in fortification can conflict with basic rights.[71]

The physical presence of barriers and fortifications, data bases, additional police, new departments and agencies, a color-coded terror alert system, and a growing number of counterintelligence agents across the country provide something material that people can observe and for which politicians can claim credit. But is this the best way to prevent, prepare for, and respond to terrorism, or are there other processes and methods that we might pursue to enhance security. If so, how would they help and what would they cost? And what might be the relationship between citizens and the homeland security effort? Should the role for citizens be limited to preparing individual residences for a possible terrorist attack—buy more duct tape? The Citizen Corp program provides one alternative, where Citizen Corps Councils at the county and local levels of government engage volunteers from the community to serve—in the event of an emergency—as responders, in medical reserve squads, and in other capacities.[72]

The challenge for the Bush Administration is to engage this discussion, and it's not an easy discussion to take on. Such a discussion would force a careful examination of the current approach and a discussion about the risks that will never be completely eliminated—not a comfortable position for elected officials focused on providing security for residents and administrators concerned that the spotlight of discussion will only bring criticism and fodder for the media. Yet, the discussion is essential.

Presidential Leadership Style and Homeland Security

Any effort to define and lead a discussion on homeland security will be conducted in the context of congressional and bureaucratic politics, efforts to secure cooperation with state and local officials and representatives of the private sector, and recognition of resource and technological limitations.[73] In addition to these political and resource-based obstacles, the president's own management style will of course play an influential role in determining how the nation will prevent, prepare for, and respond to acts of terror in this second term. Two dimensions of the president's management style are examined here: (1) his preference for programs within the executive office of the president (EOP), (2) his choice of leadership.

Building the Capacities of a New Cabinet Department

An aggressive approach to homeland security will require a DHS that is up to the task. It's unlikely, however, that the Bush Administration will invest the energy and resources to build this expertise. When the department was created, conspicuously missing were key organizations in the intelligence community that might have given the new department greater clout among other agencies.[74] The new department was given authority to analyze and distribute intelligence gathered by other agencies—a capacity that remains undefined and underutilized. The primary capacities inherited by the DHS, instead, focus on the day-to-day enforcement of immigration laws and maritime laws, maintaining and patrolling borders and ports of entry, screening passengers and luggage, allocating grants to state and local governments for preparedness and determining contracts with the private sector for research and development. In this mix, some of the twenty-two merged agencies brought strong competence, and others brought years of mission, confusion, and dysfunction. Also in this mix rests the potential for DHS to emerge as a facilitator of preparedness, a central point of distribution for intelligence gathered by other agencies, and the generator of intelligence analyses focused to determine vulnerabilities of critical infrastructure across the country.[75] But the department must first conquer its own internal struggles to coordinate, and build the needed political and administrative capacities to play a key role in intelligence—all while trying to maintain the responsibilities central to the missions of the individual agencies. The department, in short, needs resources, strong leadership, and presidential support—and it doesn't seem any of the three will be forthcoming any time soon.[76]

The bottom line is that the Bush administration supported the new department with reluctance; indeed, the administration was opposed to the new department but relented under pressure from Congress, and revelations of the mishaps leading up to 9/11.[77] Instead, the Administration's preference for homeland security was the small scale Office for Homeland Security created shortly after 9/11 and located within the (EOP). The office was to play a coordinating role among the many agencies involved in homeland security, and avoid the consolidation, or appearance of government growth that the new department inevitably represents.

The preference for an office within the EOP reflects the dynamics of the "Politicized Presidency", as analyzed by Terry Moe.[78] Expectations for presidential accomplishment, the history of reorganizations that did little to enhance presidential influence, and the drive to control programs for which presidents will be held to account, all create incentives to centralize decision-making across government agencies and departments within the White House, close to the president. In the case of the office of Homeland Security, proximity to the president was to be the primary source of power and influence to "coordinate activities, to make sure that anybody who wants to harm America will have a hard time doing so."[79] As part of the effort to maintain close presidential influence over homeland security, the Office and its accompanying Council were to be outside of congressional influence. In his initial role as director of the Office of Homeland Security, Tom Ridge was not confirmed by the Senate, and resisted any formal testimony before Congress despite tremendous pressure to do so.[80] The preference, in short, was for an office with coordinating skills and presidential clout, built on the model of the National Security Council, not for a large department that would inherit and be required to integrate a range of agencies from the competent and venerable to the dysfunctional and despised and put even the most competent and experienced managerial skills to the test. The expectation that the second Bush Administration would invest the resources and energy to build the capacities of a department whose agencies bring legacies, strong constituencies, union and management challenges that will impede if not obstruct direct presidential influence, is highly unlikely.

Choice of Leadership

The president's selection of federal appeals court judge Michael Chertoff to be the second secretary of DHS, has implications for the anticipated relationship between the administration and the department, as well as for the direction the department is likely to take in the war on terror.[81] The president's second term began with the nominations of White House staff to lead key cabinet posts, most prominently Condoleezza Rice to head the Department of State and Alberto Gonzales to head the Department of Justice. Both departments are of course key players in the war on terror and will be directed by close confidants of the President. Department of Homeland Security, on the other hand, will be led by Judge Chertoff, a former director of the Department of Justice (DOJ), criminal division with limited ties to the president. If the pattern of decision-making in the second term mirrors that of the first, close confidants of the president will help to craft the strategic homeland security policies. Most likely, Judge Chertoff will be left to manage the ongoing reorganization of twenty-two different agencies and tending to the inherited competencies of the department.

Judge Chertoff's background and professional orientation, however, could signal the priorities within the department and the ways in which the department might develop over the next few years. As a key architect of the U.S. Patriot Act, and the former director of the DOJ criminal division, Judge Chertoff will likely emphasize the prosecution and enforcement dimensions of the work of DHS. Secretary Chertoff's early decisions to fill management positions in DHS reflect this tendency, as well; several lawyers who were colleagues with Chertoff in the DOJ were selected.[82] A more rigorous emphasis upon border patrol and the enforcement of customs and immigration laws, is a likely scenario. Less likely is a strong effort to build DHS as a facilitator for preparedness among other federal agencies and across state and local governments—an outcome that would have been more likely had the Bush Administration's original nominee to fill the post, Bernard Kerik, assumed the post.[83] As the former police commissioner of New York City, Kerik had the experience of meeting homeland security priorities at the metropolitan level. Attention to the distribution and targeting of grant money, the flexibility of grant spending, and communication with state and local governments in the homeland security effort would have been FAMILIAR TO KERIK.

Conclusion

If homeland security is to become anything more than the "gas mask in the desk drawer," strong presidential leadership is essential in the second term of President Bush. A broad discussion about what the nation expects in terms of security, what that security will cost, and what the nation is willing to pay to bring about security is essential, as is some clear guidance about the ways in which we might build upon or alter the capacities of homeland security. While we can identify the potential strengths of a new DHS, recognize the potential benefits of a transparent dialogue focused on security and the costs of security, and see the logic of moving beyond the "big bumper" approach to security, it is unlikely that a second-term George W. Bush Presidency will make the investments or take risks.

Notes

1. "President Bush Reaffirms Resolve to War on Terror, Iraq and Afghanistan." Remarks by the president on Operation Iraqi Freedom and Operation Enduring Freedom, The East Room, March 19, 2004, http://www.whitehouse.gov/news/releases/2004/03/20040319–3.html.
2. The term, "connect the dots" was used extensively in analyses that detailed what went wrong, particularly in the intelligence community, leading up to 9/11. The focus was on the lack of communication and information sharing between agencies such as the CIA and the FBI related to the terrorists who planned and executed the attacks on September 11, 2001. See Gregory Treverton, "Intelligence Gathering, Analysis and Sharing," in *The Department of Homeland Security's First Year: A Report Card*, ed. Donald Kettl (New York: The Century Foundation, 2004).
3. Department of Homeland Security, *National Response Plan*, December 2004, p. 2.
4. Public Law No: 108–458
5. Stephen Daggett, *The US Intelligence Budget: A Basic Overview*, CRS Report for Congress, September 24, 2004.
6. Prior to his nomination for DNI, Negroponte served as the top U.S. diplomat in Iraq for several months, was U.S. Representative to the United Nations, and served as Ambassador to Honduras (1981–1985), Mexico (1989–1993) and the Philippines (1993–1996) and held the post of Deputy Assistant to the President for National Security Affairs (1987–1989), among many other positions. See http://www.un.int/usa/negroponte_bio.html;http://www.whitehouse.gov/news/releases/2005/02/20050217–2.html; http://www.cnn.com/2005/ALLPOLITICS/02/17/intelligence.chief/
7. Summary of Intelligence Reform and Terrorism Prevention Act of 2004, December 6, 2004, p. 1; William Branigin, "Bush Nominates Negroponte to new Intel Post," *Washington Post*, February 17, 2005, http://www.washingtonpost.com/wp-dyn/articles/A31826–2005Feb17.html.
8. Donald Kettl, *System Under Stress: Homeland Security and American Politics* (Washington, DC: CQ Press, 2004).
9. Siobhan Gorman, "Homeland Security: Second Class Security," *National Journal*, May 1, 2004.
10. Some would argue that there are qualitative differences in this approach. The examination of cargo before leaving foreign ports, for example, as well as the program—One Face at the Border—are viewed by DHS as fundamental shifts in the way terrorism is fought. It is, however, more a question of degree. One Face

at the Border does not change the approach to border control, but merely merges the activities of previously distinct entities such as immigration control and customs. Similarly, the screening of cargo at foreign ports extends the concept of examining cargo in home ports.

11. Gorman, "Homeland Security: Second Class Security," *National Journal*, May 1, 2004. For FY 2005, the net discretionary spending for the DHS rose by $1.8 billion from the FY 2004 appropriated amount. Fact Sheet: Department of Homeland Security Appropriations Act of 2005, http://www.dhs.gov/dhspublic/ interapp/press_release/press_release_0541.xml.

12. Sharon L. Caudle and Randall Yim, "Homeland Security Results Management: Missions, Capabilities, and Oversight," in *The McGraw-Hill Handbook of Homeland Security*, ed. David Kamien (forthcoming, 2005).

13. DHS, Threats and Protection, "Protected Critical Infrastructure Information (PCII) program," Frequently Asked Questions, http://www.dhs.gov/dhspublic/ display? theme=92&content=3756 DHS.

14. Metropolitan Waterfront Alliance, http://www.waterwire.net/News/ fullstory.cfm? ContId=1439.

15. Migration Policy Institute, MPI staff, May 2003, "A New Century: Immigration and the US," www.Migrationinformation.org.

16. Paul Magnusson, "America's Cities are Seeing Red over Code Orange," *Business Week* Issue 3836, June 9, 2003, p. 55; The U.S. Conference of Mayors, "Survey on Cities' Direct Homeland Security Cost Increases Related to War/High Threat Alert, March 27, 2003, http://www.usmayors.org/uscm/news/ press_releases/documents/survey_032703.pdf

17. See E. Marla Felcher, "Aviation Security," in *The Department of Homeland Security's First Year: A Report Card*, ed. Donald Kettl (New York: The Century Foundation, 2004). Felcher cites testimony of Robert Kupperman, who made the point about the "episodic" nature of terrorism and the difficulty of sustaining political focus at a 1989 Senate Hearing on responses to terrorism. Robert Kupperman, "Responses to Terrorism," Hearing of the Senate Governmental Affairs Committee, *Federal News Service*, September 11, 1989.

18. Office of the Press Secretary, November 16, 2002, "President Discusses Department of Homeland Security in Radio Address, Radio Address by the President to the Nation, Archives," November 2002, http:// www.whitehouse. gov/news/releases/2002/11/20021116.html.

19. Progressive Policy Institute, *America at Risk: A Homeland Security Report Card*, July 2003; Democratic Task Force on Homeland Security, *Federal Homeland Security Assistance to America's Hometowns: A Survey and Report from the Democratic Task Force on Homeland Security*, October 29, 2003; Donald F. Kettl (ed.), *The Department of Homeland Security's First Year: A Report Card*, (New York: The Century Foundation, 2004).

20. David Kamien, "Maritime Security: What Keeps Port Security Directors up at Night," *Homeland Security* (January 2004), pp. 10–14.

21. For example, the 2nd Circuit U.S. Court of Appeals in New York reported a backlog of 4,000 cases appealing negative decisions by immigration officials for asylum. As the number of administrative decisions rejecting asylum requests have grown, so too have the number of appeals to the federal court system. Dan Eggen, "Immigration Backlog Forces Justice to Shift Staffing," *Washington Post*, December 14, 2004, p. A11. http://www.washingtonpost.com/wp-dyn/ articles/A62070–2004Dec13.html.

22. Michael Hillyard, *Homeland Security and the Need for Change* (San Diego, CA: Aventine Press, 2003); Donald F. Kettl (ed). *The department of Homeland Securit's First Year,* 2004.

23. The Federal Emergency Management Agency (FEMA), now the Directorate of Emergency Preparedness and Response, and the Coast Guard, for example, came to DHS with strong reputations for mission accomplishment.

24. General Accounting Office, *Aviation Security: Screener Training and Performance Measurement Strengthened, but More Work Remains,* GAO-05–457, May 2005.

25. General Accounting Office, *Maritime Security: Substantial Work Remains to Translate New Planning Requirements into Effective Port Security,* GAO-04–838, June 2004.

26. James Q. Wilson, *Bureaucracy: What Government Agencies Do and Why they Do It?* (New York: Basic Books, 1989).

27. Anne Khademian, "Strengthening State and Local Terrorism Prevention and Response," in *The Department of Homeland Security's First Year A Report Card,* ed. Donald Kettl (New York: The Century Foundation, 2004).

28. Office of the Press Secretary, *FY 2004 Budget Fact Sheet Homeland Security,* October 1, 2003; GAO, *Homeland Security: Management of First Responder Grants has Improved, But Challenges Remain,* GAO-05–121, February 2005.

29. Siobhan Gorman, "Spreading the Faith", *National Journal,* October 11, 2003, C:\DHS\News and Information from Factiva.html; Paul Posner, Testimony Before the Subcommittee on Government Efficiency, Financial Management, and Intergovernmental Relations, Committee on Government Reform, House of Representatives, *Combating Terrorism: Intergovernmental Partnership in a National Strategy to Enhance State and Local Preparedness,* March 22, 2002, GAO-02–547T.

30. Office of the Press Secretary, "FY 2004 Budget Fact Sheet Homeland Security," October 1, 2003; "FY '04, U.S. Department of Homeland Security Counterterrorism Grants—State Allocations, Appendix A."

31. Mimi Hall, "Homeland Security Money Doesn't Match Terror Threat: Does Zanesville, Ohio Need to Test for Nerve Agents while NY Struggles for Funds?" *USA Today,* October 29, 2003, http://www.usatoday.com/news/washington/2003–10–29-security-cover-usat_x.htm.

32. Department of Homeland Security, Press Release, "Fact Sheet: Department of Homeland Security Appropriations Act of 2005," October 18, 2004, http://www.dhs.gov/dhspublic/interapp/press_release/press_release_0541.xml.

33. The grants, titled the Urban Area Security Initiative Grants, are allocated based upon population density, perceived threats based upon intelligence data and analysis, and the presence of critical infrastructure or key monuments.

34. Individual states submit a State Homeland Security Plan to DHS through its Office of Domestic Preparedness, that plays a crucial role in how the money is distributed and spent.

35. Eric Kelderman, "Panel Urges Anti-Terrorism Spending Guidelines," *Stateline. org,*2003.

36. Daniel Griswold, "The Immigration Issue," *The Wall Street Journal,* November 20, 2002, http://www.nationalreview.com/comment/comment-griswold112002.asp; Stephen Dinan, "Republicans Warn of Party Split over Immigration," *Washington Times,* http://www.washtimes.com/national/20041202–111826–8264r.htm.

37. Kevin Bacon, "Immigrants find High Tech Servitude in Silicon Valley, 2000, http://www.labornotes.org/archives/2000/0900/0900c.html.

38. For example, the Federation for American Immigration Reform(FAIR), released a report in 2004, *The Costs of Illegal Immigration to Californian*, which examined state costs in health care, incarceration, and education relating to the cost of each.

39. White House Fact Sheet, "Fair and Secure Immigration Reform," http://www.whitehouse.gov/news/releases/2004/01/20040107–1.html.

40. Mimi Hall and Patrick O'Driscoll, "Border Patrols Growing in Arizona," *USA Today*, http://www.usatoday.com/news/nation/2005-03-29-borders_x.htm

41. A TRAC Special Report, "Georgraphic Deployment of Homeland Security Full Time Staff by Occupation, March 2003," in *The Department of Homeland Security: The First Months*, August 25, 2003. See also, "A TRAC Special Report, New Findings: Patrolling Which Borders?" 2002.http://trac.syr.edu/tracins/findings/aboutINS/newFindings.html.

42. Migration Policy Institute, "A New Century: Immigration and the US," http://www.migrationinformation.org/Profiles/display.cfm?ID=6;Migration   Policy Institute, "US Mexico Border, US in Focus," July 2002.

43. Center for Immigration Studies, "Current Numbers," http://www.cis.org/topics/currentnumbers.html.

44. http://www.visalaw.com/04apr1/newsletter.pdf.

45. The conflicting responses to President Bush's recent proposal for a temporary worker program for potential workers outside the United States and current undocumented men and women inside the United States, illustrates the difficulty of defining policy in this area. For an overview of the proposal, see http://www.whitehouse.gov/news/releases/2004/01/20040107–1.html.

46. Katherine McIntire Peters, "Covering the Waterfront," *Govexec.com*, September 1, 2004.

47. Larry Greenemeier, "Port Security May be Aided by Electronic Container Seals, Information Week," September 14, 2004, http://informationweek.com/story/showArticle.jhtml?articleID=47205231.

48. The estimate is $795 million annually, adjusted for inflation. Greta Wodele, "Coast Guard Modernization Plan Veers off Course," *Govexec.Com*, April 8, 2004.

49. Siobhan Gorman, "Homeland Security: Second Class Security," *National Journal*, May 1, 2004; Council on Foreign Relations, Terrorism Question and Answers, "What are the priorities for Homeland Security Secretary-designate Michael Chertoff?" http://cfrterrorism.org/home/

50. Katherine McIntire Peters, "Covering the Waterfront," 2004.

51. Marla Felcher, "Aviation Security," 2004.

52. September 11 Commission.

53. Public Law No: 108–458.

54. Stephen Daggett, CRS Summary; Cummings 2004, p. 6.

55. The legislation changed the title of this program from The National Foreign Intelligence Program to the National Intelligence Program.

56. Stephen Daggett, CRS Summary.

57. Ibid.

58. Ibid.

59. Stephen Daggett, CRS Summary.

60. Sharon L. Caudle and Randall Yim, "Homeland Security Results Management: Missions, Capabilities, and Oversight," in *The McGraw-Hill Handbook of Homeland Security*, ed. David Kamien (New York: McGraw-Hill, 2005).

61. Dave Siff, "Despite Top Rank, New York Keeps Preparing," *CNN.com*, September 6, 2002, http://edition.cnn.com/2002/US/09/06/prepared.cities. newyork/

62. Anya Sostek, "Taking Action: New York's State of Mind: Out of the Twin Towers' Ashes, NY is building a World Class Terror-Fighting Machine," *Securing the Homeland: A Special Report From Governing Magazine and Congressional Quarterly*, http://www.manhattan-institute.org/html/_govmag-out_of_the_twin_towers.htm.

63. Keith Bea, *Proposed transfer of FEMA to the Department of Homeland Security*, Congressional Research Service, July 29, 2002, received through the CRS Web.

64. Ibid.

65. Ibid., p. 17.

66. National Academy of Public Administration, *Coping with Catastrophe: Building an Emergency Management System to Meet People's Needs in Natural and Manmade Disasters* (Washington, DC: NAPA, 1993); Sandra Schneider, *Flirting with Disaster: Public Management in Crisis Situations* (Armonk, NY: M.E. Sharpe, 1995).

67. Walter Pincus, "FEMA's Influence May be Cut Under New Department," *Washington Post*, July 24, 2002, p. A17, http://www.washingtonpost.com/ac2/ wp-dyn/A53075, July 23, 2002.

68. National Emergency Management Association, "Comments on Draft National Response Plan," June 6, 2003.

69. U.S. Office of Homeland Security, *National Strategy for Homeland Security* (Washington, 2002), p. 42.

70. National Academy of Public Administration, *Coping with Catastrophe*, Sandra Schneider, *Flirting with Disaster*, 1995.

71. Ellen Alderman, "Homeland Security and Privacy: Striking a Delicate Balance," *Carnegie Reporter* 2:1, Fall 2002.

72. White House Press Release, "President to Discuss New Citizen Corps Initiative," http://www.whitehouse.gov/news/releases/2002/01/20020130.html.

73. For a discussion of these dimensions of homeland security see, Anne Khademian, "The Politics of Homeland Security," in *The McGraw-Hill Handbook of Homeland Security*.

74. Gregory Treverton, "Intelligence Gathering, Analysis, and Sharing." In Donald F. Ketil, *The Department of Homeland Security's First Year*, 2004.

75. Ibid.

76. The 2005 Appropriations for DHS provide an increase in spending of $1.8 billion. However, assessments of the needs of individual agencies within DHS, alone, dwarf the $1.8 billion increase. The Coast Guard, for example, estimates billions more are needed to bring security systems to American Ports. American Association of Port Authorities, Press Release, "Port Security Council Formed to Address Security Funding Issues," May 18, 2004, http://www.aapa-ports.org/ pressroom/may1804.htm.

77. Donald Kettl, *System Under Stress*, 2004.

78. Terry Moe, "The Politicized Presidency," *New Directions in American Politics*, ed. John Chubb and Paul Peterson (Washington, DC: Brookings Institution Press, 1985).

79. Elizabeth Becker and Tim Weiner, "A Nation Challenged: Homeland Security. New Office to Become a White House Agency," *New York Times*, September 28, 2001, Friday, Section B, Column 4, National Desk, p. 5.
80. Ibid.
81. Pete Williams, "Bush Nominates Judge to Head Homeland Security," *MSNBC*, January 11, 2005, http://msnbc.msn.com/id/6812230
82. John Mintz, "Chertoff's DHS has a Justice Department feel," *Washington Post*, May 25, 2005, p. A 25; http://www.washingtonpost.com/wp-dyn/content/article/2005/05/24/AR2005052401363.html.
83. Mike Allen and Jim VandeHei, "Homeland Security Nominee Kerik Pulls Out," *Washington Post*, December 10, 2004, p. A01, http:// www.washingtonpost.com/wp-dyn/articles/A56247–2004Dec10.html.

Chapter Eleven

The Best Defense? Iraq and Beyond

Tom Lansford and Jack Covarrubias

Introduction

The Bush administration has worked toward making wide spread changes within the Department of Defense in how it has planned for future military operations. The need to reorient a Cold War era military establishment to take into account post–Cold War realities has been and continues to be an agenda item for the current administration. Bush 41 and Clinton failed in many ways to wrest control away from bureaucratic minded senior military officers that had become risk aversive to the point of undermining the ability to project and protect U.S. interests. Over the course of Bush's first term and what is expected to continue during the second term, Bush and his hand-selected staff have worked to bring a slow changing military bureaucracy into new realities.

This chapter is constructed in two movements. The first movement examines the main elements of the Bush administration's security and defense policy within the context of contemporary domestic and international influences and constraints. The chapter begins by placing the administration's policy in the framework of broad and longstanding historical trends in U.S. security strategy, including the use of short-term and ad hoc "coalitions of the willing." Specifically, an examination of continuities with previous administration's efforts to develop and implement innovations in strategy and tactics and deploy new weapons systems demonstrates that Bush has embraced past Republican positions as well as taking into account new international realities. The movement concludes by analyzing the president's choice for senior defense positions, including the Secretary of Defense and top military officers, and surveys the chief executive's relations with these officials and leading members of Congress who exercise influence over defense policy.

The next movement of the chapter explores the impact of contemporary military operations, such as Afghanistan and Iraq, on both military doctrine and weapons development. Central to this analysis is an overview of the tactics and weapons employed in both recent major campaigns. For instance, the military predominance of the United States allowed a quick victory in

Operation Enduring Freedom, but Bush's decision to deploy narrow military coalitions had a negative impact on his later efforts to develop a coalition during the Iraq campaign. In the Iraq campaign, the post-Saddam insurgency undermined public support, both in the United States and in allied capitals, for future military operations. This section of the chapter will explore the emergence of what has been termed the "Iraq syndrome" on the ability of the president to build security coalitions. The conclusion of the chapter will survey the major international security threats facing the president in the next term and the capability of the U.S. military to respond to these dangers.

U.S. Defense Policy and the Presidency

In the United States Constitution of 1789, the president has the most far-reaching powers in the realm of foreign and security policies.[1] These powers come from Article II, Section 2 of the Constitution, in which the President is designated "Commander in Chief of the Army and Navy of the United States" and of the state militias when they are called into federal service.[2] Section 2 also grants the president broad control of the nation's diplomacy, including the sole power to negotiate treaties (subject to confirmation by a vote of two-thirds of the Senate) and to appoint ambassadors (subject to confirmation by a simple majority of the Senate).

The authority to declare war is vested in the hands of Congress through Article 1, Section 8, but the president may deploy forces and engage in combat for up to 60 days without congressional approval under the terms of the 1973 War Powers Resolution. The law was designed to limit the capability of the president to use U.S. troops in combat in response to the Vietnam War. It also increases the oversight ability of Congress, however, contemporary history has shown that the measure does not significantly impede the chief executive's ability to use military force.[3] For instance, John Hart Ely has argued that the War Powers Act reduces Congress to

> simply hemming and hawing, sidetracking resolutions to start the sixty-day clock with incomprehensible "points of order," passing resolutions to similar but not identical effect in the two houses and then being "unable" to reconcile them until the war was over, or more often, just doing nothing. Of course this is just a reversion to pre-resolution form—letting the President initiate military action while retaining for Congress the options (depending on how the war went) of pointing with pride or viewing with alarm.[4]

In addition, the National Security Act of 1947 reorganized the security agencies and departments of the government in such a way as to increase the direct influence of the chief executive, especially through the creation of the National Security Council.[5] Furthermore, American foreign policy is rooted in the notion of the "sole organ theory" which holds that the president is the "sole" source of foreign and security policy.[6]

In addition to the explicit constitutional and legal foundations of presidential security powers, a variety of factors, including tradition, necessity, and interpretations of the Supreme Court have expanded the boundaries of executive authority. The traditional freedom given to U.S. presidents to use military force without a congressional declaration of war has come to be seen as a manifestation of executive privilege.[7]

The use of force is also a manifestation of Wildavsky's concept of "two-presidencies" in which one "chief executive" represents domestic policy while the other represents foreign and security policy.[8] Wildavsky identified five main reasons for the concentration of power:

(1) since foreign policy and security issues often need "fast action," the executive rather than the legislative is the more appropriate decision-making structure;

(2) as aforementioned, the Constitution grants the president broad formal powers;

(3) because of the complexities involved voters tend to delegate to the president their "trust and confidence" to act;

(4) the "interest group structure is weak, unstable and thin"; and

(5) the legislature follows a "self-denying ordinance" since tradition and practicality reinforce the power of the chief executive.[9]

Wildavsky's work is echoed by many scholars, including Mark Logan who contends that in Western democracies, "the mass public consciously or unconsciously cedes influence" to politicians and policy elites.[10]

Contemporary Presidents and the Use of Force

One manifestation of this concentration of power in the office of the chief executive has been the repeated use of the U.S. military throughout the nation's history without a formal congressional declaration of war. There has also been a marked increase in the preference by both the executive and the legislature for such actions.[11] Even during those periods in which the United States experienced divided government, with the White House controlled by one political party and all, or one chamber, of the Congress controlled by the party in opposition, the executive was able to utilize force with only limited constraints.[12] The air campaign in Kosovo and the military operations in Bosnia are examples of this trend in the 9/11 era. In the resolution authorizing force in Afghanistan, only one member of Congress, Representative Barbara Lee, voted against granting the President the authority to deploy troops.

Given the nature of the terrorist groups that attacked the United States on 9/11, such policy trends proved useful to the Bush administration since a formal declaration of war was seen as problematic in terms of the specific identification of the foe and the ability of the Bush administration to expand combat operations beyond Afghanistan to countries such as Iraq. Instead, the president was able to deploy military forces and initiate a campaign, backed by the congressional resolution, within one month of the terrorist attacks. Bush further had broad bipartisan support in the resolutions authorizing the use of force in Afghanistan and Iraq (the Iraq resolution passed in the House 296 to 133 and 77 to 21 in the Senate). The results of the 2002 midterm elections, which ran counter to historical trends, bolstered the president's political capital since the Republican gains were interpreted as a manifestation of public support for the administration's security policies.

The president was also able to gain support for his broader defense goals by supporting or implementing policies popular with senior Congressional leaders. For instance, Bush's decision to abrogate the Anti-Ballistic Missile (ABM) Treaty had wide support among Republicans. For instance, Representative Bob Stump (R-AZ), Chairman of the House Armed Services Committee stated that "The Administration has chosen, in Secretary Wolfowitz' words, to 'move beyond' the [ABM] treaty. I believe this is a wise decision. We should seek to do so cooperatively with the Russians, but unilaterally if necessary."[13] "Senator James Inofe (R-OK) noted that President Bush is showing decisive leadership in backing the deployment of a missile defense system and breaking free from the outdated ABM Treaty. . . . Missile defense is an urgent national priority."[14] The administration also bolstered its congressional support through other policies, including increased U.S. support for Taiwan and broad NATO expansion to include seven countries from the former Soviet bloc in Central and Eastern Europe. These actions reinforced support for the military operations associated with the broader war on terror.

Defense Policy and Military Force

The scope and nature of the campaigns in Afghanistan mirrored broader strategic efforts undertaken by the United States in the post–World War II era, even though the battlefield tactics integrated the latest technology and military innovations. Since World War II, U.S. security policy has consistently revolved around the use of military alliances and coalitions. Noted Cold War historian John Lewis Gaddis contends that this trend began during the early period of the Cold War as the Truman and Eisenhower administrations understood that U.S. capabilities might not be enough to counter the Soviet Union. Instead, "the United States would also need the manpower reserves and economic resources of the major industrialized non-communist states."[15] Eisenhower's Secretary of State, John Foster Dulles, even stated that security arrangements had greater importance than nuclear deterrence and that such alliances were the "cornerstone of security for the free nations."[16]

The majority of military coalitions deployed by successive U.S. administrations were "coalitions of the willing." Rather than develop formal alliance systems, American presidents often chose to develop informal coalitions of those nations willing to bandwagon with the United States on a specific issue or against a particular threat. Even formal treaty alliances such as the

North Atlantic Treaty Organization had enormous flexibility in terms of specific operations and worked on the principle of internal coalitions.[17] This strategy minimized leadership issues and problems associated with mission scope. Such coalitions of the willing generally increased the effectiveness of the U.S.-led arrangements, although not all problems were eliminated.[18] Successful examples of such coalitions included the grand coalition of the first Gulf War and the succession of NATO-led operations in the Balkans.

The success or failure of coalitions of the willing revolves around the role and importance of U.S. leadership.[19] As G. John Ikenberry points out, leadership in the international arena is really about "power": "To exercise leadership is to get others to do things that they would not otherwise do."[20] Throughout the Cold War period, the United States exercised considerable hard and soft power in such a manner as to both attract and coerce allies through a combination of rewards and punishments.[21]

The military operations of the first administration of George W. Bush reflected this preference for coalition warfare as a means to ensure U.S. leadership, and to bolster both domestic and international support. The success of the administration's first coalition in Afghanistan, in both military and political terms, bolstered the willingness of the administration to undertake other military operations as part of the broader war on terrorism. It also brought together longstanding trends in American defense strategy and ongoing reforms within the Department of Defense and the broader American security infrastructure.

Second Terms and U.S. Defense Policy

Throughout the twentieth century, presidents who gained a second term often found themselves concentrating more on foreign and security policy than domestic issues. While Congress typically becomes more assertive during the second term, especially following the midterm elections, the president's freedom of action in security matters remains broad. Therefore, successive presidents have endeavored to use their second term to create a historical legacy centered around foreign and security policy. During the 2004 presidential elections, the Bush campaign team endeavored to use the war on terrorism and national security matters as issues toward this trend.

The expanded use of military operations or national security issues during the second term occurs concurrently with a rise in unilateralism, as administrations become less inclined to accept the constraints imposed by coalitions or alliances. For instance, during the Clinton era, U.S. policy toward Iraq became increasingly unilateral in nature, although there was steady military support from the United Kingdom. Meanwhile, military missions in the Balkans confirmed the utility of unilateral action or at least coalitions only of the willing. During the military actions in Bosnia and Kosovo, U.S. military officials faced multiple problems as they sought to plan missions and decide on targets through consensus with the allies.[22] Specifically, U.S. officers asserted that their European allies frequently let political considerations overcome military issues during the day-to-day operations.[23] A National Defense University symposium concluded that "National (parochial) decisions constrained Allied Operations" and that "the constraints imposed on the planning process were the inhibitions of those nations doing the planning."[24]

George W. Bush and U. S. Defense Policy

Even before 9/11, George W. Bush sought to reorient U.S. defense policy away from the post–Cold War tendencies of the two previous administrations. Bush wanted a more efficient and flexible military that focused on the core threats to American interests. Central to this goal was the appointment of Donald Rumsfeld as Secretary of Defense who was given a broad mandate to reform the Department of Defense (DOD) after identifying key needs, capabilities and threats.

Rumsfeld had two main tasks. First, he was asked to transform the military from its Cold War, machine-heavy, conventional-war orientation to a more flexible and adaptive structure that incorporated the increasing information advantages that the United States possessed. Second, Rumsfeld was ordered to restore civilian authority over a Pentagon that many analysts perceived had become "too cautious . . . during the Clinton years" as a result of the Powell Doctrine.[25]

Once in office, Rumsfeld achieved an odd mixture of success and failure. On one hand, he aggressively pursued the elimination of unneeded or redundant weapons systems and procedures within the Pentagon. On the other hand, his management style alienated many senior officers. While he accomplished his immediate goals, he also became a lighting rod for criticism of the administration, both by domestic groups and within the international community. For instance, Rumsfeld exacerbated tensions between the United States and some of its European allies when on January 22, 2003, he made a series of comments which underlined the administration's policy of trying to develop a coalition of willing European states in regards to Iraq:

> Now, you're thinking of Europe as Germany and France. I don't. I think that's old Europe. If you look at the entire NATO Europe today, the center of gravity is shifting to the east. And there are a lot of new members. And if you just take the list of all the members of NATO and all of those who have been invited in recently—what is it? Twenty-six, something like that?—you're right. Germany has been a problem, and France has been a problem.[26]

Security Strategy

Concurrent with the DOD reforms was a parallel initiative through the National Security Council to redefine security policy. On one level, the initiative involved new threat assessments, including a reexamination of the potential harm to national interests from terrorism. Even prior to the terrorist attacks of 11 September 2001, National Security Advisor Condoleezza Rice and CIA Director George Tenet had reevaluated contemporary policy and were in the process of developing new recommendations which placed greater emphasis on the threat posed by international terrorism.[27] Nonetheless, the attacks dramatically reoriented this effort and led to the refocusing of energy into the global campaign against anti-U.S. terrorism. Following the successful overthrow of the Taliban, the administration sought to develop a multifaceted, global campaign against terrorism. Key to the new strategy was the promulgation of the National Security Strategy.

On January 29, 2002, in his State of the Union Address, Bush identified Iran, North Korea and Iraq as members of an "axis of evil." The administration also began to increasingly refer to Iraq as the next logical step in the U.S.-led war on terror. Bush further began to state publicly that he would take preemptive military action.[28] This doctrine of preemption would later be codified in the National Security Strategy.[29] Meanwhile, Bush authorized increases in covert aid to anti-Saddam elements while his national security team worked through the late summer of 2002 to develop specific policy options. Secretary of State Colin Powell emerged as the foremost advocate for building a strong coalition, while Vice President Dick Cheney and Secretary of Defense Donald Rumsfeld argued for immediate action, even if it meant unilateral military strikes. Powell was able to sway the President who used a September 12, 2002 UN speech to launch the diplomatic effort.[30]

Afghanistan

Concurrent with this shift in U.S. defense policy, the shift in importance of the war on terror both within the administration and within the world allowed for unprecedented influence of the DOD in how the Afghanistan conflict would be handled. While efforts to gather a coalition of the willing proved to be successful, how this coalition would be used would seemingly leave U.S. coalition partners out of the limelight. Leadership in the U.N. mandated operation to free Afghanistan from the Taliban and eliminate elements of Al Qaeda would be under U.S. control. This largely diminutive role for the coalition partners would meet with little resistance until the Iraq campaign. Central to U.S. decision making in not utilizing volunteered assets more fully in the campaign rested on the technological sophistication of the weapons that would be utilized and the simple fact that the United States could go it alone.[31]

The military response to the attacks on 9/11 would be called Operation Enduring Freedom. The planning of the operation would account for the difficult history of the terrain. Tommy Franks, the American commander of U.S. Central Command, understood fully that this nation of obstacles cost the Soviet Empire over 14,000 dead and 35,000 wounded as well as a great deal of national pride and stamina.[32] The technological strength of the Soviets over the Afghanistan resistance during their eight-year campaign was muted by the guerrilla tactics faced and the environmental difficulties of operating in the desert and mountainous regions.[33] The southwestern plain is a barren desert while the plain region in the north is grasslands. The other two-thirds of Afghanistan is mountainous.[34]

The Coalition

After the 9/11 attacks, the U.S. had a great deal of support amongst the nations of the world. The quick decision by the Bush administration in both determining the organization responsible, Al Qaeda, and in demanding Taliban cooperation in ending their assistance to the Al Qaeda network served to deepen the pledges of support given to the nation.

This was to be a war against all terrorism, according to Bush administration rhetoric. Afghanistan was only the opening salvo. As such, cooperation in both military and non-military areas was requested. By the opening of combat operation in Afghanistan on October 7, 2001, all of the major powers of the world had indicated their support.[35] In effect, the coalition of the willing model utilized by past presidents was culminated in the campaign in Afghanistan. A problem occurred in that military necessity was allowed to unbalance political considerations in how that coalition would be utilized.

Military Campaign

The harsh environment involved, as well as political considerations led General Franks to prefer an air campaign of bombardment of key strategic positions backed by Special Forces operations and utilizing the indigent anti-Taliban Northern Alliance that had occupied about 20 percent of the country.[36] The goal of this strategy was to prevent a repeat of the mistakes of past attempts. The lesson from the Soviet experience in Afghanistan was to work with the internal resistance movements and avoid getting locked into a full-scale ground invasion.

In order to accomplish this task, the multinational force utilized a vast arsenal of combat and logistical support platforms capable of sustaining around the clock air coverage in the region. By coordinating efforts across the political-military spectrum, multiple fronts could be open simultaneously preventing the Taliban and Al-Qaeda forces from gaining an initiative without needing a full-scale ground invasion.[37]

Air platforms such as the B-1, B-2, B-52, Tomahawk cruise missiles, AC-130 gun ships, as well as various fighter/bombers and unmanned aerial vehicles allowed for the precision targeting of over 70 percent of targets struck within the campaign.[38] When combined with small elite forces of U.S. troops, virtually all command and control abilities of the Taliban leadership were neutralized by October 20, 2001, some two weeks after the beginning of the air campaign. On December 22, 2001 an interim Afghan government was set up. On May 2, 2003 Secretary of Defense Donald Rumsfeld announced the end of combat operations in Afghanistan.

How Useful Was the Military Coalition?

The limited number of ground troops needed for the campaign combined with the large technological lag of U.S. allies to U.S. capabilities limited the usefulness of the alliance. While a great deal of political support was necessary, defense decision-makers in the American government preferred to minimize the sharing of command and control functions of the campaign. From past experience, American commanders preferred a more utilitarian method of operation. The consensus style of decision-making that encapsulated European military thinking, particularly NATO, was viewed as too slow for American doctrine and placed too many constraints on the effective use of force.[39]

Also at issue was the technological gap between U.S. and non-U.S. forces. Since the end of World War II, the United States has consistently outspent its European allies at all levels of defense spending. For example, in 2001 the United States spent 85 percent more on defense than the combination of its allies.[40] Both in quantity and quality, U.S. spending over an extended period of time has decreased the gap of interoperability amongst the Western allies.[41] The Secretary General of NATO, Lord Robertson has referred to his own organization as "a military pygmy" referring to the widening gap in capabilities.[42] In an op-ed piece in the New York Times, Thomas Friedman succinctly put it:

> As a result, we are increasingly headed for a military apartheid within NATO: America will be the chef who decides the menu and cooks all the great meals, and the NATO allies will be the busboys who stay around and clean up the mess and keep the peace—indefinitely.[43]

The United Kingdom was the only consistently interoperable force pledged.[44] While the international pledged support to the cause was high, the usefulness of the units involved was significantly lower than what was available in U.S. or U.K. arsenals. The United Kingdom was willing to release command and control to the United States and provided a substantial air and sea package of air-refueling support, reconnaissance, heavy lift and a carrier task force. In addition, the United Kingdom and the United States have a significant history of combined operations.[45] For these reasons, with the exception of a few key capabilities, the United States did not desire or request substantial military assistance from the coalition with the exception of the United Kingdom.

Lesson Learned and Political Implications

From the standpoint of the U.S. military, Operation Enduring Freedom was an overwhelming success. The combination of an overwhelming U.S. force with the political backing of the world at large proved to be a potent combination for the tasking at hand. This lesson would be carried forward to the campaign in Iraq. However, there was a political cost in minimizing the participation of the coalition in the operation. For instance, the French offer of a significant intervention force was rebuffed by the Bush administration and led to a great deal of embarrassment for the Chirac government.[46] In the end, coalition members knew full well that the United States did not need nor necessarily want help.

Perhaps the lesson with the most impact for the future was one forgotten. On the campaign trail in 2000, Bush expressed his view of how the nation should act: "If we are an arrogant nation, they'll view us that way, but if we are a humble nation, they'll respect us."[47] Afghanistan seemed to bring perceptions of this arrogance to light for the world. However U.S. power may be defined, its problem is not American arrogance as much as it is its overwhelming presence on the international stage.[48]

Afghanistan Security: U.S. Concerns

The primary concern for the Bush administration regarding Afghanistan is improving security and reconstruction efforts. As part of this overall plan, the continued hunt for Taliban and Al Qaeda members will be continued. For the second term of the Bush administration, the capture of Usama bin Laden could play an important role in substantiating the continued war on terror as well as relieving the international pressure associated with the back lash of the Iraq conflict. However, a return to wide spread violence or the collapse of the newly elected Karzai administration could back peddle American prestige further than it has already fallen.[49]

The structure of the postwar security relies on (1) the continuation of Operation Enduring Freedom; (2) The success of the International Security Assistance Force;[50] (3) The training and equipping of an Afghan National Army; (4) The training of national guard and police units.[51] Furthering international cooperation along these lines will serve the United States well in both preventing the collapse of Afghanistan and in maintaining strong ties with its Allies in these trying times.

Concurrently, massive relief and reconstruction efforts are being tackled by both the United States and Coalition members. In March of 2004, International donors met in Berlin to pledge their financial support to this goal. Of the US$27.5 billion thought needed for the next several years, some US$11.1 billion had been pledged.[52] It is with successful reconstruction and relief efforts that the security situation and the ultimate success of the Bush administration policy in Afghanistan will be successful in the next term.

Iraq

In the lead up to the beginning of military operation against Iraq on March 19, 2003, the United States had been under considerable pressure from the international community. The impact of the 9/11 attacks on U.S. policy made the United States much more willing to be proactive on the world stage. Beginning with the State of the Union address in January of 2002, the Bush administration demonstrated an interest in regime change in Iraq by including Iraq in Bush's now famous Axis of Evil speech.[53] The process of developing a coalition for this new campaign encountered stiff resistance.

It is interesting to note that the success in Afghanistan without large military contributions by America's allies can be viewed as having a negative impact on the ability of the United States to form a coalition for regime change in Iraq. It has been said that the quick and decisive victory in Afghanistan brought to the political forefront the capacity and willingness of the U.S. military machine to operate without substantial help from the world community. The willingness of the Bush administration to utilize this capacity created fears of a growing U.S. unilateralism. The post–Cold War compliancy appeared to be replaced with one of engagement and preemption. The only superpower seemed to view the world as friend or foe and had the capacity and willingness to act upon this new American Grand Strategy.[54] In part, this acted to push states into taking staunch positions against removing a dictator that no one should have called a friend.

The run up to the invasion of Iraq provided the catalyst for this increasing fear of American power. The viewpoint difference between many in the world community and the Bush administration was stark. The statement by Deputy Secretary of State Richard Armitage seems to epitomize this idea of American exceptionalism: "We've got influence, power, prestige and clout beyond any nation in the history of the world; it brings forth a certain amount of envy."[55]

However, this is a very different perception than what was felt in the international community. The opinion of many seemed to rest upon the perception of an American administration unwilling to take their opinions and concerns into account. This opinion seemed strongest amongst the nations of Western Europe, which, as Fukuyama put it, were beginning to view opposition to American policies as the chief passion of global politics.[56] Much of this stems from three main points that Fukuyama mentions:

1. Weak states understandably want stronger ones constrained by norms and rules, while the world's sole superpower seeks freedom of action.
2. Like former smokers, [Europe] wants everyone else to experience their painful withdrawal symptoms from sovereignty.
3. Americans confuse their national interests with universal ones. Europeans, by contrast, regard the violent history of the first half of the twentieth century as the direct outcome of the unbridled exercise of national sovereignty.

Part of the reasoning can be found in a certain amount of imperial jealousy amongst weaker states. The other, perhaps in what was viewed as an illegitimate formulation of preemptive doctrine. Again, another reason was for domestic political reasons or economic reasons.[57] At the beginning of the invasion, the United States found itself as having already lost the political battle. It's staunchest ally, the United Kingdom, was suffering political backlash as well. The large coalition formed for the task of tackling Iraq was politically tainted as being coerced or American lapdogs.[58] The invasion of Iraq without the backing of many of the major powers or the United Nations only further exacerbated the opinion that the United States a growing hegemonic bully.

The Network Centric War

As far as the campaign itself is concerned, U.S. doctrine worked superbly and with little or no surprise. American capability soundly destroyed the ability of the Iraqi Army to operate or maneuver. The beginning of the campaign relied heavily on American and Allied air superiority and the introduction of ground forces. The initiation of what was coined "shock and awe" took place on March 21, 2003.

> More than 400 Tomahawk cruise missiles were launched from US and British ships and submarines. Additionally, about 100 air-launch cruise missiles were fired, and 700 precision guided munitions were dropped by coalition aircraft on targets throughout Iraq.[59]

By March 23, Coalition forces had flown some 6,000 sorties over Iraq.

The strategy for the campaign had more to do with decapitating command and control functions of the Iraqi regime in order to send their forces into disarray. In essence, cut off Iraqi units from one another and neutralize them with either air or ground forces. To this effect, U.S. doctrine of Network Centric Warfare worked superbly. Network Centric Warfare is defined as:

> the effective linking or networking of the war fighting enterprise. It is characterized by the ability of geographically dispersed forces to create a high level of shared battlespace awareness that can be exploited via self-synchronization and other network-centric operations to achieve commanders' intent.[60]

From a practical standpoint, it is the mechanism by which a commander can selectively task mission to platform in a rapidly evolving environment. If everyone is on the same page and knows what others are doing, momentum can be built by the shear speed at which decisions can be made and executed. It has been termed as the massing of effect versus the massing of arms. In essence, it is the ability to synchronize effects within the battle space, achieve greater speed in command, and increased effectiveness, survivability, and responsiveness of individual components linked within the network.[61]

Network Centric Warfare is still within the development phase; however it has already been termed the next revolution in military affairs. This transition rests upon three broad based themes.[62] The first is a shift in focus from the platform to the network. By focusing on the needs of a fully networked force, each individual component can be tailored towards fulfilling a specific function within the broader picture. The second theme rests upon viewing individual players within the battlespace as part of a "continuously adapting ecosystem." Much like our natural environment, the battlespace is composed of many parts each affecting the whole. By increasing awareness amongst the parts an asymmetric information advantage is achieved.[63] This in effect acts towards lifting the "fog of war." The final broad theme rests upon how decisions are made to cope with a changing ecosystem.

By the end of major combat operations on May 1, 2003, coalition fighters and bombers had flown about 20,700 sorties of which approx 90 percent of the weapons used were guided.[64] This is in comparison to the 10 percent used in the 1991 campaign. Vice President Cheney commenting on the military victory in Iraq specified several technological advances that helped enable U.S. victory.[65] For example, with only two-thirds of the aircraft deployed in Desert Storm the United States was able to strike twice as many targets. Ten different types of Unmanned Aerial Vehicles ranging from tactical to strategic systems were used. Information sharing at all levels was accomplished using military email servers. Real time targeting photos were sent to bombers already inflight and to ground commanders.

The Iraq Syndrome

Before the dust had settled from the end of major combat operations, the United States came under attack both domestically and abroad for not having a plan for postwar occupation, for not finding WMDs, and more physically, by insurgents. Even at this juncture, the United States was not going to be given the opportunity to fully vindicate its efforts.

The message from Iraq seems to be that "any large scale U.S. intervention abroad is doomed to practical failure and moral iniquity" without the support of the international community and the domestic audience.[66] This Iraq syndrome, whether true or not, will plague future endeavors by this administration or future administrations unless a successful outcome can be managed.

Indeed, the situation is not a new one in the American experience. Over the years clear expectation for American involvement in international conflicts have arisen. To begin, Americans tend to understand war but know little of protracted low-intensity conflicts.[67] The military is viewed as a weapon to be used and then put away. The Vietnam experience left a poor taste in the mouths of many Americans toward long-term occupation duties. Missions of short duration with little national impact have become the expected norm.

A second issue is Americans tend to view international problems in a very black and white fashion. President Bush annunciated this with his "you're with us or against us" statement. America's allies have tended to have a broader view. The unconventional conflicts of the post 9/11 era have left areas of gray that have limited international and domestic support for military action.

One final issue is that Americans expect quick and simple decisions to often complex problems that may or may not have a solution. While these three issues are not the end all for limitations on American military affairs, problems begin to arise when facts on the ground do not add up to the rhetoric preached. In a world of imperfect information, leaders are destined to face the price of not having the correct knowledge with the correct answers. The audience costs an American president faces for projected international involvement have worked to limit American involvement abroad. As America's stature in the international community has increasingly grown to include an international audience, so have the costs of international commitments.

To sum, the United States is ill-prepared for occupation duties. Its capabilities on the field of battle are unmatched both practically and doctrinally, however its answer to foreign pacification has always relied more on dollars than brawn.[68] Following the Afghanistan model, the United States had hoped for an international peace keeping force and a substantial inflow of reconstruction capital to help rebuild Iraq. However, the force of international troops that were supposed to provide postwar security never materialized.[69] This has left the United States to deal with a growing insurgency and a domestic population that increasingly dislikes the American presence.[70]

While the January 2005 elections in Iraq were a good sign of a possible new future, much is still left to be done. With a new constitution due in August and a new general election scheduled for December, there are significant signposts ahead signifying success or failure.

In the next four years the Bush administration should move the country toward a greater cooperation with its European allies in Iraq regardless of the political cost it may incur. This cooperation should lie along four key considerations:

1. The establishment of an effective government that incorporates the many factions within Iraq. The general election scheduled for December 2005 will be the tell tale sign that will ultimately determine the time line for an eventual American downsizing.

2. The creation of an indigenous self-defense force and police force: no effective government can be formed unless security can be guaranteed.[71] While the number of coalition forces promised to Iraq never materialized, training of the new Iraqi defense force has taken on a more international effort.

3. Providing a substantial influx of aid and debt relief, as well as reconstruction efforts.[72]

4. The securing of borders and oil resources.

Conclusion

It seems improbable that the United States will have to take on a major player militarily in the near future. However, the ability to do so is drastically curtailed by the tempo of current operations. The United States has close to 400,000 troops deployed around the world with Iraq and Afghanistan being the most prominent . . . for the moment.[73] At a force level of near 150,000 troops, Iraq is proving to be a significant drain on the ability of the United States to project force.[74]

The Bush administration has worked hard at increasing the transformation of the military for future conflicts. Doctrinally, it is clear that the United States has the most powerful military around. However, the political ability to effectively deploy the military seemingly rests upon the cusp of success in both Iraq and Afghanistan. This limits the options available to the United States and paradoxically increases the possibility of smaller brushfires occurring. Some recent examples, albeit not that small, include the tensions in Iran and North Korea over nuclear weapons development.[75]

Specifically focused coalitions of the willing appear to be the policy model for future military and reconstruction efforts. However, the usefulness of foreign militaries operating alongside the United States will continue to be an exercise in politics instead of one of need. As defense budgets around the world continue their decline even as U.S. budgets rise, the ability to operate together will continue to shrink. With that, the United States must make a greater effort to not alienate the world around them. In short, the Bush administration, as well as future administrations, must excerpt political necessities while allowing the military the room it needs to do its job.

Notes

1. See L. Fisher, *Presidential War Power* (Lawrence: University Press of Kansas, 1995).
2. U.S., *The Constitution of the United States of America* (1789).
3. See E. Collier, *The War Powers Resolution: Twenty Years of Experience* (Washington, DC: Congressional Research Service, 1994).
4. John Hart Ely, *War and Responsibility* (Princeton, NJ: Princeton University Press, 1993), p. 49.
5. See C. Shoemaker, *The NSC Staff: Counseling the Council* (Boulder, CO: Westview, 1991); Gerry Argyris Andrianopoulos, *Kissinger and Brzezinski: the NSC and the Struggle for Control of U.S. National Security Policy* (New York: St. Martin's, 1991); and Lord Carnes, *The Presidency and the Management of National Security* (New York: Free Press, 1988).
6. C. Lehman, *Making War: The 200-Year-Old Battle Between the President and Congress Over How Americans Go to War* (New York: Scribner's, 1992).
7. D. Adler, and L. George, eds., *The Constitution and the Conduct of American Foreign Policy* (Lawrence: University Press of Kansas, 1996).

8. A. Wildavsky, "The Two Presidencies," in S. Shull, ed., *The Two Presidencies: A Quarter Century Assessment* (Chicago, IL: Nelson-Hall, 1991), pp. 11–25.

9. Ibid., pp. 14–17.

10. M. Logan, "Elite Analysis of Democracies' International Policy," *Perspectives on Political Science* 29(1) (2000), p. 5.

11. See, for instance, E. Keynes, *Undeclared War: Twilight of Constitutional Power* (University Park: Pennsylvania State University Press, 1982).

12. G. Silverstein, *Imbalance of Power: Constitutional Interpretation and the Making of American Foreign Policy* (New York: Oxford University, 1996).

13. Bob Stump, House Armed Services Committee, Hearing on Missile Defense Policy (19 July 2001), quoted in Congressional Statements on Missile Defense and Nuclear Weapons Policy, online at http://www.ceip.org/files/projects/npp/resources/Congressnukesnmd.htm.

14. Senator James Inhofe, Press Release (1 May 2001), quoted in Congressional Statements on Missile Defense and Nuclear Weapons Policy, online at http://www.ceip.org/files/projects/npp/resources/Congressnukesnmd.htm.

15. John Lewis Gaddis, *Strategies of Containment: A Critical Appraisal of Postwar American National Security Policy* (New York: Oxford University Press, 1982), p. 152.

16. John Foster Dulles, "Policy for Security and Peace," *Foreign Affairs* 32 (April 1954), pp. 355–357.

17. Tom Lansford, *All for One: Terrorism, NATO and the United States* (Aldershot: Ashgate, 2002), pp. 60–62.

18. Mark Schissler, *Coalition Warfare: More Power or More Problems?* (Newport: U.S. Naval War College, 1993).

19. For an examination of theories on international leadership, see David P. Rapkin, ed., *World Leadership and Hegemony* (Boulder, CO: Lynne Rienner, 1990).

20. G. John Ikenberry, "The Future of International Leadership," *Political Science Quarterly* 111(3) (Fall 1996), p. 388.

21. Hard power is "a country's economic and military ability to buy and coerce" while soft power is "the ability to attract through cultural and ideological appeal"; Joseph S. Nye, Jr., "Redefining the National Interest," *Foreign Affairs* 78(4) (July/August 1999), p. 24. Nye argues that in the post– Cold War "information age soft power is becoming more compelling than ever before"; ibid., p. 25.

22. Suzanne Daley, "NATO Quickly Gives the U.S. All the Help That It Asked," *The New York Times*, October 5, 2001.

23. See Wesley Clark, *Waging Modern War: Bosnia, Kosovo, and the Future of Combat* (Washington, DC: Public Affairs, 2001).

24. Institute for Strategic Studies, "After Kosovo: Implications for U.S. and Coalition Warfare–Executive Summary" (Fort McNair: NDU, 1999).

25. Vernon Loeb and Thomas Ricks, "Rumsfeld's Style, Goals Strain Ties in Pentagon," *Washington Post*, October 16, 2002, p. A1.

26. Donald Rumsfeld, "News Transcript: Secretary Rumsfeld Briefs at Foreign Press Center," Department of Defense News Transcripts, January 22, 2003.

27. Bob Woodward, *Bush at War* (New York: Simon & Schuster, 2002), pp. 3–4.

28. In the speech, Bush declared that "I will not wait on events, while dangers gather. I will not stand by, as peril draws closer and closer. The United States of America will not permit the world's most dangerous regimes to threaten us with the world's most destructive weapons"; George W. Bush, "The President's State of the Union Address" (January 29, 2002), online at http:// www.whitehouse.gov/news/releases/2002/01/20020129-11.html.

29. Specifically, the new strategy document notes: "While the United States will constantly strive to enlist the support of the international community, we will not hesitate to act alone, if necessary, to exercise our right of self defense by acting preemptively against such terrorists, to prevent them from doing harm against our people and our country"; U.S. National Security Council, *The National Security Strategy of the United States* (September 17, 2002), online at http://www.whitehouse.gov/nsc/nss.html.

30. Woodward, pp. 334–335.

31. Lansford, *All For One*, 2002.

32. Lester W. Grau and Ali Ahmad Jalali, "The Soviet-Afghan War: Breaking the Hammer and Sickle," as viewed at www.vfw.org on January 1, 2005.

33. General (Ret) Mohammad Yahya Nawroz and Lester W. Grau, "The Soviet War in Afghanistan: History and Harbinger of Future War," in *Military Review* (Sept/Oct 1995).

34. Center for Army Lessons Learned (CALL), Handbook No. 02–8 "Operation Enduring Freedom: Tactics, Techniques, and Procedures," *U.S. Army*, p. 5.

35. Lansford, *All For One*, 2002.

36. "Operation Enduring Freedom and the Conflict in Afghanistan: An Update,"*International Affairs & Defense Section House of Commons Library* (Oct 2001).

37. "Operation Enduring Freedom-Afghanistan," as viewed at globalsecurity.org on January 15, 2005.

38. Joseph Fitchett, "High Tech Weapons Change the Dynamics and the Scope of the Battle," *International Herald Tribune*, December 28, 2001.

39. For example, a 1999 piece quoting General Clark speaking on NATO decision-making during the Kosovo air campaign as saying "the alliance was hamstrung by competing political and military interests that may have prolonged the conflict"; William Drozdiak, "War Efforts Restrained by Politics," *The Washington Post*, July 20, 1999.

40. *U.S.A. Today*, "Military Weakness Threatens Enlarged NATO," November 20, 2002.

41. Steven Erlanger, "Military Gulf Separates U.S. and European Allies," *New York Times* March 16, 2002 A few of the short falls identified in *Operation Allied Force*, the air campaign over Kosovo, included precision-guided munitions, laser-designator capability, heavy lift, night vision, secure interoperable communications, high-fidelity identification friend or foe systems, electronic warfare capabilities, air defense threat warning systems, and intelligence collection and dissemination. "Kosovo" Lessons Learned from Operation Allied Force," *Congressional Research Service*, November 19, 1999.

42. Steven Erlanger, "U.S. Officials Try Assure Europeans on NATO," in *The New York Times*, February 3, 2002.

43. Thomas L. Friedman, "The End of NATO?" in *The New York Times*, February 3, 2002.

44. For a review of the U.K.–U.S. relationship, see John Drumell, *A Special Relationship: Anglo-American Relations in the Cold War and After* (London: Palgrave, 2000).

45. Lansford, *All For One*, 2002.

46. Ibid.

47. As viewed in Joseph S. Nye, *The Paradox of American Power: Why the World's Only Superpower Can't go it Alone* (Oxford, New York: Oxford University Press, 2002).

48. Timothy Garton Ash, "The Peril of Too Much Power," *New York Times*, April 9, 2002.

49. Hamid Karzai was elected on October 9, 2004 in what was largely regarded as an orderly event. Parliamentary elections are scheduled for spring of 2005 but may be postponed until the fall. See Congressional Research Service RS21922, *Afghanistan: Presidential and Parliamentary Elections*. Also see *Afghanistan: From Presidential to Parliamentary Elections, International Crisis Group Asia Report 88*, November 23, 2004.

50. For more information on the ISAF see Anthony Davis, "Afghanistan: Stability in View," in *Jane's* December 14, 2001 or "International Security Assistance Force-ISAF4," at globalsecurity.org.

51. See "Afghanistan: Post-War Governance, Security, and U.S. Policy," *Congressional Research Service*, December 28, 2004.

52. Ibid.

53. President George W. Bush, "The State of the Union Address," January 29, 2002.

54. Peter Slevin, "The Word at the White House: Bush Formulates His Brand of Foreign Policy," *The Washington Post*, June 23, 2002.

55. Glenn Kessler, "Diplomatic Gap Between U.S., Its Allies Widens," *Washington Post*, September 1, 2002.

56. Francis Fukuyama, "U.S. vs. Them: Opposition to American policies must not become the chief passion in global politics," *The Washington Post*, September 11, 2002.

57. For example, Sabrina Tavernise, "Oil Prize, Past and Present, Ties Russia to Iraq," *New York Times*, October 17, 2002.

58. Sarah Anderson, Phyllis Bennis, and John Cavanagh, "Coalition of the Willing or Coalition of the Coerced: How the Bush Administration Influences Allies in its War on Terror," *Institute for Policy Studies*, February 6, 2003.

59. U.S. Department of Defense News Briefing, March 22, 2003.

60. VAdm Arthur K. Cebrowski, U.S.N., and John J. Garstka, "Network Centric Warfare: Its Origin and Future," Proceedings of the Naval Institute 124(1) (January, 1998), pp. 28–35.

61. Network Centric Warfare: Department of Defense Report To Congress (July 27, 2001).

62. Vice Admiral Arthur K. Cebrowski, U.S. Navy, and John J. Garstka, "Network-Centric Warfare," *Proceedings* (January 1998).

63. John J. Garstka, "Network Centric Warfare: An Overview of Emerging Theory," Phalanx 33:4 (December 2000).

64. U.S. Department of Defense press briefing, May 9, 2003.

65. Remarks by the Vice President to the Heritage Foundation, *Office of the Vice President* (May 1, 2003). Available online at http://www.whitehouse.gov/news/releases/2003/05/20030501-9.html.

66. Lawrence Freedman, "Rumsfeld's Legacy: The Iraq Syndrome?" *The Washington Post*, January 9, 2005.

67. Sam C. Sarkesian, John Allen Williams, and Stephen J. Cimbala, *U.S. National Security: Policymakers, Processes, and Politcs* 3d ed. (Boulder, CO: Lynne Rienner Publishers, Inc., 2002).

68. Gen. Wesley Clark, "America's Virtual Empire," *Washington Monthly*, November 2003.

69. Michael Gordan, "Catastrophic Succes: The Strategy to Secure Iraq did not Foresee a Second War," *The New York Times*. October 19, 2004.

70. Anthony Cordesman, "The Developing Iraqi Insurgency: Status at End-2004," *CSIS* December 22, 2004, Working Draft.

71. Part of the insurgency currently occurring is the fault of U.S. authorities completely disbanding the Iraqi military after the fall of the regime. These out of work soldiers turned to what they know how to do.

72. While this is the largest aid effort the United States has undertaken since the Marshall plan, it is not enough. Greater international assistance is necessary. Further, the insurgency has hampered reconstruction efforts and has forced the withdrawal of various aid groups from the country.

73. "World Wide Military Deployments," *GlobalSecurity.org* as of January 18, 2005.

74. Troop levels have been boosted for the upcoming elections. See "Pentagon Boosts Forces in Iraq to Highest Level," *MSNBC*, December 2, 2004.

75. "N. Korea, Iran: Twin Nuke Troubles," *CBS News*, September 11, 2004. Also see Unclassified Report to Congress on the Acquisition of Technology Relating to Weapons of Mass Destruction and Advanced Conventional Munitions, July 1, through December 31, 2003, *CIA*.

Chapter Twelve

Problematic Policies Toward the Middle East

Ann M. Lesch

Two arguments are frequently made about second-term presidencies. The first is that the president may have exhausted his agenda and his personnel and therefore not be able to project and implement new ideas and new approaches. A second, contrasting argument is that second-term presidents may suffer from hubris and overreach themselves, with negative consequences for their policies as well as their political legacy.

President George W. Bush shows no evidence of having exhausted his agenda. Indeed, in both the domestic and foreign policy arenas he is vigorously promoting new policies, on the unstated assumption that his mandate is stronger now than after the first election. However, he has reconstructed his policy-making team in a way that fails to add new faces. Instead, he is recycling his previous advisors in order to tighten his control over the policy-making process.

Concerning the second argument, one could argue that the Bush presidency already suffered from hubris during the first term and that the declared aims of the second term are even more expansive domestically and internationally. Given the president's apparent lack of intellectual curiosity, his sense of self-righteousness, and his lack of self-reflection,[1] the consequences of such hubris could further inflame the crises in the Middle East and in relations with U.S. allies, not to speak of the Korean peninsula and elsewhere in East Asia. Despite the possibility of some forward movement on the Israeli-Palestinian front, the tensions in the wider Middle East are unlikely to abate and, if U.S. policy does not alter meaningfully, they are likely to deepen.

The First Term

U.S. actions during the first term had a highly polarizing impact internationally. Although Washington no longer confronted the Cold War, senior officials remained focused on maintaining the United States' preeminent role internationally. They asserted the U.S. right to act without restraint in a unipolar world. In that regard, National Security Council advisor

Condoleezza Rice emphasized that the "United States has a special role in the world and should not adhere to every international convention and agreement."[2] The administration's rejection of the Kyoto Treaty to control global warming, the treaty of the International Criminal Court, and canceling of the Anti-Ballistic Missile Treaty with Russia are merely three of the most publicized cases of its refusal to abide by international agreements. The assumption was that the United States' unmatched economy and vast armed forces would enable Washington to go-it-alone, managing its affairs in splendid isolation. (That was in stark contrast to the first Bush administration's concept in 1991 of a "new world order.")

Until 9/11, the dominant impulse was isolationism, notably, withdrawal from involvement in the Balkans and from active diplomacy in the Palestinian/Israeli arena. Iraq was the key exception. As early as the first meeting of the National Security Council in January 2001, destabilizing and potentially overthrowing the Iraqi regime was the centerpiece for the White House.[3] In contrast, little attention was paid to al-Qaida during those initial months. National Security Council director Condoleezza Rice let Cabinet-level coordination of anti-terror efforts lapse, and the president did not activate any special measures when the CIA warned him in August 2001 that al-Qaida was planning attacks on U.S. soil.

The 9/11 attacks on the United States' financial and political-military capitals transformed the mission of the Bush presidency, while deepening its unilateralist assumptions and approach. One can even say that the administration only acquired a real foreign policy mission at that time. The president's biblical language—"with us or against us"—underscored that mission and reinforced Bush's dichotomized view of the world. The administration quickly struck at a logical target: Taliban-ruled Afghanistan, which harbored Osama bin Laden's training camps and al-Qaeda's headquarters. However, that was merely the initial target in a world-wide and unending "war" against "terror," an unseen but ubiquitous enemy. Suddenly, essentially nationalist and ethnic conflicts (e.g., in Chechnya, the Basque nationalists in Spain, Israel/Palestine, and Uighur nationalists in China) morphed into components of that war on terror, a perspective that legitimized military (rather than politico-diplomatic) actions by those governments against dissident groups.

Instead of withdrawing from this hostile world environment, the United States—the sole superpower—would fight on behalf of "civilized" values, on its own, if necessary. This interventionist approach suited Vice President Dick Cheney and Secretary of Defense Donald Rumsfeld, who articulated the doctrine of "pre-emption", meaning the right to attack before the enemy has the capacity to strike. They brushed aside Secretary of State Colin L. Powell's efforts to build diplomatic coalitions, cooperate with the United Nations, and find non-military means to contain North Korea, Iran, Iraq, and other potentially hostile countries.

The doctrine of preemption was also applied to Iraq, their decade-long nemesis. And this doctrine was linked to the war on terror, which provided a rationale for ousting the Iraqi regime. Since Saddam Hussein's government could not be blamed for 9/11 and had no credible links to al-Qaeda, the definition of the war on terror had to be altered in order to encompass regime-change in Iraq. Therefore the presence (or potential for) weapons of mass destruction (WMD) was added to the definition of the war on terror, focusing on the risk that WMD might be employed by the regime—or transferred to a terrorist group—in order to attack the United States. The United States would then have the right to launch a "preventive" or "pre-emptive" attack on the WMD-deploying country. Moreover, at least some policymakers—notably Paul Wolfowitz of the Department of Defense—viewed removing Saddam Hussein's regime in the context of "liberating" the Middle East from dictators: Once the United States would transform Iraq into a democracy, neighboring countries would also be transformed politically, whether by example or by force. This, in turn, would enhance the United States' strategic control over the Middle East and Central Asia, underpinned by a network of U.S. military bases and politico-military alliances.

The Likely Impact of Changes in Personnel

Changes in personnel at the senior ranks in the administration may well have a significant impact upon its foreign policy orientation in the Middle East and elsewhere. The departure of Secretary of State Powell is the most obvious change. Powell was the good-soldier who nonetheless managed to mitigate some aspects of the White House's unilateralism through his efforts to keep alliances from fraying and work toward negotiated solutions in Iraq and Israel/Palestine. He was a voice of caution in behind-the-scenes policy debates. We now know that, on the day that he resigned, he reiterated his longstanding warning to President Bush and British Prime Minister Tony Blair that "we don't have enough troops [in Iraq]. We don't control the terrain."[4]

Powell's departure means that the government has lost a reasoned voice expressing the concerns of career diplomats and career military officers. With his departure, the cabinet is likely to speak with one voice. That fits the style of presidency promoted by Bush: Policy is run out of the White House, with the cabinet serving as a "chorus of support for the White House policies and [providing] technical expertise for implementing" those policies.[5] That approach had worked, during the first term, in regard to socio-economy policy, once Paul O'Neill and Christie Whitman were removed from the cabinet. In national security and foreign policy, however, the administration had spoken with loud, often-clashing voices (although mostly from a hawkish perspective).

The president intended to end that dissonance during the second term. Shifting Condoleezza Rice from the National Security Council to the Department of State, with her like-minded assistant Stephen Hadley stepping into her former position, strengthened the White House's control over the national security apparatus and its global "message." (Making Karen Hughes, the president's close aide and former press officer, Under Secretary of State for Public Diplomacy further underlined the focus on projecting one message.) Rice, in her initial travels to Europe, the Middle East, and Asia, remained on target in her calls for spreading freedom: whether religious freedom in China (where she attended a church service), political freedom in Egypt (to which she canceled her planned visit, when a leading democratic activist was jailed),[6] women's rights in Saudi Arabia (about which she called for women to have the right to vote in the municipal elections), labeling North Korea an "outpost of tyranny," or trying to isolate Syria by withdrawing the U.S. ambassador after former Lebanese Prime Minister Rafik Hariri's assassination in February. Rice also demanded that Syrian troops withdraw from Lebanon, which occurred for a constellation of reasons by May. Rice was silent, however, about human rights violations in Libya, where the United States ended sanctions after Mu'ammar Qaddafi ended its WMD program, and about democratization in Pakistan and Uzbekistan, close U.S. allies in the "war on terror." Concerning Pakistan, Rice contented herself by noting cryptically that President Musharraf had "come a long way."[7]

Other appointments underlined the uniformity of policy and ideology fostered by the Bush administration. White House counsel Alberto Gonzales' appointment as Attorney General placed in a pivotal position the proponent of holding detainees indefinitely, without access to lawyers or courts. Gonzales also authored controversial presidential findings that claimed that anything short of permanent physical disablement was not torture, maintained that the Geneva Conventions do not apply to the "war on terror," and argued that the president has the right to waive anti-torture laws and international treaties that protect Prisoners of War. (When he was legal aide to then Governor Bush, Gonzalez had been a strong proponent of the death penalty.)

The new Secretary for Homeland Security, Michael Chertoff, had previously oversaw the detention of foreign nationals in his capacity as assistant attorney general. Despite initial publicity over these security "coups," virtually all these persons were detained (and often deported) for immigration violations, not for security offenses.

Porter Goss, moving from chair of the House intelligence committee to director of intelligence, ensured that the White House would tame the CIA. This was especially the Vice President's concern, as Cheney had mistrusted the intelligence reports on Iraq ever since the CIA assured the first Bush administration, in 1990, that Iraq would not invade Kuwait. Goss's committee had denounced the CIA as "dysfunctional,"[8] words that were echoed by Bush in his rejection of the CIA's National Intelligence assessments. With the appointment of Goss, the White House guaranteed a political housecleaning of the CIA staff and ensured that it would receive only the information and conclusions that Bush wanted to hear.

This was reinforced by the appointment of John D. Negroponte, then Ambassador to Iraq, as the director of the new national intelligence office that would oversee the CIA, Department of Defense, and other intelligence bodies, and would handle the daily intelligence briefing for the president. Negroponte, as ambassador to Honduras in the early 1980s, had managed the Contra operations against the Sandinista government in Nicaragua, working closely with the controversial General Alvares (head of the notorious death squads) and used back channels to assist CIA director George Casey's efforts to circumvent the Congressional ban on aid to the Contras.

Two other appointments were equally controversial: those of John Bolton to be Ambassador to the United Nations and Paul Wolfowitz to be president of the World Bank. Bolton, the abrasive former Under Secretary of State for Arms Control, had exacerbated tensions with North Korea, alienated Secretary of State Powell, and angered career officers who refused to bend their findings to his ideology. While Vice President Cheney argued that putting this White House loyalist in a key diplomatic post would enhance the United States' ability to force changes in the United Nations,[9] there was concern that his combative style could undermine Rice's efforts to be more inclusive and to reach out to recently alienated allies. Even President Bush, during his post-election trip to Europe, sought to soft-peddle disagreements concerning Iraq and to meet at length with the leaders of Germany, France, and Russia, who had sharply criticized U.S. policy in the Middle East and elsewhere.

Wolfowitz's appointment to head the 184-member World Bank was equally startling, but had more intrinsic logic. Although Wolfowitz was identified with the ideologically driven message pressed by the neoconservatives in the Middle East, he had played a subtle role as ambassador to Indonesia in the early 1980s in fostering economic openness, promoting agriculture, and criticizing graft. While, behind the scenes, he sought political reform, he only called for political openness in his last public statement as ambassador. It is too soon to tell whether his propensity toward linking economic and political development, through long-term institution-building programs will come to the fore, or rather, his propensity toward stressing U.S. priorities and instituting a system of rewards and punishments for U.S. allies and enemies.

Policy Toward Israel/Palestine

During the first term, Bush's bible-based approach to the Middle East prioritized Israeli political claims over Palestinian claims. The president was cool to the Mitchell Plan of May 2001 and to the Road Map articulated by the diplomatic Quartet, and was not interested in persuading Israel to undertake proposed confidence-building measures (CBMs), whereas he pressed the Palestinian Authority (PA) to implement CBMs. While supporting the idea of a Palestinian state, Bush ignored the territorial issue. During the spring of 2004, in an exchange of letters with Israeli Prime Minister Ariel Sharon, the president explicitly endorsed the presence of nearly all the Jewish settlements and Israel's permanent control over 60 percent of the

West Bank and all of Jerusalem. In other words, a Palestinian state would be formed only in the Gaza Strip and in non-contiguous enclaves comprising at most 40 percent of the West Bank. Meanwhile, the president insisted that the Palestinians institute political reforms and curb the power of PA President Yasir Arafat by appointing a prime minister, cutting back on the multiple security forces, and instituting measures to ensure accountability and transparency in the PA's finances.

Most importantly, following 9/11, the Bush administration viewed the conflict through the lens of the war on terror. It accepted Prime Minister Ariel Sharon's definition of Arafat as the #1 terrorist, agreed to Israel's military reoccupation of the West Bank in 2002 as an act of self-defense against acts of terror against Israeli civilians, and endorsed its construction of the wall separating Israel from the West Bank as a component of the war on terror. From the Israeli government's perspective, this support meant that negotiations on a final peace accord were placed in "formaldehyde": Freezing the peace process would "prevent the establishment of a Palestinian state" much less resolution of the issues of refugees, Jerusalem, and final borders.[10] Although the White House might talk of an eventual Palestinian state, realities on the ground would rule that out.

Arafat's death just after the U.S. elections altered those dynamics, to a degree. The Bush administration—as well as Sharon—had used Arafat's presence as an excuse to avoid addressing fundamental diplomatic issues. The emergence of the moderate politician Mahmoud Abbas, who had long opposed Palestinians' use of violence against Israel and who had chafed under Arafat's personalized rule, meant that the Israeli government had a serious negotiating partner. Bush welcomed the election of the new Palestinian president on January 9, 2005. During the Palestinian transition Bush reiterated his emphasis on "the need for a Palestinian democracy" as the "heart of the matter."[11] In Bush's calculations, democracy and action against terrorism remained key to solving the Israel/Palestinian conflict, rather than pressure on Israel in regard to settlements and borders. (This contrasted with the European approach that negotiations on final status issues should begin immediately and that an Israeli-Palestinian peace was a prerequisite for wider political reform in the region.)

Abbas responded to U.S. and Israeli pressure by employing his security forces to stop militants from firing rockets into Israel as well as negotiating with Hamas to institute a moratorium on attacks inside Israel. Abbas, however, is not in a position to "uproot" or "strike" Hamas and young militants from his Fatah movement, as Israel and the United States have demanded. In his words, "they are part of our people" and must be included politically, rather than excluded.[12] Despite Abbas's efforts to tame militant movements and consolidate his position, Fatah was roundly defeated in the January 2006 legislative council elections, which swept Hamas politicians to power.

Meanwhile, Israeli military incursions into the Gaza Strip and the West Bank continued, as did the destruction of houses in Gaza, the letting of tenders to construct housing on the West Bank, the building of the wall to seal off

Israel from the West Bank, and the expropriation of Palestinian land in Jerusalem and the West Bank. Those actions make it difficult for Abbas to gain public support. Moreover, as negotiations did not resume on long-term political issues, Abbas's credibility was severely undermined. The political power of Abbas and the Fatah old-timers waned: Hamas swept several of the municipal council elections as well as the legislative council elections, largely on an anti-corruption platform, and the young guard in Fatah challenged its elders. Furthermore, Hamas could claim, with considerable accuracy, that its violence caused Sharon to pull settlers and troops out of Gaza in August 2005.

Thus, the signals from the second term are that the U.S. approach will remain too limited to have an impact on the fundamental aspects of the Israel/Palestinian conflict. So long as the administration prioritizes 'terror' and 'democratization' in a diplomatic and political vacuum—while downplaying issues of land, settlements, and statehood, and ignoring the crucial questions of the refugees and Jerusalem—it will be impossible for the Palestinian Authority (PA) to gain credibility, much less stability. Ignoring the nationalist roots of the conflict and the reality of ongoing Israeli military occupation enables Sharon's government to further entrench itself in the West Bank and Jerusalem, and stifle Palestinian aspirations for political and economic independence. So far, the second Bush administration has benefited from the serendipitous departure of Arafat and his replacement by the pliable Abbas.

Absent active U.S. diplomacy that addresses fundamental issues, this opportunity will be lost. Sharon's government will not undertake serious negotiations with the PA without firm U.S. insistence. The PA does not have the strength to undertake those negotiations alone. This will require modification in the administration's stance toward settlements and other final status issues; otherwise, the United States will act not as an honest broker but as the partisan of Sharon. The likelihood of the administration modifying its policies is quite low, given its preexisting sympathy for Israel's policies and its close strategic relationship with Israel. Rice was unable to obtain an unequivocal commitment to a ceasefire from the Israeli and Palestinian governments at the Sharm al-Sheikh summit on February 8 or establish a clear role for the United States as monitor of the disengagement process in Gaza. And, prior to Sharon's April 2005 visit to the United States, Rice admitted that the United States had not "reached closure" on an agreement to freeze settlements.[13] During that visit, whereas Bush cautioned Sharon not to expand controversial settlements such as Ma'aleh Adumim, Sharon explicitly emphasized the importance of that settlement and its strategic link to Jerusalem.[14]

The Situation in Iraq

There is an extraordinary disconnect between the goals and assumptions of the Bush administration and the realities on the ground in Iraq. Secretary of

Defense Donald Rumsfeld, a notable holdover from the first term, derides "naysayers and doubters" and depicts the U.S. fight in Iraq as one of "the battlefields of the global war on terror [which] are everywhere one looks."[15] Former Deputy Secretary of State Paul Wolfowitz continued to view the struggle as a contest for democracy. Even former Secretary of State Powell commented that successful elections in Iraq would turn the situation around and lead to the "ultimate victory, when Iraqis control their own destiny."[16]

Officials no longer refer to the link between Iraq and WMD. The search for WMD ended quietly in December 2004, empty handed. A new link with terrorism has emerged, however, as violence escalates inside Iraq. The National Intelligence Council (NIC)—the CIA's think-tank—stated baldly that Iraq is now a magnet for international terrorist activity, with Iraq replacing Afghanistan as the training ground for the next generation of terrorists. In Iraq, the NIC concluded, terrorists can train, recruit, and enhance their technical skills, in part using weapons caches that U.S. troops left unprotected after they occupied the country.[17] Ironically, al-Qaeda had lacked a presence within Iraq before 9/11; prior to the U.S. invasion, Ansar al-Islam had been contained in a tiny corner of the country, from which it attacked Kurdish targets; and Ansar al-Sunna had been a political-religious movement without an armed wing. Now those three movements have the capacity to attack at will in large sections of the country, not just in the "Sunni triangle." A Christian Iraqi living in Baghdad complained on Christmas eve: "The Americans said they came to fight the terrorists, but the terrorists came when [the Americans] came . . . Both sides destroyed our country."[18]

U.S. forces have never been able to control the situation on the ground, and their potential for doing so eroded sharply in late 2004 and early 2005. When "major combat operations" ended in May 2003, the United States had already failed to secure the country. They did not prevent the looting of government ministry buildings, oil refineries and oil fields, national archives and universities, archeological digs, and even munitions dumps. Rumsfeld's cavalier attitude toward the looting, coupled with Coalition Provisional Authority (CPA) head Paul Bremer's disbanding of the Iraqi army meant that there was no organized Iraqi force to maintain order, whereas hundreds of thousands of discontented, unemployed, and armed men were available to support an insurgency.

The deterioration on the ground was so acute that, by 2005, the U.S. embassy banned the use by U.S. personnel of the ten-mile highway from the Green Zone to the Baghdad airport, and attacks took place inside the heavily guarded Green Zone as well as at its entry points. By October 2004 at least seventy attacks took place daily around the country, a third more than before an interim Iraqi government was established on June 28. (Despite a brief dip following the January 2005 elections, attacks remained thereafter at the level of 50–60 a day.) Of those, a third took place in Baghdad alone, despite interim Prime Minister Iyad Allawi's depiction of Baghdad as "safe" and Bush's assertion that the insurgency was only in "small pockets."[19] For the average Iraqi, this amounts to total insecurity and unbearable day-to-day conditions: lack of electricity, escalating fuel prices, hours waiting at gasoline stations, and untreated sewage in the streets on top of chronic joblessness and the continuous fear of kidnapping or assassination on the way to school or to work.

Military operations by U.S. forces alienate the broad public. During "sweeps" of village houses soldiers punch in doors and ransack cupboards, hooded "informants" identify individuals to be arrested, family members—including women—are taken hostage until the wanted person turns himself in, and detainees are roughed up and even tortured by Iraqi police and U.S. security personnel. The confidential Herrington Report, commissioned by Major General Barbara Fast, concluded that these sweeps "make gratuitous enemies" of people.[20]

The scorched-earth fighting in Falluja in November 2004 destroyed entire blocks in the city. Only 50,000 of the 300,000 residents remained during the invasion; by mid-March 2005, only 60,000 lived there, under night-time curfew and blocked from access to the rest of Iraq. The water, electricity, and telephone systems remained largely unrepaired, and only 40 of 25,000 families had received compensation for property damage.[21] The Iraqi Director of National Intelligence stated bitterly: Falluja is now "an empty city, almost destroyed," from which insurgents have flooded to other cities.[22] Moreover, the U.S. invasion of Falluja triggered mass violence in Mosul. Immediately erupted into mass violence. Armed men controlled the streets and burned government offices and police stations, leading to the collapse of the entire 6,000-man Iraqi police force and compelling the United States to rush troops back to that city of 1.8 million residents, the third largest in Iraq.[23]

These patterns indicate that 'pacification' by the foreign occupier has fueled the insurgency, rather than dampened it down. In January 2005, the aforementioned Iraqi Director of National Intelligence concluded that at least 200,000 Iraqis smuggle weapons, provide safe houses, and serve as part-time fighters alongside more than 40,000 hard-core insurgents. That is double the number of insurgents that U.S. officials had stated and amounts to a total far greater than the 130,000 U.S. troops, who were hastily increased to 150,000 in January 2005. The same Iraqi national intelligence director—who described the loose alliances of convenience among Ba'athists, Abu Musab al-Zarqawi's al-Qaeda affiliate, Ansar al-Islam, Ansar al-Sunna, and other groups—concluded that Washington is in "denial" concerning the breadth and depth of the insurgency.[24]

A key argument used by U.S. officials has been that, once an elected (and therefore legitimate) government and national assembly are in place and once Iraqi police and national guardsmen are trained, U.S. troops will be reduced and the American presence can fade into the background. Bush asserted that, once elections are held, the "myth" will be destroyed that insurgents are fighting a foreign occupation; rather, they will be fighting "the will of the Iraqi people."[25] The January 30, 2005, elections were therefore designed to elect a 275-member national assembly that would write a constitution; by the end of 2005, a referendum would be held on that constitution and then a government would be elected.[26]

However, the United States' scenario has not worked out as planned. The U.S. officials had hoped that some 22 Sunni cities could be reoccupied during the fall of 2004 by means of negotiations with local leaders or, should that fail, by force so that insurgents would be 'evicted' and Iraqi troops would control them prior to the elections. They assumed that, since most residents opposed the bombings and assassinations that accompanied the insurgency, they would welcome having U.S. troops reoccupy these cities. That assumption proved false. Moreover, U.S. troops were spread too thin to reoccupy so many cities at once. Indeed, as soon as troops were removed from one seemingly quiet area (such as Mosul) to quell 'troublemakers' in another city, security deteriorated in the previously pacified region.

Just as Plan A (based on the assumption that Iraq would remain calm after the spring 2003 invasion) was proven false, so has this Plan B proven false. After the interim government was instated in June 2004, violence against Iraqis and foreigners escalated throughout central Iraq and in much of southern Iraq. (Only the Kurdish areas remained relatively quiet, but the U.S. forces' use of a Kurdish battalion to attack Falluja runs the risk of inciting a violent backlash against Kurds living outside Kurdistan.) Interim Prime Minister Allawi's Iraqi National Accord, funded by the CIA since the mid-1990s (when the CIA gave up on Ahmad Chalabi's Iraqi National Congress), lacked legitimacy within the country and Allawi himself lacked the troops to enforce order. Young men joined the police and national guard in search of employment, but found themselves subject to continual attack: car bombs and mortar attacks at recruiting stations, training centers, police stations, and against those on patrol; the assassination of recruits on home leave, of police outside their homes, and of intelligence officers driving to work. In fact, attacks on the fledgling security services increased by more than fifty percent after June 28. And, as noted in Mosul, police desert their posts when threatened and when under direct attack. The only battalion willing to fight alongside U.S. soldiers to reoccupy Arab-populated cities was a Kurdish battalion, rather than battalions with Arab recruits.

Government officials are equally targeted. The governor of Mosul was killed in the summer of 2004, followed by the governor and deputy governor of Baghdad during the winter. Many other deputy governors, police chiefs, judges, and middle-ranked officials have been killed as collaborators with the occupation. Translators, truck drivers, and women who work as maids on bases are equally suspect, not to mention candidates for the election and members of election committees. Other assassinations have reflected political tensions within Iraq, notably the assassination of Shi'i and Kurdish politicians by the largely Sunni insurgents. The murder of a female MP from Allawi's party outside her home in Baghdad on April 27 was the first killing of a recently elected political figure.

The war has had a severely corrupting impact on U.S. soldiers, military intelligence, and prison guards. What was initially thought to be an isolated instance of violence against and humiliation of detainees in Abu Ghraib prison by ill-trained and undisciplined military police is now known to have been a small part of a system legitimized from the top of the Bush administration. This includes White House Counsel Gonzales' assertion that the president was above international law, his redefinition of torture to allow severe beatings, and the presidential finding that he drafted that stated: "I [the president] determine that none of the provisions of [the] Geneva [conventions] apply to our conflict with al-Qaida in Afghanistan or elsewhere throughout the world."[27] They extend to Secretary of Defense Rumsfeld's memorandum of December 2002 (subsequently modified) that authorized harsh interrogation techniques in Guantanamo prison that included using dogs and removing clothes; techniques that had migrated to that prison camp from Afghanistan and that were subsequently encouraged by Guantanamo's commander for use in Iraq to "set conditions for successful interrogations."[28] Torture techniques included leaving the person in a straightjacket or shackles in the sun while hooded, dehydrated, and lying in his own faeces; mock executions, hetero- and homo-sexual abuse, beating detainees on the kidneys and other sensitive places, parading them naked in public areas of the camp, and photographing them while wrapped in Israeli flags.[29] *The Lancet* and the *New England Journal of Medicine* reported that some medical personnel were complicit in this torture, with army doctors and medics reviving beaten detainees, not treating wounds caused by torture unless the detainee cooperated with the investigation, participating with interrogators in the deprivation of sleep and restrictions on food, and falsifying medical records for death certificates.

The fighting conditions have a severely negative impact on American soldiers' morale. While many still express their determination "to do my part here for the global war on terror,"[30] others express disillusionment with the war effort. Isolated from the people in their Humvees, soldiers find the situation incomprehensible and terrifying, and cannot differentiate between "civilians" and "insurgents."

In one striking example, the U.S. military spent $10 million in Abu Ghraib town (a suburb west of Baghdad) to reconstruct the municipality, business center, firehouse, library, youth center, and children's playground. Those buildings were all ransacked and burned as soon as the reconstruction was finished. Even the new computers and air conditioners were stolen from the youth center. Insurgents killed five town councilors and kidnapped two others in Abu Ghraib; they also killed eight national guardsmen.[31] In other places, public works projects cannot even be completed, as contractors flee death threats and armed attacks.

The conditions under which the soldiers fight have not eased their morale. Tours of duty, which normally do not exceed twelve months, are now routinely extended. The government wants to extend the tours of national guardsmen, who now constitute 45 percent of the combat units in Iraq, for up to 24 months, with the possibility of an unlimited number of call-ups. As a result, National Guardsmen worry that the fifteen combat units are nearly "tapped out" and the head of the Army Reserves has expressed concern that the tremendous burden has reduced the reserves to a "broken force."[32] Indeed, in the case of Montana alone, 1,500 of the 3,500 members of the National Guard and most of their helicopters were in Iraq in spring 2005, leaving the governor unable to prepare to fight forest fires or cope with other potential emergencies. With reenlistment in the regular armed forces down and a sharp reduction in the number of volunteers joining the National Guard, the capacity of the armed forces to sustain a 150,000-troop level has become highly questionable.[33]

Moreover, troops complain that many Humvees and trucks are un-armored or insufficiently armored. Some have scrounged for scrap metal with which to reinforce their vehicles; others have appealed to their families at home to send metal strips. Although Rumsfeld's response to these complaints was dismissive during his visit to a base in Kuwait,[34] Army reservists who refused to transport fuel because their trucks had no protective armor were not court-martialed, an implicit recognition that their complaints were valid. This takes place just as the administration's aggressive budget cuts result in a reduction in staff in the Veterans Administration, thereby delaying responses to medical benefits claims, as well as a reduction in qualified medical personnel in the field at a time when there are very severe injuries and substantial post-injury trauma.[35]

Implications for U.S. Policy in Iraq

During 2004 and into early 2005, the mood of pessimism increased in the CIA, Defense Intelligence Administration, State Department, and Army officer corps. The CIA termed the actions in Iraq "a disaster" that was resulting in the United States "digging the hole deeper and deeper."[36] The July 2004 National Intelligence Assessment could not develop any "rosy" scenario; its worst case scenario involved the country dissolving into civil war. The CIA station chief in Baghdad, upon completing his tour of duty, cabled home that the bleak situation at all levels was likely to deteriorate even further unless an effective Iraqi government could be put in place.[37]

Army historian Major Isaiah Wilson III pointed out that the United States had failed to develop a stabilization plan until November 2003, six months after the occupation began. Wilson stressed that the armed forces (and, by implication, the senior policymakers) still did not recognize that they faced a people's war, a nationalist war against a military occupation.[38] Indeed, a planner at the U.S. Army War College commented laconically: "The intensity of nationalism on the part of the Iraqi people" was greater than expected.[39]

Overall, there seems little recognition of how U.S. military operations play into the insurgents' hands—a scenario that the controversial former weapons inspector Scott Ritter depicted bluntly: "The insurgents harassed UN and NGO personnel to the point that they fled the country, which thus required the US to use increasing force to 'restore' order; that in turn generated more anger and more recruits to the insurgency, which led to more violence and more use of force by the US troops."[40] The war, in his vivid language, was like "squeezing jello": "When you attack one place, the fighters slip away and attack elsewhere. US operations therefore serve insurgents' aims of creating chaos and (the insurgents' hope) ultimately forcing out the US contractors, officials, and troops."[41] (In the meantime, thugs and other lawless groups take advantage of the chaos to carjack, kidnap for ransom, and loot.)

These critiques should lead to a fundamental reformulation of the war goals. However, that is not yet in evidence. Bush stuck to the scenario that the Marines could deliver a "severe blow" to the insurgents that would allow the Iraqis to hold "free elections" and transform their society into a full-fledged democracy.[42] Although a senior military officer was sent to Iraq in January 2005 to assess the situation on the ground, published reports indicate that the United States expects to maintain its troop level at the current 150,000 (or no less than 120,000) for at least two years, and to remain on the ground for many more years.

There does not appear to be a Plan C if elections do not calm the situation and if strife among and within the Iraqi political forces escalates. The legitimacy of the elected national assembly and the new government has been called into question by many Iraqis, not only Sunni Arabs or members of Moqtada Sadr's Mahdist Army, but also by average citizens who question rule by politicians who came to power as a result of foreign occupation.[43] In any event, once constitution-writing is underway, serious schisms among the political forces may emerge, with Kurdish claims to autonomy and special rights potentially challenged by Shi'i and Sunni Arabs, with disenfranchised Sunni Arabs continuing to reject the new regime, with differences emerging within the majority Shi'i community, and with secular and feminist voices increasingly marginalized. So far, Iraqi political forces have managed to cobble together a government, after nearly three months' maneuvering, but its ability to function remains questionable. United States involvement is more apt to exacerbate those tensions than manage them, particularly if it takes side on the contentious issues.[44] But the government is unlikely to even agree on whether and when U.S. armed forces should depart, given the uncertainty of whether they could remain in power without that U.S. presence.

There are serious danger signs in Bush's stubbornness, his sense of self-righteousness, and his apparently willful disregard of realities on the ground. These signs are exacerbated by his current effort to ensure that only 'loyalists' lead the CIA and State Department as they already do in the Department of Defense and the White House. Former President Jimmy Carter's National Security Council advisor for the Middle East William Quandt commented in the run-up to the November 2004 elections: The president must *want* good intelligence; these actions indicate that Bush deliberately does not want to anchor decisions in fact.[45]

Bush insists that he is fighting for democracy and moral values, which he alleges al-Qaeda and Iraqi insurgents "hate." But the issue is not one of Arabs or Muslims hating freedom and democracy; rather, they hate U.S. policies in the region. Moreover, the administration's assertions of the right to "transform" a wide range of Middle Eastern regimes (notably Iran and Syria) increases Arab cynicism about the true purpose of Washington's claim to spread democracy. Without a serious effort to resolve the Israeli/Palestinian conflict, without an exit strategy in Iraq, and without an end to U.S. detention policies that challenge international conventions, U.S. claims to uphold moral values ring false. The United States also lacks the means to carry out its expansive ambitions. With the wars in Iraq and Afghanistan costing $1 billion a week, with virtually no allied support in Iraq,[46] and with the United States ignoring the strategic and economic interests of its major allies, the Bush administration is deepening its isolation globally as well as regionally. Israel may be ready to attack Iranian nuclear weapons sites on behalf of the United States and itself, but no other ally supports those expansionist war aims. And there appears to be no willingness on the part of the U.S. administration to turn to its allies and the United Nations in meaningful ways to institute policies based on internationally supported norms and legal principles.

Bush galvanized popular fear of Iraq based on false assertions related to WMD and he continues to call for "perseverance" based on false assumptions. He does not appear able to admit that he must scale down his aspirations globally, much less within Iraq. But he ultimately requires an exit strategy; if not, there will be enormous human and dollar costs. The assertion noted initially that a second-term president may suffer from hubris and overreach himself appears borne out by the opening moves and the personnel shifts in the opening months of Bush's second term. Whether mid-course corrections can be made appears questionable given the tightly knit composition of the Bush policy team.

Notes

1. See, for example, Paul O'Neill's views, as presented in Ron Suskind, *The Price of Loyalty* (New York: Simon & Schuster, 2004).
2. *Foreign Affairs*, December 2000.
3. Suskind, *The Price of Loyalty*, 2004, 70–75.
4. *Washington Post*, December 24, 2004.
5. Unnamed former official, *Washington Post*, November 5, 2004.
6. Ayman Nour, the young head of the Ghad (Tomorrow) party, was stripped of his parliamentary immunity and jailed on January 29, 2005, three days before the governing National Democratic Party and opposition leaders were scheduled to meet. Shortly after Rice canceled her visit, President Hosni Mubarak announced on February 26 that the constitution would be amended to permit competitive elections for the President in September 2005. Nour, who announced while he was detained that he would run for president, was released on March 12. Rice subsequently traveled to Cairo, where she delivered a hardhitting speech calling for democratic reforms. Nonetheless, Nour was rearrested shortly after the presidential elections, scheduled for spring 2006, were postponed for another two years.
7. *Washington Post*, March 26, 2005.

8. *Washington Post*, November 13, 2004.
9. *Washington Post*, March 23, 2005.
10. According to Sharton's close aide Dov Weisglas, *Washington Post*, October 7, 2004; *Financial Times*, October 8, 2004.
11. *Washington Post*, December 2, 2004.
12. *International Herald Tribune*, January 4, 2005.
13. *Washington Post*, March 26, 2005.
14. Al-Jazeera and *Washington Post*, April 12, 2005.
15. *Washington Post*, December 25, 2004.
16. *Washington Post*, September 27, 2004.
17. *Washington Post*, January 14, 2005.
18. *Washington Post*, December 25, 2004.
19. *Washington Post*, September 26, 2004.
20. *Washington Post*, December 1, 2004.
21. Knight Ridder news agency, March 21, 2005.
22. *Daily Star*, January 4, 2005.
23. *Washington Post*, November 11, 2004.
24. *Daily Star*, January 4, 2005.
25. *Washington Post*, December 7, 2004.
26. Members of eighteen provincial councils and the special legislature for the Kurdish region were also elected. The National Assembly met on March 15 for its first session, to take the oath of office, and then did not meet again until March 29. In April, the members appointed Jalal Talabani (head of the PUK) President, with Adel Abdul Mahdi (interim finance minister, Shii) and Ghazi Yawar (interim president, Sunni Arab) vice presidents. They named Ibrahim Jafari prime minister; he was head of the pro-Iranian Dawa Party, an exile in London until mid-2003, and a physician by profession. It was not until late April that he announced the 32-member cabinet, with seventeen Shii (including Interior Minister), eight Kurds, six Sunni Arabs (including the Defense Minister), and one Christian. Seven were women. There were slated to be up to four deputy prime ministers, including Ahmad Chalabi. (*Washington Post*, April 28, 2005) It remains uncertain as to whether the Sunni slots will be filled, given the Shii alliance's rejection of some Sunnis who had served under Saddam Hussein and the small number of "cooperating" Sunni politicians' resentment that they cannot select their own representatives. Interim President Yawar therefore boycotted the ceremony to install the government.
27. Secret finding, December 2002, cited in *The Guardian*, September 13, 2004.
28. *Washington Post*, August 30, 2004.
29. As casualties mounted in the summer of 2003, the U.S. Army Military Intelligence memorandum of mid-August 2003 (send to all military intelligence officers in Iraq), declared that "gloves are coming off" and called on those officers to suggest interrogation techniques (*Washington Post*, April 19, 2005). General Sanchez himself authorized twenty-nine such techniques in a memorandum the same year (*Washington Post*, March 23, 2005). The Herrington Report, noted earlier, written by a veteran of U.S. counterinsurgency in Vietnam, warned that harsh tactics imperil U.S. efforts in Iraq. Documents released to the ACLU and other organizations, under federal court order, also revealed widespread abuses during arrest and interrogation. See *The Guardian* September 13, 2004, and *Washington Post*, December 1, 22, and 26, 2004, among other sources.
30. Marine helicopter pilot, op. ed. in the *International Herald Tribune*, August 24, 2004.

31. *Washington Post*, December 9, 2004.
32. *Washington Post*, January 6 and 7, 2005.
33. The Army and Marines failed to meet their recruitment targets in February, March, and April 2005 (*Washington Post*, March 24, 2005). In fact, the Army stood at half of last year's recruitment level for combat brigades.
34. *Washington Post*, December 9, 2004.
35. *The Los Angeles Times*, December 11, 2004, citing the New England Journal of Medicine.
36. Former senior CIA analyst to the *Washington Post*, September 29, 2004.
37. CNN, December 7, 2004.
38. *Washington Post*, December 25, 2004.
39. *Washington Post*, September 29, 2004.
40. Al-Jazeera, November 9, 2004.
41. Ibid.
42. *Washington Post*, December 7, 2004.
43. Initial reports indicated a high voter turnout in the Kurdish regions, substantial turnouts in parts of Baghdad and in largely Shi'i central and southern towns, but little or no turnout in largely Sunni cities such as Ramadi, Samarra, and Falluja. The election resulted in 140 seats of 275 going to the United Iraqi Alliance (Shii parties), seventy-five to the Kurdish alliance (PUK and KDP), and forty to interim Prime Minister Ayad Allawi's party (secular Shii, professionals, with some Sunni Arab support). The UAL, lacking a majority, had to form a coalition with the Kurds, but had less immediate need to ally with Allawi's party and smaller groups.
44. United States officials have expressed concern that the civil code for family status issues might be replaced by religious laws (a move that Kurds and secularists oppose), that Shii political forces could want a clerical-government, and that purges of Baathists could weaken the newly trained police and security forces and lead to another major upsurge in the revolt. They also worry that Kurdish politicians will overplay their hand by demanding control over Kirkuk, which will trigger an Arab and Turcoman (and also Turkish) backlash.
45. Lecture at the American University in Cairo, October 11, 2004.
46. At its peak, thirty-eight countries sent troops to Iraq. As of spring 2005, 20,000 troops from twenty-three countries supplement the 150,000 U.S. troops. Portuguese (120), Dutch, Bulgarian (362) and Ukrainian (1,500) troops are pulling out in 2005; the 1,700 Polish contingent will leave by early 2006; and the 3,000 Italian troops will start leaving in fall 2005. That will leave British and South Korean troops as virtually the only allied forces. Bush stressed new NATO support in his meetings in Brussels in spring 2005, but this really amounts to the twenty-six NATO members agreeing to help to train Iraqi police and national guardsmen, outside Iraq, not on Iraqi soil.

Part VI

Presidential Leadership

Chapter Thirteen

George W. Bush: A Transformational Leader at Midterm

Stanley A. Renshon

The 2004 presidential election represents President Bush's third iteration of his controversial presidency. From the first, pre–9/11, he struggled for traction and seemed to loose ground. The second stage began on 9/11, as a result of which, he and his presidency were transformed and Bush went from having a vision to embracing a mission. The third act of his presidency began with his modest, but decisive reelection victory. The question is: What will he do with it? One purpose in this paper is to look both back and ahead to answer where this president is going, how he intends to get there, and what this means for American politics and policy.

The key frameworks for this analysis are leadership and transformation. What is the nature of this president's leadership and how it developed? What was the impact of 9/11 on him and his leadership style? What role did character and leadership play in the election? What does this suggest about the president's leadership with his newly earned political capital during his second, and final term?

The second key concept is transformation. In a recent book, I have described President Bush as a transformational leader.[1] Is this an accurate characterization, and if so what are its implications for President Bush's second term? What kind of leadership will be needed to be successfully transformative? Is it possible to be a transforming leader, in practice, in a society that is still sharply divided?

Before turning to those questions, it is useful to spend a brief time on the framework and method of this analysis. The analysis of a president's approach to his work lies at the intersection of psychology and presidential leadership. It raises questions regarding the psychological infrastructure of a president's decisions and what their choices mean for their presidencies, the country, and the world.

Assessing a President's Psychology

A question that often arises is how one learns about a president's psychology. The answer is that you can learn a lot about a president, or any person, by looking carefully at them over time and across circumstances. This requires that you immerse yourself in a president's history and public life. You listen to what they say, watch what they do, examine their circumstances and the choices they make within them, read the reports/analyses that are relevant to their choices, assess what others have to say about them, and do all that day in and day out. Then you blend these ingredients, putting all this information into a framework that seems to make sense and helps explain what you have found.

These tasks are more than a filling exercise. They are chances of discovering new relationships and odd elements that can become the basis of a useful formulation. Let me give one example: A single, unconventional occurrence—Mr. Bush's decision to spend his last 2000 campaign hours in Al Gore's home state which thereafter became the starting point of a psychological pattern that I labeled—*right back at you*.

It is a pattern that runs counter to the expectation that the person will do the conventionally approved thing and avoid exacerbating what is already a tense situation in the hope of quietly getting by. So, when George W. Bush went to the United Nations to ask support for disarming Iraq, the expectation surrounding this difficult task was that he would need to make his case and make a *plea* for action. He did. Yet, he also chose to directly challenge the relevance and courage of that organization—asking it "to show backbone" That galvanized the United Nations, but only briefly, before the organization's standard operating procedure reasserted itself.

The same *right back at you* psychology was evident in his introduction of the his four tax cut packages, his renomination of Judge Pickering to an Appellate Court position, and in his decision to put gaining control of the Senate front and center in the 2004 midterm elections at a time that he was preparing the public for a possible war with Iraq, and others. It was on display again more recently when he went out of his way to praise Donald Rumsfeld rather than soft peddle his support,[2] and when he renominated the judges that the Democrats had filibustered in his last term. It is as well reflected in his determined pursuit of social security change, specifically individual retirement accounts[3] and his support of John Bolton to the position of ambassador to the United Nations.[4]

Herein lays both a substantive and a methodological point. The substantive point is that unlike his, father George W. Bush obviously doesn't avoid conflict. The dynamics of this psychological element in George W's leadership style also has to do with his stance toward others—mostly his ability to stand apart from allies and enemies alike—, and his willingness to go after want he wants—a necessary ingredient of having the courage of your convictions. And recall, all this started out with a single fact—that ran counter to traditional nominee behavior.

The methodological point is that once you have gained an appreciation of a president's psychology, and this is especially true of George W. Bush, it provides a firm grounding for the further analysis of his presidency.

The Presidential Psychology of George W. Bush

Washington Post columnist David Ignatius recently said of George W. Bush that he was a man "whose character remains at once transparent and opaque."[5] I think not, especially the opaque part. To an unprecedented degree, Mr. Bush's presidency is one whose basic policy stance toward many issues is surprisingly clear and well defined, even when they are, as indeed is the case for many of them, controversial. The same is true, not surprising, of the president himself.

This Bush's presidency is a very strong reminder that the awesome powers of that office are set into motion and guided, or not as the case may be, substantially by the psychology of the man who occupies it. It is his ambitions, his judgments, his understanding of his circumstances and what he decides to do about them that provide the motivational fuel, the policy compass and the public psychology anchor.

So what can we say abut this president's basic psychology? One approach is to depend on typologies, in which presidential psychology is shoehorned in neat conceptual categories like whether he is "active" or "passive," likes his work or doesn't.[6] There are however, enormous problems with such an approach, including the issues of inferring too much psychology from the categories themselves, the issues of "mixed" category types, and the tendency to draw too much of a direct link between categories and global assessments of a presidency.[7]

Another approach is to develop a framework for the analysis of character psychology at the clinical level of analysis, one that applies to people in general, as well as presidents. Such a framework would consist of the psychological elements that are relevant to every person's development, and certainly in twenty-first century America. Elsewhere, I've suggested those core psychological frames are ambition, character integrity, and relatedness.[8] Ambition is simply the reach of your aspirations in relation to your capacities to realize them. Character integrity reflects the ideals and values that guide a person through life's currents and their fidelity to them in difficult circumstances. And finally, relatedness is a term that covers a person's basic psychological stance towards others.

What can be said of George W. Bush regarding these three character elements? With regard to the first, one clear fact is that for George W. Bush personal and political ambition were not fused at an early age as they were for Bill Clinton, Lyndon Johnson, John Kerry, and many others. One consequence of the developmental separation of personal and political ambition is that that self-esteem is not entwined, one might say enmeshed, in gaining and keeping power. Winning is something, especially for a competitive man like George W. Bush raised in a competitive family, but it isn't everything, and above all in taking risks you could loose, his emotional life doesn't depend on it.

George W. Bush grew up in a family with a strong history of accomplishment. He also grew up idealizing a very successful father, chose to follow in his footsteps, but spent roughly four decades working hard, but never filling much less surpassing those shoes. Other people in these circumstances would have given up, but not George W. Bush. He kept plugging away at his life's motivation, which literally was to find his place in the shadow of his father's accomplishments in the world more generally.

The story of that struggle need not concern us here except to say, that in a psychological sense George W. Bush is a self-made man. His focus and determination were the eventual instruments of his own salvation, from lackluster business success and a drinking problem. It is not surprising that they are, as well, the instruments of his political success.

Personally, the ambition that mattered to George W. Bush was to find his own place and make something successful of himself. Politically, his ambitions are quite different.

Psychology → Leadership → Transformation

Leadership is one of the two core tasks of presidential responsibility. But what is it exactly? Political leadership is relational. It involves mobilizing, orchestrating, and consolidating the efforts of others for common purpose. Sometimes leaders mobilize latent public sentiments like courage and optimism, as Winston Churchill did in leading England through the dark days of the Battle of Britain. Sometimes, as was the case with Ronald Reagan, the leader comes to symbolize the rising ascendancy of a particular group or view. Sometimes, as is the case with George W. Bush, a leader seeks, by inclination or necessity, to transform the policy and political paradigms that stand in the way of what he views as the country's best path to safety and prosperity.

I characterize George W. Bush as a transforming president for a simple reason. He wants to fundamentally transform American domestic and foreign policy. In domestic politics he wants to replace the command and control interest- group liberalism model with a right center model that emphasizes freedom of choice, and responsibility. In foreign affairs, he frames American national security policy through the lens of national interest that he has coupled with a view of America as a model and a spur for democratic national development in regions heretofore considered inhospitable. Few realize that the president's efforts to transform American domestic institutions have their direct parallel and counterpart in his efforts to do the same with international ones. These ambitions were clear before 9/11, but they have literally gone from a vision to a mission in the wake of that horrendous attack.

Bush critics were surprised at the size of Bush's first term agenda. After all, how could a spoiled, passive dunce who endlessly parroted a few limited ideas fed to him by the real powers behind his throne, variously depicted as Karl Rove, Donald Rumsfeld, or Dick Cheney be taken seriously? This was both factually wrong and psychologically inconsistent. Bob Woodward's extensive interviews with the senior administration advisors about the decisions to invade Afghanistan and Iraq made perfectly clear that Bush was in charge.[9] Moreover, the idea that Bush, who had struggled all his life to find his occupational footing would on obtaining hard-won success by effort, resolve, and skill simply hand over the reigns of his office to someone else makes no psychological sense.

Yet, old habits die hard and after President Bush won re-election pundits called attention to "second term curses," the need to mend fences with allies and critics, and the wishful thinking of liberals like E.J. Dionne that George W. Bush might use his Inaugural Address to list his mistakes and cancel his most cherished policies.[10] Of course, anyone with even a passing understanding of the George W. Bush's psychology would know that such behavior would be entirely out of character. Not surprisingly, his second Inaugural[11] and State of the Union[12] addresses were filled with lofty transforming ambitions, spreading freedom throughout the world, redesigning social security, and continuing the transition in Iraq from tyranny to a version of democracy reflective of Middle Eastern culture. Mr. Bush clearly has large visions of what he would like to accomplish. But visions and ambitions alone are not enough to make a transformational presidency.

His critics are now, it seems, very slowly coming to grip with the second major dimension of Bush's character, his determination to see his visions, ambitions, and principles through. President Bush does not wholly ignore politics; no president can. His calculations on the steel industry protection show that he obviously considers politics, as every president must. What is true however, is that to an extent that is rare in public life and certainly in the modern presidency, Mr. Bush has developed very strong convictions about strategic and policy issues, is willing to say where he stands, and contrary to the subterfuges of triangulation strategy, is willing to follow through.

Lastly, in analyzing Mr. Bush's character and psychology is the issue of relatedness. Critics charge that Mr. Bush is an arrogant unilateralist with no need for, or interest in others. The truth is more complicated. He is a man who wears his feelings on his sleeve and they are often tender towards those who have been hurt (like the missing intern Chandra Levy's parents, or the devastated family members after 9/11 with whom he spent many hours in a vast sea of emotional devastation, or the service men he has routinely and quietly visited.

Bush has developed a lifetime of close friendships, from every stage of his life. He likes people and is drawn toward them, but, and this is a crucial distinction, he does not need to be liked. One of his key traits is an ability to stand apart from friends as well as opponents. Proof? His support for: a large expansion of government, increased government spending, a new Medicare drug entitlement, his support of generic drugs for which large drug companies sued his administration, more funding for the United Nations, funneling AID's money to groups that also promote abortion, a plan to regularize the status of illegal immigrants, imposing hefty new penalties for makers of diesel engines that don't comply with clean air standards among many other initiatives. It is easy for leaders to satisfy their friends and frustrate their opponents; it is very much less easy to do the reverse, which is one reason why the ability of a leader to stand apart from his supporters is a strong measure of character integrity.

Paradoxically, while George W. Bush is criticized for being a unilateralist, a case could be made that he *sometimes* invests too much trust prematurely in others. He thought he could see into Russian President Vladimir Putin's soul,[13] and so conflated limited and specific areas of policy agreements with a more general alliance, and was forced to reassess the relationship.[14] When the Soviet foreign Minister complained about Bush's trips to former Soviet satellite countries Latvia and Georgia, Mr. Bush went anyway.[15] He added a pointed reminder to Mr. Putin that the sovereignty of the newly democratic state of Georgia "must be respected by all nations."[16]

He was traduced by his good amigo Vincente Fox on the issue of amnesty before he had even had his own immigration people in place.[17] Five days later 9/11 reframed the immigration debate. By May of 2005 Mexico was sending a diplomatic note of protest to the United States regarding the passage of legislation, signed by the president, which included provisions to build an extension of a barrier between the countries and a crackdown on driver's licenses being given to illegal aliens.[18] And of course there was the debacle of Bernard Kerik whose larger than life persona trumped a careful analysis of his history.[19] In each of these cases, rather than confirming to the caricature of man unable to think, work, or care about others, it was his occasional tendency of premature identification and natural friendliness that got him into trouble.

Generally however, his interpersonal style could best be characterized as, observe, then trust. Once you loose his trust like Yasser Arafat did, you are done. But if you earn his trust you have gained wide latitude. The administrations' internal debates, especially in foreign policy in his first term, have been frequent and fierce. David Sanger wrote in the *New York Times* that "Mr. Bush, more than most recent presidents, has tolerated—even encouraged— a constant battle in his administration over how to shape its approach to the world." Mr. Bush dislikes long memos and briefings, but he does relish debates. They are his preferred vehicles for getting the information he needs.

There is much more that could be said about Mr. Bush's character and psychology. Yet, in reality, any discussion of this or any other president as a transformational leader must examine another part of the leadership equation, public psychology. Both are critical to an understanding of a president's second-term prospects.

Public Psychology and the Great Divide

Much has been written about the divides that separate Americans. Americans are increasingly divided by party, though less so by ideology.

Much has been made of the red-blue divide. Less noticed, and more critical is the leadership divide. Americans now desire two different kinds of presidential leadership: *heroic* and *reflective*.

Briefly: *Heroic* leadership envisions the president as struggling against, and overcoming through determination, courage or otherwise heroic efforts, the circumstances he must surmount. Its archetype is Franklin Roosevelt, its metaphor the hierarchy, and its motto: Decide and command.

Reflective leadership, unlike heroic leadership, seeks to develop common, horizontal ties, not direct and hierarchical ones. Its prototype was Bill Clinton. Its metaphor is the prism, and its motto is: Select and reflect. It is not reflective in the sense of being introspective. Rather, it is reflective in the sense of gathering the disparate elements of frayed or fractured political and cultural consensus and mirroring them so that publics can see the basis for their common purposes. Americans want a president who is one of them, not above or beyond them.

Not surprisingly, Americans now want both in their president. They want two different presidents: one that will lead the charge to protect them in a world they now understand is very dangerous, while reassuring them as he does it; and one who will reunite the long frayed strands of the American national community, even as he solves their domestic policy concerns.

When, right after 9/11, Mr. Bush said of himself that he was "a loving guy, but he had to a job to do,"[20] he captured in almost perfect pitch two aspects of his own psychology, and the two aspects of his leadership style, *heroic* and *reflective*. He's focused and determined, but he genuinely does care about people. Yet, the softer reflective side faded from public view in the aftermath of 9/11 and the tough decisions on Iraq.

And therein lies a difficult problem. Mr. Bush wants to transform American policy in the context of an epic heroic struggle. By definition, he wants to forge a new consensus, but to get there he has to do so over the fight to the death resistance of a fading paradigm and its supporters. Paradoxically, George W. Bush can't unite America without first dividing it.

A Transforming President

George W. Bush stands poised to become the first truly transformational president since FDR. Indeed, if he succeeds in his quest he will have accomplished something FDR never lived long enough to do, transform America *and* the world. And if he succeeds at that, or even comes close, he will surely be considered a president of the first rank.

Mr. Bush's role as a transformational leader is somewhat paradoxical. He is not by nature, nor did he give much evidence prior to 9/11 of being, a heroic leader. As late as the 2000 presidential campaign, he touted himself as a "Reformer with Results."[21] Yes, he had clear views and followed through on them. But that only made him honest, not heroic.

Transforming What?

Embedded within many of Mr. Bush's policy remarks and position papers his campaign issues were some truly transformational ideas. He wanted to link education to performance not expenditures and was serious about closing the racial performance gap. He thought tax cuts, not large-scale government programs were the key to economic stimulus. He wanted to revamp social security so that younger workers could really own part of their retirement savings. He wanted to substitute cap and trade market mechanisms to reduce pollution in place of government command and control regimes. He wanted to involve religious organizations in helping the government to reclaim damaged lives.

Democrats, of course, violently disagreed with these policies and preferred what they felt were the time-tested successes of large scale-command and control government policies. Think government mandates, freedom, responsibility and choice were the key concepts behind Mr. Bush's new right-center policy frame. Think I-Pod.

In foreign policy, candidate Bush did favor a policy of limits. We could not be the world's policeman, nor rebuild all the Haiti's of this world. But he also said, "A president must be a clear-eyed realist. There are limits to the smiles and scowls of diplomacy. Armies and missiles are not stopped by stiff notes of condemnation. They are held in check by strength and purpose and the promise of swift punishment."

Yes, Mr. Bush said he wanted to work with our allies, but he also said protecting America must be the first duty of a president, a priority enshrined in his oath of office. Mr. Bush took that, like other things he said, seriously. His critics didn't.

He wanted the United States and its allies to be protected by an anti-missile defense system. He would not sign treaties like the Chemical Weapons Convention that obligated the United States without enforcement mechanisms to catch or deter cheaters. He would not sign on to the International Criminal Court so long as the United States was often called on to keep the peace, but left its soldiers and leaders subject to lawsuits while doing it. And he wouldn't sign the Kyoto Climate Accords so long as it exempted major polluting countries like India and China and as written would cause substantial harm to the U.S. economy.

Democrats here too violently disagreed with Mr. Bush's policies. They preferred to put their faith and America's fate in international institutions and treaties. Mr. Bush thought that a bad bet.

About the only transformational policy idea not put forward by then-candidate Bush was his doctrine of preemption, or more accurately preventive war. Yet, even that policy grew directly out of Bush's stated pre–9/11 view of the world that "America has determined enemies, who hate our values and resent our success" and that "The [Soviet] Empire has passed, but evil remains."[22] September 11 provided a dramatic confirmation of Bush's view. Moreover, given that he thought his first and primary responsibility was to "preserve and protect," preventive war or preemption was hardly a radical step.

Mr. Bush's new policy initiatives reflect an emphasis on individual choice, personal responsibility, and institutional accountability. Internationally, the president's initiatives reflect a clear-eyed, tough-minded assessment of national interest coupled with a Wilsonian desire to make the world a better and safer place. What distinguishes both sets of initiatives is that they reflect large ideas, involve considerable risk for Mr. Bush personally and politically, and are aimed at changing the way Americans think and understand their world.

The transformations in the international sphere are going to require Americans to change how they understand themselves and their relationship to the world. Americans are well known internationally for being open and friendly, and we like others to like us. These are hard times for that strand of American psychology as that wish coexists with the realization that the friendship of others won't necessarily protect us, and too much of such reliance may even lead to disaster.

Domestically, Mr. Bush's proposed changes will also take some psychological adjustment on the part of Americans. He is offering more choice, not everyone is comfortable with making them. He is offering more freedom; not everyone is comfortable exercising it. He is asking for more personal discipline and responsibility. Not everyone wishes to, or is able to, exercise it. President Bush, to repeat, has his work cut out for him.

So, Mr. Bush did embrace large transformational ideas, but didn't embrace a heroic leadership stance in calling for them, at least at first. That changed on September 11. Mr. Bush undertook a heroic task, and took the heroic leadership stance necessary to accomplish it. transformed the Bush presidency and Mr. Bush personally was 9/11.

That attack refocused the administration in a fundamental way on the national security risks the United States faced. A key distinction, between domestic and foreign policy, between "over there" and there collapsed. As for Mr. Bush, he now had not only a vision, but also a mission. The heroic task that Mr. Bush had now acquired was to save the United States from the deadly consequences of catastrophic terrorism. His personal characteristics—focus, resolve, and determination were now fully engaged in this heroic task and in the process Mr. Bush became a heroic leader.

Transforming How?

A major question remains however: How does Mr. Bush hope to succeed in the transformations he is undertaking? He came into office the first time by the slimmest of margins and his second victory was solid but by no means a landslide public endorsement. Forget all Mr. Bush's talk about a mandate. Yes, he won and so is authorized to govern, but what he has really earned is an audition.

Change from the familiar is psychologically difficult, even when it is not working well. Trying new ways of policy thinking or new policies, which may or may not work better than the old ones, also makes the public nervous. Mr. Bush has his work cut out for himself reducing public anxiety about his new paradigm efforts, and that work won't be accomplished quickly or easily.

Yet, he does have assets to bring to his task. It is not well understood that Mr. Bush's character psychology are his greatest personal and political resources. The 2004 exit polls showed that clear stands on the issues and strong leadership were seen as the most important qualities in a president. Among Bush voters 87 percent, thought he was a strong leader and 79 percent thought he did take clear stands on the issues.[23] A January, 2005 *AP-Ipsos Reid* poll found that the two-thirds of the electorate described Bush as likable, strong and intelligent. A majority of Americans think that he is dependable and honest.[24] The January 2005 *NBC/Wall Street Journal* poll confirmed these facts.[25] The public doesn't yet support all of his policy initiatives, but their trust in Mr. Bush personally is likely to get him a real hearing.

Mr. Bush's transformation, if it happens will owe much to his psychology and the psychology of his leadership, but transformations are not accomplished by psychology alone, however powerful, Mr. Bush has clearly taken Richard Neustadt's advice about the importance of self-help to heart,[26] but he is also the beneficiary of some trends that have applied to his quest.

First, the dominant paradigm, interest group liberalism, which has been in decline since it reached its heydays in the 1960s. Its adherents have grown convinced that the answers they provide are superior and beyond debate. Yet, Democrats and liberals have steadily been loosing market shares on many policy questions.

Second, a counter paradigm has arisen: call it the right-center paradigm that found its effective spokesman in Ronald Reagan but its roots in decades of idea development at think tanks like the Heritage Foundation and funding sources like the Bradley Foundation. Interest-group liberalism has gone from a requirement to an option. It is not longer the sole policy or moral foundation of the republic.

Third, political institutional power has shifted. It has shifted in Congress, in the States, more slowly in the federal agencies like the U.S. Civil Rights Commission, in quasi-public institutions like PBS, in the south and as the 2004 presidential election demonstrated among voters.

Fourth, cultural institutions are in flux. There are now alternatives to the major news networks that have broken the near monopoly on political commentary. *Fox News* and talk radio have now been joined by a large community of bloggers, plugged into larger communities of experts. The news has become politically diverse and democratized. The political tilt of university faculty is becoming more a matter of debate.

Does Transformation Equal Realignment?

Following the conceptual work of Burnham,[27] realignment has become equated with dramatic historic shifts in a single election. In his theory such elections result in large scale changes of voter allegiances from one party to another, providing stable, governing majorities for decades. Over time it has become clear that there are a number of difficulties with that theory.[28]

One issue is the definitional requirement that such a transformation takes place as a result of a single decisive election as Burnham insists happened in 1800, 1860, and 1932. This neglects the possibility of "rolling realignment," that is realignment that does not takes place in one or two key, dramatic elections.[29] This appears to be an accurate description of the gradual rise to parity, and then ascendancy of the GOP's right-center paradigm.[30]

A second issue concerns the precise psychological mechanisms by which transformation occurs. Burnham's theory focuses on the cataclysmic events like the Great Depression and the public's clamor for leaders to do something about it. One that didn't (Hoover) lost, one that did (Roosevelt) won. The assumption of Burnham's model is that the lever of change is policy. My argument is that there is something else going on underneath those policy preferences that are the real level of transformational change.

Third, the question arises whether realignment must entail whole scale change in the composition of the party strengths. Is it possible for the country to have a governing realignment without a wholesale change in each party's relative numerical strength? Evidence suggests it is.

So, there are two questions before us. Is there a transformation of some kind underway? Will Mr. Bush's transformations, if successful, result in historical shifts in the relative strengths of the political parties? The answers to these questions are: maybe, and not necessarily.

In order to address these questions, we must first reach an understanding of the nature of transformation.

Political transformation is, in its most essential form, an alteration and shift in the framing, understanding, and associated expectations surrounding policy issues. These changes lead, as a result, to a change in what people think and their support for new policy paradigm options. It is a paradigmatic shift first and a party allegiance shift second.

This definition points away from an exclusive focus on policy support and certainly a focus on wholesale shift in party numbers. Rather, it focuses on a more psychological level, one that examines reframing and expansion of policy understanding as the key fulcrum of realignment transformations. It follows, therefore, that it is quite possible for Mr. Bush to achieve his transformation without turning most Americans into Republicans.

Change in Mr. Bush's direction could come about in other ways as well. Americans could change the way they think about policy, and in the process force the Democratic party to shift as well to remain competitive. There is some evidence that this process is already under way. Gearing up for the 2004 presidential campaign, Democrats said they would not seek to dismantle all of Bush's policy initiatives, for example, his emphasis on measuring results in the No Child Left Behind Act. Democratic presidential nominee John Kerry alluded to the fact that Democrats had learned some lessons, presumably from Mr. Bush. More recently, some in the Democratic Party have called for it to reexamine its lock- step commitment to abortion under every circumstance[31] and become truly strong on defense issues.[32] The grounds of political debate are showing signs of shifting!

No paradigm change is possible without new ideas that provide an alternative. Yet, as noted, trading in the old for the untried requires a leap of faith. Such leaps require trust to overcome the understandable anxiety that accompanies paradigm change. If the public loses confidence in Mr. Bush as a leader, his transformations will falter. If he is able to retain their trust, he will have a critical lever by which to help make the transformations he envisions.

FDR's Realignment: A Misleading Model?

Political scientists waiting for any evidence of realignment as the foundation of transformation generally look to FDR's experience. However, I want to suggest here that a focus on that model is misplaced. Electoral landslides are not the only way transformations are accomplished.

In the classic formulation, as noted, realignment involves the wholesale switching of political party allegiance and the coming together of a new stable coalition that provides a new national governing majority. The only modern example of this is the FDR election in 1932 at the height of the Depression, in which Democrats gained the presidency and swept both houses of Congress. In the process, the Democratic Party won the allegiance of white southerners, Catholics, and organized labor. In the 1936 presidential election, Roosevelt further cemented his coalition with the addition of African Americans and Jews. That coalition held at the presidential level until 1968, when disaffected southerners began their migration out of the Democratic Party by voting for George Wallace.

There are a number of elements that are central to the FDR realignment model and critical for a consideration of George W. Bush's chances to repeat history. Most accounts of the FDR model stress the wholesale change and consolidation of voters' allegiances. From the standpoint of the political horse races and scorecards this is understandable.

Yet that focus obscures several key elements of the realignment. First, it obscures the fact that at its core was a national trauma. Second, it obscures the important fact that the president at the helm was a pragmatic optimist who offered hope, and was willing to take enormous personal and political risks to change policy direction. The results are with us to this day.

It is important not only to focus on the fact that voters changed their allegiance; but to ask *why* they did so. The change in perspective and policy thinking was the key. The public was desperate for hope and answers. They wanted something, anything, put in the place of nothing. Roosevelt provided that change in perspective and expectation by substituting an activist government with a central role in providing economic stability and growth in a laissez-faire economic policy in which government was essentially an economic bystander.

George W. Bush's problem however, is in important ways, quite different. If he is to succeed he has to replace a very powerful, entrenched paradigm with substantial public and institutional support. He is not replacing a failed paradigm that failed catastrophically like the government as an economic bystander did during the depression. Rather, he is trying to replace a paradigm that has had its successes, but whose failures and limits have become increasingly evident in the last three decades.

From the standpoint of political institutions and democratic process, FDR's shift in framing was not revolutionary. He did not change the form of government. Key American public institutions remained intact. But instead of having nowhere to look for economic help, the people recast their gaze and expectations and looked to the government for economic answers, not to business or the market. They expected solutions that worked, or at least that were tried. Above all, they expected government action. The refocus on the government as a first responder reflects a profound shift of expectation and focus.

That policy paradigm in its basic form is still with us today. The New Deal coalition may have broken apart, but the change in policy paradigm has remained in tact. This suggests an important lesson: *The two are not synonymous. Or to restate the point more directly, it may be possible to have transformation without major realignment.*

Is George W. Bush the new FDR? Is 9/11 the public psychology equivalent of the Great Depression? Some clues come from examining the nature of the critical role that FDR played in the New Deal Transformation. He rejected a laissez-faire approach and in doing so rejected what was then the dominant "mainstream" thinking. *His* shift in thinking preceded and stimulated the public's shift in thinking. The changes from that shift in perspective have cascaded across almost every corner of America in decades since, but it is important to keep in mind that they began with a shift in perspective in the mind of one person and his advisors. It was their judgment that broke with convention and set in motion that frame of understanding, expectation, and presidential behavior that is today's mainstream and now thoroughly conventional orthodoxy.

Roosevelt's paradigm shift involved economics and politics, not culture. President Roosevelt had nothing to say about what it meant to be an American, whether a commitment to this country and its institutions were worthwhile, or whether one's identity as an American ought to be replaced by ethnic or racial identities. All of these things were not a matter of real debate, as they are now. Thus, any discussion of changing the dominant paradigm today must take into account that the divisions to be breached are cultural and political rather than economic and political as they were for FDR.

Finally, there is the matter of the president's psychology. There is FDR's optimism, willingness to take risks, his capacity not to be deterred by failure, and above all his determination to find something that would work. Few scholars credit FDR's alphabet programs with ending the Depression. They do credit World War II. Yet his administration's programs did help, and they did result in a shift and realignment of perspective that is with us today. Those programs were driven by his psychology.

These character traits find their echo in Mr. Bush's psychology and mission. He has been seized by a fierce and steely determination that began before 9/11 and was crystallized by it. This was added on top of an already legendary ability to focus and a willingness to engage and fight on behalf of his beliefs. If Mr. Bush succeeds in his transformation, he will owe it as much to his psychology and the psychology of leadership as to his policies.

Yet, it is also true that 9/11 had a profound effect on American public psychology and thinking. The idea that, "it can't happen here," proved to be demonstrably false. Not only could it happen here, it did. And, it could very well do so again. The presumption of comfortable security and "business as usual" was no longer tenable. In foreign policy, Mr. Bush pushed for a new tougher stance and the public substantially supported his leadership in the war against terror. Having established this bond, he will be more able to call upon it in his second term for his major domestic battles including the redesign of social security. The 9/11 tragedy set the stage for transformation, but it is the psychology of Mr. Bush's leadership that will be instrumental in any successful efforts.

A Charge to Keep

Showing British reporters around his White House office, Mr. Bush singled out a picture on his wall titled "A Charge to Keep." It was a picture that he had chosen to hang in his governor's office in Texas, and he had, at the time, sent a memo to all his staff to come in and look at it. It's the title of his campaign autobiography as well. It is quite clear the picture has special significance for Mr. Bush.

The picture is based on a Methodist hymn, and speaks to "serving something larger than yourself in life," and the president said it "speaks to his spirituality." Yet the picture itself suggests both another more worldly meaning and a deeper psychological one.

The picture shows three rugged horsemen taking a steep and rough trail at a gallop. One horseman is clearly in the lead with the other two just behind him. They have almost, but not quite, made the crest of the hill, though it is clear that given their effort, they will do so. They are unflagging in their uphill struggle.

In many ways, the picture captures some essential features of Mr. Bush's psychology and his approach to leadership. The quest, or whatever it is that motivates the horsemen, is an uphill battle. The path is strewn with rocks, dead branches, and the remains of forest decay.

The path is steep and there is risk in not doing it at a more leisurely pace, but the horsemen are having none of that. They are charging up the hill at what seems full speed. There is urgency to their speed. They must get somewhere important, and the clock is ticking. It is indeed a charge to keep in the double sense of that phrase. There is a rendezvous with purpose and destinies on the other side of that hill, somewhere in their futures. And in order to get there they have to keep charging, hard. This can be no charge of half measures.

The horseman in the foreground and leading the charge is a horse-length in front of the others. He clearly is part of the threesome, but not bound by their pace. His eyes look straight ahead. His face is etched with concentration. He is part of the group, but apart from it as well—a parallel to Mr. Bush's character and relationships in real life. There are three men in the picture and we can't tell if more are following. Perhaps they are the vanguard of a larger group. Perhaps the success of their quest depends on them alone.

One can see much of Mr. Bush's principles of leadership in that picture, and it is one reason why it resonates so deeply for him. Of that lead rider Mr. Bush said, "he's riding a tough trail. You don't know how many horsemen are behind him, you know at least two. It could be 2,000. You just don't know. But you do know it's a pretty rough looking trail, and *there is absolutely no question in your mind he's going to make it.*"[33]

It is not a picture you could imagine his father choosing. George W. Bush's strong identification with the picture reflects his preference for leading rather than governing. The exact reverse was true of his father. A charge to keep is, in the many senses of that phrase, reflective of that fact. The call to service that George W. Bush speaks of alludes to another part of his leadership after 9/11; Mr. Bush as New World prophet alerting Americans to mortal danger.

When considering Mr. Bush's hard-charging style it is well to remember that circumstances as well as psychology play a role. In both the domestic and international arenas the president's transforming agenda must contend with powerful, entrenched, and hostile interests arrayed against him. That is why a hard charge may be necessary to get you up and over the hill, but a weak one is not likely to make much headway.

Conclusion: Second-Term Blues of Another Kind

Second terms inevitably bring vindication and decline. A president has, for whatever reasons, been reelected, and his policies and leadership are sufficiently validated to have done so. But inevitably the clock on the president's post-office status has started ticking, and many are counting the days. His opponents both domestically and internationally can hardly wait, and the same is true for those of his own party who would like to replace him in office.

Second presidential terms are notoriously difficult for a number of reasons that the editors have helpfully identified in their opening chapter. Some are structural like the loss of policy momentum and ideas, the lack of a clear public mandate, and the president's "lame duck" status and thus clout. To these the editors add the familiar staples of second-term scandals and a tendency to overreach. Small wonder that at least one pundit has stated categorically, "Presidential second terms usually end in failure."[34]

Yet, if we look at the above list of second-term curses, several points come immediately into view. First, in many ways the curses of a second term in Bush's case, are little different than the obstacles confronting him in his first. Consider the lack of a clear public mandate and the tendency to overreach, both of which have characterized the Bush administration from its first day in office. Mr. Bush did not gain an obvious public mandate for his policies, when gauged by the strength of his electoral win in either 2000 or 2004, yet that did not dissuade him from pitching a large and ambitious agenda at the start of both terms. If one requires an agenda proportional to one's measure of electoral victory, this then is as well, an operational definition of overreaching.

Mr. Bush has not run out of policy ideas. On the contrary, his second-term ambitions to reform social security and immigration policy, and continue the spread of democracy to the Middle East and Eastern Europe are, by any measure, historical level undertakings. If Mr. Bush's second term falters, it will not be because he ran out of big policy ambitions or lost a commanding mandate he never had.

Nor does Mr. Bush have to worry about a vice-president with one part of his existence firmly rooted in the ambition to become president. Mr. Cheney may or may not be a dark horse contender for the 2008 election. However, he has made it abundantly and honestly clear that he harbors no such ambitions.

Finally there is the specter of second-term scandals. George W. Bush is no Bill Clinton. Whatever Id impulses his unconscious may or may not hold they have clearly been tamed by decades of personal exertions of will, determination, and success in finding and forging his pace in the world. It is impossible to see him risk his place and his critical position as leader of this country's critical interests in the service of self-aggrandizing impulses, as Bill Clinton did.

Whatever scandals have come his way as a result of administration policies (Abu Ghraib) or political associations (Enron) Mr. Bush has deftly managed to get out in front of the problems and associate himself with their solution. He is also insulated to some degree by the fact that he has been usually frank about his policy views, and is considered by most to be generally honest and straight-forward. What remains in considering this president's second-term blues is a factor that is, in some ways truly unique: He is engaged in a fight to the political death.

The death of political empires is never easy, and the possible demise of interest-group liberalism is no exception. Democrats have lost ground in almost every political area. They are in a fight to the finish for that most important political commodity: power. No one of course will be killed, but people and ideas will be vanquished.

Democrats have found unity, though not political revitalization in opposition. They are unanimous in their opposition to Bush's social security plans, while offering no policy solutions on their own. They have effectively used the filibuster to stymie Bush's appointments to the Appellate Court system, and they have made the president's appointment of John Bolton as U.S. Ambassador to the United Nations an excruciating mixture of policy disagreement, character mud slinging, and political venting.[35] Commentators, eager to showcase conflict and the potential for dire results, have written a great deal about the Bush administration's second-term agenda being in trouble[36] or "stalled."[37]

Yet, it is unclear how much these setbacks will be translated into actual policy defeats. A Senate compromise forced by the Republicans has cleared three Appellate Court judges to take their positions, and more will no doubt follow. Mr. Bolton may have been delayed, but he was conformed. And, even if he isn't Mr. Bush's right back at you psychology promises that another tough U.N. critic will take Mr. Bolton's place. And while Mr. Bush's social security plans are in trouble, it is much too early to count them dead.

In the meantime, in the first 120 days, the Bush administration has passed comprehensive bankruptcy reform, class action lawsuit reforms, immigration and border control reforms, and set a budget framework that allowed oil drilling in Alaska and cut the growth rate for Medicaid expenses and other entitlements. Internationally, Bush is still stymied by North Korea and Iran's nuclear ambitions, but it is unclear just how exactly these issues can be successfully addressed. In any event, nothing much has changed on these important matters since Bush's first term.

Meanwhile, Iraq has reached another milestone after an historic democratic vote by selecting its own nationally representative leadership. Syria has withdrawn from Lebanon, the movement toward a democratic Palestinian state inches forward, and almost totally uncommented upon, Mr. Bush has won U.N. agreement to exempt American peace keeping troops from the International Criminal Court.[38]

Second terms, like first terms, have their successes, triumphs, setbacks, failures, and lulls. This makes hard to develop an overall assessment, especially after only 100 days of a full four-year second term. Mr. Bush had an enormous first- term legislative success record. In his second term, he has even more political resources in the form of fellow party members controlling Congress and all of the personal characteristics—his large policy ambitions, his determination, his political agility, and his pragmatism that he had during his first term. For those reasons, it would be a mistake to confuse the Bolton flap with a major setback to the administration's plans. And those plans, remember, revolve around changing the policy discourse so that right-center ideas become part of the accepted wisdom.

It is true that Mr. Bush's quest still faces many substantial and powerful barriers. But it is also true to quote Bob Dylan, "The times they are a changing."

However, whether these factors, coupled with the president's drive and determination are enough to tip the scales is still unresolved. Mr. Bush faces determined enemies at home and abroad who will stop at little or nothing to defeat him. On the other hand those who have repeatedly bet against him have been on a loosing streak.

Notes

1. Stanley A. Renshon, *In His Father's Shadow: The Transformations of George W. Bush* (New York: Palgrave, 2004).
2. Thom Shanker, "As Criticism Grows, Bush Offers Support of Rumsfeld," *New York Times*, December 21, 2004.
3. Jackie Calmes, John D. McKinnon and Brody Mullins, "Bush's Embrace of New Initiatives Gains House Social Security Ally," *Wall Street Journal*, May 4, 2005, p. A4.
4. Sheryl Gay Stolberg, "In Face of Opposition, Bush Renews Support for Bolton," *New York Times*, May 14, 2005, p. A1.
5. David Ignatius, "Bush's Next Test," *Washington Post*, January 19, 2005, p. A19.
6. James David Barber, *The Presidential Character: Predicting Performance in the White House* (New Jersey: Prentice-Hall, 1972).
7. Alexander George, "Assessing Presidential Character," *World Politics* 26(2) (January, 1974), pp. 244–245.
8. Stanley A. Renshon, *The Psychological Assessment of Presidential Candidates* (New York: Routledge, 1988).
9. Bob Woodward, *Bush at War* (New York: Simon & Shuster, 2002), pp. 145–146. At one point Woodward asks Bush in an interview whether he let his National Security Advisor, Dr. Rice, know that he intended to press the members of his National Security Council on several matters to which Bush replied, "Of course, not. I'm the Commander-in-Chief, see I don't need to explain-I do not need to explain why I say things." This does not sound like a president willing to give up his authority and decision role to others.
10. E.J. Dione, "What Bush Could Say," *Washington Post*, January 18, 2005, p. A17.
11. George W. Bush, "Transcript- President Bush's Second Inaugural Address," *Washington Post*, January 20, 2005; see also Elisabeth Bumiller and Richard W. Stevenson, "Bush, at 2nd Inaugural, Says Spread of Liberty Is the Calling of Our Time," *New York Times*, January 21, 2005.
12. George W. Bush, "Text-President Bush's State of the Union Address," *New York Times*, February 2, 2005; see also Todd S. Purdum, "Yet Another Bold Stroke," *New York Times*, February 3, 2005.
13. Elizabeth Cliff, "Seeking Putin's Soul," *Newsweek Online*, December 17, 2004.
14. Peter Baker, "Dealings With Putin Discussed," *Washington Post*, December 12, 2004, p. A24.
15. Elisabeth Bumiller, "Russia Objects to Bush Visit to Neighbors; Rice Replies," *New York Times*, May 6, 2005, p. A8.
16. Elisabeth Bumiller, "Bush Encourages Georgia With a Warning to Russia," *New York Times*, May 11, 2005, p. A3.
17. Editorial, "Mr. Fox Comes to Washington," *New York Times*, September 6, 2001.
18. "Mexico protests to U.S. in immigration furor," *Reuters*, May 18, 2005.

19. Mike Allen and Peter Baker, "On Kerik Nomination, White House Missed Red Flags," *Washington Post*, December 15, 2004, p. A04.

20. George W. Bush, "Remarks In a Telephone Conversation With New York City Mayor Rudolph Giuliani and New York Governor George Pataki and an Exchange with Reporters," (September 11, 2001) *Weekly Compilation of Presidential Documents*, (September 17, 2001), 37(37) p. 1308.

21. Terry M. Neal, "Bush Energized by S.C. Victory," *Washington Post*, February 20, 2000, p. A11.

22. George W. Bush, "A Distinctly American Internationalism," Ronald Reagan Presidential Library, Simi Valley, California, November 19, 1999.

23. CNN, "U.S. President/National/ Exit Poll," November 5, 2004.

24. Will Lester, "Americans Hopeful on Second Bush Term," *Associated Press*, January 16, 2005.

25. Hart/Mcinturff, "SurveyNo. 51," NBC/*Wall Street Journal*, January, 2005.

26. Richard E. Neustadt, *Presidential Power* (New York: John Wiley, 1960).

27. Walter Dean Burnham, *Critical Elections and the Mainsprings of American Politics* (New York: Norton, 1970).

28. David Mayhew, *Electoral Realignments: A Critique of an American Genre* (New Haven, CT: Yale University Press, 2002).

29. Andrew E. Busch, "Rolling Realignment," *Claremont Review of Books*, (Winter, 2004).

30. This is not an argument that the GOP right-center paradigm, has not itself evolved. Certainly Ronald Reagan's leadership and policy stance were different than that of Senator Barry Goldwater whose electoral drubbing by Lyndon Johnson marked the low point of conservative pubic acceptance. So too, George W. Bush differs from Mr. Reagan in a number of ways that are beyond the scope of our focus here. The point here is that the right-center paradigm has evolved and developed.

31. Patrick D. Healy, "Clinton Seeks Common Ground on Abortion," *New York Times*, January 25, 2005.

32. Peter Bernard, "Fighting Faith: An Argument for a New Liberalism," *The New Republic*, December 13, 2004.

33. Brett Hume, "Raw Data: Text of Bush Interview," *Fox News*, September 22, 2003.

34. Dick Morris, "How Second Terms Fail," *New York Post*, January 19, 2005.

35. Yochi J. Dreazen and David Rogers, "Senate Democrats Engineer a Delay of Vote on Bolton," *Wall Street Journal*, May 27, 2005, p. A3.

36. Howard Fineman, "Food Fight in the Big Tent," *Newsweek*, May 24, 2005.

37. Harold Meyerson "Arnold Meets His Match," *Washington Post*, May 25, 2007, p. A27.

38. Warren Hodge, "U.N. Votes to Send Any Sudan War Crimes Suspects to the World Court," *New York Times*, April 1, 2005, p. A6.

Index